DUALITY

Prepare Yourselves and Your Children
for the Age of Artificial Intelligence

DUALITY

Prepare Yourselves and Your Children for the Age of Artificial Intelligence

Bernard GOLSTEIN

ISBN: 9781071374863
This version: Full - paperback - EN - v1.1 – June 9th, 2019

All inquiries to be sent to: duality@golstein.com

To Eva, Nathan,
and all the children
who will build
the age of Artificial Intelligence

Contents

Introduction

Prepare while there is still time

I t was a beautiful day in October 2018, at NUS, Singapore's most prestigious university. We had just discussed the Future of Work for two hours in a packed lecture theatre. The Master's students did not miss a word of the discussions, captivated by the immense transformations awaiting jobs: guaranteed obsolescence for some, inevitable drastic evolution for others. We were joking about the much better use that students were making of their time with us, thinking about the future, than across the hall, where some of their classmates were taking courses in accounting and finance – a very precarious choice. Nevertheless, our discussion highlighted the context of unbridled change, calling for a complete redefinition of life priorities and a healthy reflection on career choices. A young man then raised his hand and said to us, looking depressed: "I completely understand the flood of changes that is looming, but I am still under pressure from my parents and society to become a lawyer or a doctor." An awkward silence ensued. The young man had just pinpointed the poignant contradiction between well-wishing parents and a world dashing at full speed, whose trajectory is completely out of their control.

Since then, variations of this scene have played out at each of my conferences and workshops. Members of the public, whether adults, university students, secondary school students or primary school children, question me during the general discussion or come immediately afterwards for a private conversation. The same question is asked week after week: what should we learn? People are eager to get answers, after being confused by inconsistent advice from their friends and mentors or being sorely disappointed with the obvious lack of credible information.

This gave rise to the idea of this book: to enable parents to provide informed and relevant advice. The first task was to inform them about the ins and outs of Artificial Intelligence, and to provide them with substantiated forecasts about the future of work. It didn't take long before another objective was added: to offer a framework to prepare their children for the age of Artificial Intelligence. The target included all children, not just those who intended to work in Artificial Intelligence itself.

The task at hand didn't look easy. What could be taught to children today that would be relevant and useful when they turned twenty or forty years old? How could we nurture competent and informed users of Artificial Intelligence who could make the most of its considerable advantages, while shielding them against its undeniable dangers? What would be the state of society in a few decades, and how could we foster the emergence of individuals capable of steering it positively? What would this technology, having greatly contributed to shaping society, look like? For the time being, how could we disentangle the real from the fake, the hype or the denial in the current state of the said technology? The permanence and magnitude of the change to come, which were the only things that we could take for granted, never failed to remind us of their existence. How many times, while writing this book, did we see the sudden realisation of what was previously considered impossible? Suddenly robots, which were still staggering the day before, started walking along a brick path while doing a balancing act! Our amazement increased day after day, when word processing software prompted us not to discriminate on the basis of gender, when a AI biochemist solved the difficult problem of protein folding, or when a virtual personal assistant managed to book a table at a restaurant by phone without giving itself away...

This acceleration of change quickly proved to be a major focus of this book. By the end of the century, we will probably succeed in creating Artificial General Intelligence. Simply put, this intelligence will surpass us in every way. The world will be disrupted and only profound changes in our societal models will prevent unmanageable chaos. Is that a remote date? Certainly not; it's only a few generations away, virtually tomorrow morning on a geological scale. The effects have already started being felt. All you have to do to convince yourself is to go to the warehouse of a large retailer: there are hardly any employees left, since almost everything is automated. Some still claim that this is only the fate of a few trades, rather than a solid trend. Unfortunately, denial is the most common attitude. People's natural reaction is to believe their own profession is shielded from transformation. Little do they know.

In its early stages, change, even exponential change, is almost imperceptible. It is slow and seems completely harmless. At some point, a stronger signal attracts our attention. Things suddenly start speeding up, gaining momentum, and quickly getting out of control. We are left puzzled and wondering why we could not react in time.

Would you like an illustration? Imagine yourself on the sideline of a basketball court, in a large covered arena, watching your children play a game. At the beginning of the thought experiment, an imaginary tap releases a drop of water. The next minute, two drops flow out. The next minute, four drops, and so on. This is an exponential acceleration: the volume of water discharged doubles every minute. At the end of the first ten-minute quarter of the game, no one notices the presence of the water – its total volume would fit into a small coffee cup. At the end of the second quarter, the ground seems wet. At the end of the third quarter, your feet are in the water: it is 12 centimetres deep. One minute later, the water reaches your ankles. The next minute, it covers your knees; then your waist one minute after that. One more minute and you're underwater. Two more minutes and there are no more air pockets in the arena. You're drowning! Disaster seems to have struck in just five minutes, when in fact it had been brewing since the beginning of the game. Yet you didn't notice anything until the last moments, when you were already in great distress.

Does that ring a bell? Climate change, perhaps? As early as the 1970s, some knew. But at first, no one wanted to listen. Then no one was ready to believe. Above all, no one was willing to change. In the most advanced countries, we retained our lifestyle; elsewhere, others adopted it. We continued to release massive emissions of greenhouse gases into the atmosphere. Some commitments were made, barely implemented, almost with no effect. The situation has deteriorated exponentially, bringing us dangerously close to the Earth system's tipping points. When they are reached, disaster will be inevitable. It took a 15-year-old child, the young Swedish Greta Thunberg, to sound the alarm and tell world leaders at COP 24 that she was disgusted: "You only speak of green eternal economic growth because you are too scared of being unpopular. You only talk about moving forward with the same bad ideas that got us into this mess, even when the only sensible thing to do is pull the emergency brake. You are not mature enough to tell it like is. Even that burden you leave to us children. But I don't care about being popular. I care about climate justice and the living planet."

Fortunately, Artificial Intelligence, unlike climate change, will first and foremost be a considerable source of progress and well-being. It is already at work in many initiatives to fight climate change. But like all technologies, it is double-edged. Some of its effects will be positive and others negative. If we are not careful, it will bring about disruptions of comparable magnitude to climate change.

However, unlike climate change, there is still time to prepare for the era of Artificial Intelligence. That is also why we are writing today. We have the luxury of still being able to think calmly and take the necessary decisions. Yes, there is still time. But this window of opportunity will not remain open for long. Let's not wait for it to close.

Part I of this book aims to provide complete, accurate and easy-to-understand information on Artificial Intelligence. The first chapter tells the story of how it appeared to the general public and became a household name after a few games of Go. Chapter 2 demystifies AI, explaining its purely algorithmic nature and very simply describing how it is trained. That said, we highlight its extraordinary potential within a few generations. Chapter 3 draws a comparison between artificial and human intelligence, clearly describing their respective capabilities and the likely evolution of AI. Chapter 4 reviews some of the promises of Artificial Intelligence to improve our daily lives and address the great challenges facing humankind. Chapter 5 highlights the dangers of Artificial Intelligence and discusses the ethical approaches that have been put in place to minimise them.

Part II is entirely devoted to the future of work. This will be the largest of the disruptions from Artificial Intelligence. Chapter 6 presents four very different visions of the future of work, ranging from the most optimistic of scenarios to the most pessimistic, including a historical perspective and a vision of radical transformation. Chapter 7 rigorously analyses the potential for automation, within 20 years, of all the tasks that make up jobs. Chapter 8 goes a step further by dissecting the potential for automating jobs themselves. Chapter 9 explores 23 examples of professions that are destined to be automated... or not. Chapter 10 summarises the framework for systematic job analysis and provides additional guidelines for comprehension and career choice.

Part III deals with the changes to be brought to education in the age of Artificial Intelligence. Chapter 11 describes the end of the educational paradigm born in the 19th century and highlights three fundamental trends. Chapter 12 introduces the 21st Century Compass, an educational reference for children and adults. The components of the Compass are discussed in greater detail in the following chapters. Chapter 13 sets out the fundamentals of the Compass, namely the ability to learn, the moral North and foundational knowledge. Chapter 14 explores the Compass's socio-emotional competencies, specifically resilience, empathy and collaboration. Chapter 15 covers cognitive skills, with a focus on critical thinking, creative thinking and interdisciplinary thinking.

The conclusion summarises what parents need to know and do to prepare their children for the era of Artificial Intelligence.

May this book be of help.

Part I

Artificial

Intelligence

Chapter 1. A brutal awakening

"I am confident I will win 5–0"

I t is March 2016, and Lee Sedol, on the eve of his tournament against AlphaGo in a luxury hotel in Seoul, declares his absolute confidence. And why wouldn't he? The world Go community, somewhat amused by the challenge to its champion, shares his certainty. Not a single dissenting voice is heard.

It is true that AlphaGo, a piece of Go game software developed by DeepMind, beat a professional player for the first time nine months earlier. But the victim, Fan Hui, being a European champion, ranks light years behind his Asian counterparts: he is only 2nd dan. Upon his defeat he was even mocked for having "forgotten his Go" at the age of 18, when he left China for France. As for Lee Sedol, 9th dan, he is a true legend well beyond his field: a real national hero in Korea. They call him the Roger Federer of Go. He is an 18-time world champion and has completely dominated his art for about ten years. His popularity and prestige are immense.

Moreover, Go is not chess. Twenty years ago, IBM's Deep Blue succeeded in defeating chess champion Kasparov by *brute force.* It explored up to twenty moves downstream at the frantic rate of 200 million positions evaluated per second. In addition, it had access to a wealth of algorithmic heuristics and libraries of chess-specific moves, meticulously refined by a panel of grand masters. Such a brute-force strategy is not possible with Go. Although this board game, invented in China 2,500 years ago, has very simple rules, the immense difficulty lies in the sheer number of combinations: with a board of 19 rows by 19 columns, there are more possible configurations of stones on the Go board than atoms in the universe. In other words, although anyone can learn to play the game, most people would be confused when having to play the next stone because there are so many choices. When a professional player is asked about his decision to play one move rather than another, he may simply answer that it "just feels right"[1]. He can offer no explanation beyond a mysterious intuition. So much so that Go has become the Holy Grail of Artificial Intelligence research. Solve the mystery of Go and you will have taken a giant step forward in AI[2].This is all it took for DeepMind to decide in 2013 to design AlphaGo, in its longer-term quest for Artificial General Intelligence. Make no mistake: no expert expected any concrete result for at least another decade.

The stage is set in a function room at the Four Seasons Hotel in Seoul, as if a ring had been prepared to host a legendary boxing match. A panel of judges sits on an elevated platform. In front of them, the Go board is placed on a small square table. On one side sits Lee Sedol and on the other side, a lucky DeepMind employee plays the stones as AlphaGo commands are displayed on the side screen. AlphaGo itself is present at the table via a laptop computer that does not look like much; some caught a glimpse of it during the preparations, but it is now hidden by the tablecloth. A few dozen privileged spectators are gathered in the room, including Lee Sedol's family. Elsewhere in the hotel, commentators from all over the world have taken up residence. The game is broadcast live on the Internet. It is displayed on the giant screens of Korea's skyscrapers as well as on the walls of Go clubs around the world: young players are getting ready to scrutinise every move of their idol battling with this strange opponent.

The champion's rout

The first game doesn't start auspiciously for Lee Sedol. AlphaGo does better than resist. As the moves go on, Lee Sedol starts wincing. He's gradually losing some of his self-confidence. On the TV sets to the side, Korean commentators count and recount the points live and stare in disbelief: it seems that AlphaGo has taken the lead. Lee Sedol finally

---

[1] Remarks by Demis Hassabis, founder and CEO of DeepMind, reported in Greg Kohs' film "AlphaGo" (2017) [5].
[2] AI and Artificial Intelligence will be used interchangeably.

concedes victory after 186 moves and nearly three and a half hours of fighting.

Lee Sedol arrives at the post-game press conference in a packed room with cameras flashing all over the place. Yet he sees his defeat as nothing more than a regrettable faux pas. He says he was surprised to lose and blames his defeat on an error at the beginning of the game that he could not overcome until the end. But it's a wake-up call. The next day the world's press makes headlines on the grand master's unexpected defeat against the machine.

At the beginning of the second game, the pressure seems to have increased a notch for Lee Sedol. At the 36th move, he leaves his chair and goes to smoke a cigarette on a private terrace of the hotel. As for AlphaGo, it sees nothing, hears nothing, feels no pressure, doesn't know that Lee Sedol is gone or even who he is; it just plays the 37th move. A few minutes later Lee Sedol comes back and sits down. His face changes all of a sudden, distorted and puzzled, when he sees AlphaGo's move. He even gives something approaching a smile. Undoubtedly, he thinks he is out of trouble. AlphaGo's move is inhuman. No human being would have played it because... it is common knowledge that it should be avoided, at any cost, because the risk incurred is far too high. An immutable rule that humans have applied religiously since the dawn of time, even if they do not really remember why. And yet. As the game continues, Lee Sedol's position deteriorates and the master seems more and more depressed. When he resigns on the 211th move, a veil of sadness covers the Four Seasons and barely masks Lee Sedol's state of shock. "Yesterday I was surprised," he says, "today I am speechless. He later added: "Move 37 was really original and beautiful".

Lee Sedol is given a day off. Four professional players come to comfort him and try to analyse the two lost games with him. Short of ideas, Lee Sedol decides to adopt an unusual style of play for him in the hope of surprising AlphaGo. Unfortunately, the third game proves disastrous. From the fiftieth move, AlphaGo takes a clear lead that can no longer be reduced. The defeat is bitter. The tournament is also lost, because AlphaGo is already 3–0 up. The DeepMind team do not even have the heart to rejoice because Lee Sedol's distress is so apparent. At a press conference, the fallen champion is on the verge of tears. "I must first ask you for forgiveness. I know I've disappointed many of you. I apologise for my helplessness". He seems to carry the suffering of the whole world on his shoulders. The prospect of a 0–5 rout is looming on the horizon.

A symbolic win

On the fourth day, the game starts very badly for Lee Sedol. Observers are shaking with fear. He is cornered, the chronometer scrolls; no one thinks he has much of a chance. After two hours and forty minutes of struggle, Lee Sedol freezes and plunges into a state of intense reflection. Six long minutes go by. The wait seems endless. Suddenly Lee Sedol emerges from his thoughts and pulls a stroke of genius out of his hat. Some commentators even call this 78th move "God's play" because it is so unexpected. AlphaGo also finds the move totally improbable; it struggles to reply. Something looks broken. Is it a bug? The machine seems to be losing its mind. It makes a series of completely absurd moves, provoking general hilarity. The crowd starts to believe in human victory; observers mimic a boxer's gestures in raging support of their reborn champion. Lee Sedol finally wins and says in a whisper: "At least I will have won one game". His victory is greeted by an atmosphere of indescribable jubilation. During the press conference, he is given round after round of applause. "Never have I been so congratulated on a victory," he says. In the streets people run, sing and dance. It seems that the entire human race is celebrating his victory over the machine.

On the fifth day, Lee Sedol loses again despite a much better start. But the atmosphere is more relaxed. The world willingly forgives him. It took up the cause of the human champion who raised his level of play in the fourth game.

The tournament brings about a remarkable rebirth of the game of Go. Champions are led to examine their game in a new light. AlphaGo games are carefully analysed. Like move 37 in the second game, positions that were thought to be proscribed are adopted as new strategies and taught in Go schools. The game evolves under the influence of the machine. Fan Hui, who after his initial defeat joined the DeepMind team, significantly changes his playing philosophy and progresses in the world rankings. Retailers sell out of Go boards. The thousand-year-old game is experiencing a second youth under the effect of Artificial Intelligence.

It is everywhere

With AlphaGo's victory, the media hype around Artificial Intelligence explodes. It is talked about everywhere, seen everywhere. A business research and consulting institute ranks *Machine Learning* at the top of its *Media Hype Cycles*, a report on areas where expectations for technology are most unrealistic, for 2016[3]. The AI Vibrancy Index[4], which is a synthetic measurement of AI-related scientific publications, university enrolment and venture capital funds, doubles in 2016 compared to 2014 and quintuples compared to 2010.

Mischievous commentators recycle Dan Ariely's 2013 tweet: "Artificial Intelligence is like teenage sex: everyone talks about it, nobody really knows how to do it, everyone thinks everyone else is doing it, so everyone claims they are doing it."

So what is Artificial Intelligence? In its most general sense, it is the ability of machines to mimic human intelligence. If we want to avoid a simplistic and somewhat lazy definition that refers to human intelligence, we might agree that Artificial Intelligence refers to machines that can sense their environment, think, learn, and act, in response to what they sense and their programmed objectives[5].

---

[3] Gartner Hype Curve 2016 (https://www.gartner.com/smarterwithgartner/3-trends-appear-in-the-gartner-hype-cycle-for-emerging-technologies-2016/)
[4] AI Index 2018 annual report, p56
(http://cdn.aiindex.org/2018/AI%20Index%202018%20Annual%20Report.pdf) [13].
[5] This is the definition used in the joint report of the World Economic Forum (WEF) and PWC [7].

Artificial Intelligence is very real and is progressing at a rapid pace. Other areas that capture the public's attention, beyond DeepMind, include autonomous cars, which are much talked about with Tesla or Waymo[6].

Elsewhere, advances are visible in medical diagnosis, notably with IBM Watson, or the detection of malignant tumours with a success rate that no longer pales in comparison with the best oncologists. Microsoft announces that its AI exceeds human performance for speech recognition. A team led by Geoff Hinton surpasses humans in visual object recognition[7].

YouTube statistics go berserk with Boston Dynamics' robots. The humanoid Atlas opens doors and goes for a walk in the snow. It later resists the multiple assaults of a man trying to bring it down in a hangar – and after eventually falling, it manages to stand up again without losing its temper.

Artificial Intelligence makes forays into art: DeepBach composes choirs in the style of Bach[8] and Sony's Flow Machine writes songs in the style of the Beatles. Vincent AI paints in the style of Van Gogh. A novel written by an AI passes the first round of a literary competition in Japan – it is aptly named "The Day a Computer Writes a Novel".

There is often a significant gap between the achievements of a research laboratory and their application to everyday life. Weren't the first autonomous cars built in the 1980s[9]? To successfully apply Artificial Intelligence in real-life conditions, it is obviously necessary to have the right infrastructure, engineers, data and algorithms – these finite and precise sequences of operations that should lead to the solution of the problem at hand. Above all, it is necessary to sustainably solve the

---

[6] The increased media coverage of accidents is a little unfair when comparing their statistics with those of human drivers.

[7] These points will be developed in the section on perception.

[8] 50% of an educated audience cannot distinguish the original from the imitation https://qz.com/864199/you-probably-cant-tell-the-difference-between-bach-and-music-written-by-ai-in-his-style/ .

[9] This reminder is made by Rodney Brooks in *Architects of Intelligence* [1]. The car had driven 10 miles on a highway near Munich.

thousand small issues that, in a lab, can be bypassed or treated in an ad hoc manner. None of this is simple. None of this is simple.

But, again, the world realises that the advances of Artificial Intelligence have indeed begun to enter into daily life. Amazon's disconcerting ability to suggest the next book to read or Netflix's ability to predict the movies you'll like? It's Artificial Intelligence. Facebook offering to automatically tag your friends and recognising them more and more often? It's AI again. Smart speakers from Google, Amazon or Apple? That's right, Artificial Intelligence. The suddenly improved quality of Google's machine translation modules? AI again.

Meanwhile, in the corporate world, we see marketers gaining the ability to predict demand for a given product or service with unparalleled accuracy, enabling the optimisation of the entire supply chain. Companies begin to use chatbots to manage customer relations. Administrative back offices become increasingly automated. Stock market traders are replaced by software. Robots take over warehouses and factories. Multiple start-ups focus on very narrow but diverse issues such as sorting ripe fruit and vegetables or extracting relevant content from a legal document. Examples abound.

It is also brought to everyone's attention that old techniques that are now well accepted are also Artificial Intelligence: your email's spam filter, your bank's monitoring system that checks for likely fraudulent transactions, and even the automated recognition of postal codes that appeared in the 1990s.

In this era-defining year of 2016, therefore, AI seems to be everywhere. And we now know that this is only the beginning: 2017 is to be even more intense.

Invincible

One year after defeating Lee Sedol, the DeepMind team takes on the ultimate challenge. They decide to confront AlphaGo with the world number one in the very birthplace of the Go game: China. Ke Jie is 19 years old. He won his first tournament at the age of 5, has been a professional since the age of 10 and got his 9th dan at 17. He has an unparalleled reading of the game and plays fast: nothing can resist him, not even Lee Sedol, whom he knocked down several times. His arrogance is commensurate with his talent: during the match between Lee Sedol and AlphaGo, Ke Jie did not hesitate to say that he would have beaten the machine.

The match is eagerly awaited in China, where it has been actively promoted on social networks. 60 million Chinese watched Lee Sedol's first game against AlphaGo online, and 280 million watched the entire tournament. But a sudden turn of events pours cold water on the expectations of Chinese spectators: two days before the start of the tournament, Chinese television cancels the broadcast. As for Internet retransmission, it is only allowed on YouTube, which is inaccessible in China. The disappointment mirrors the high level of anticipation. The popular interest ends up nowhere near the excitement of the tournament against Lee Sedol.

Why has Chinese censorship manifested itself so radically? First of all, because China is in a delicate situation with Google, DeepMind's parent company since its acquisition in 2014. Google's activity is prohibited in China, and the press conference about the tournament will not mention the name of the American company once. But there is also a deeper reason. In a country where saving face is essential, China wants to avoid the direct and large-scale broadcasting of the likely upcoming humiliation.

Indeed, the situation has changed a lot since Lee Sedol's tournament. At the time the surprise was almost total because no one knew of AlphaGo. But the machine is now out of the box. It is said to have made significant progress since then. In December 2016 and January 2017, a mysterious player using the name Magister and then Master played and won 60 games online against the world's greatest players. Master played fast and without taking a minute's rest. On January 4th DeepMind revealed that Master was none other than AlphaGo Master, the latest avatar of their Artificial Intelligence software. So now Ke Jie, having been himself beaten during the online tournament[10], knows what to expect. Perhaps

---

[10] Ke Jie had been discreetly informed of Master's identity.

the $300,000 guaranteed for his participation alone and the $1.5 million promised in the event of a victory convinced him to take part in the Summit on the Future of Go in May 2017 in Wuzhen.

Ke Jie's preparation is reminiscent of that of a very high-level athlete. He has carefully analysed the Master games and then determined his best chances of winning. His efforts do not go unnoticed and are not entirely in vain: he does not demerit during the first game. At the end of an epic battle lasting more than four hours, he loses by only half a point. Once the match is over, he concedes that AlphaGo now has the status of God among the Go players. Over the next few days he resigns in the last two games and loses the tournament 3–0. Outside China, the world seems almost jaded by the victory of Artificial Intelligence over man.

Yet it is a remarkable performance, even beyond victory. To beat Fan Hui, the European champion, AlphaGo Fan reached an Elo ranking of 3144 but required the considerable power of 40kW[11]. AlphaGo Lee – the version that beat Lee Sedol – rose to an Elo ranking of 3739 with a power consumption four times lower than its predecessor. As for AlphaGo Master, Ke Jie's executioner, it reached an Elo ranking of 4858 with a power consumption about 10 times lower than that of Alpha Go Lee[12]!

Early retirement

At the end of the tournament, DeepMind solemnly announces AlphaGo's retirement from professional tournaments. AlphaGo is just four years old. It no longer has anything to prove and the company wants to focus on real-world problems such as protein folding or energy efficiency. However, AlphaGo's research career does not end there.

The AlphaGo Zero version is released a few months later. Three days into its training, it defeats AlphaGo Lee with a final score of 100 games to nil. After 21 days, it matches AlphaGo Master's level, and exceeds it

---

[11] Thermal Design Power (TDP) *strictly speaking* represents the maximum thermal power that must be dissipated by the processor to avoid overheating. This is an approximation of the power consumed by the processor.
[12] https://deepmind.com/blog/alphago-zero-learning-scratch/

for good at the end of its 40-day training. The nature of the algorithmic changes is even more impressive. AlphaGo Fan, the first version, was initially trained by absorbing 160,000 professional Go games so that it could learn from these masters' play and imitate them. The rest of its learning consisted of games played against itself. AlphaGo Zero, on the other hand, learned to play Go alone, without any knowledge of the field or human intervention other than communicating the rules of the game. Starting from scratch and playing randomly at first, AlphaGo Zero learns by playing millions of games against itself. In doing so, and without any human bias, AlphaGo very quickly rediscovers certain proven human strategies, and uncovers new ones which it often ends up giving preference to. Its ability to do without human interventions, which are necessarily limiting because of their scarcity, their price and their ineffectiveness, is a major step forward.

Some time later, AlphaGo Zero becomes Alpha Zero[13]. The new avatar of the Alpha family now knows how to play chess and shoji[14]. Alpha Zero has extended its range of skills thanks to an even more general algorithm and still without human intervention. The less specific the algorithm, the more significant the progress is in fundamental research in Artificial Intelligence. In barely 4 hours of training, Alpha Zero is introduced to chess... and beats Stockfish, the most powerful chess software in the world, with a score of 28 wins, 72 draws and no defeats[15]. Commenting on the fact that this result was obtained without having benefited – or suffered – from any human interference, or from the priorities nor the prejudices of human computer scientists, Kasparov claims that Alpha Zero's style "reflects the truth"[16].

---

[13] https://deepmind.com/blog/alphago-zero-learning-scratch/
[14] A Japanese chess game more complex than chess as practised by Westerners.
[15] Further research published in Nature a year later, in December 2018, will silence the last critics who had criticised the methodology used previously [48].
[16] Chess, a drosophila of reasoning (Science, vol 362 issue 6419 page 108).

The stung giant

In China, Ke Jie's defeat does not go down well, even though its visibility is considerably limited by censorship.

During the same week, interspersed between its different games against Ke Jie, AlphaGo also beats a team of 5 great Chinese masters. AlphaGo's only partial defeat occurs when playing against... itself. In the confrontation between two hybrid man–machine teams, it unavoidably loses on one side by winning on the other. As for Demis Hassabis, the founder and CEO of DeepMind, sitting at the end of the tournament alongside the defeated local players, one could not help but notice his strikingly small figure and his apparent isolation on the huge stage of the Wuzhen conference room. When he hands a trophy to the eight Chinese champions AlphaGo just crushed, the embarrassment only gets worse. He may call Ke Jie a "great genius" several times, trying by all means to save his face, but no one is fooled. China has just suffered a real insult on its own territory – the very cradle of the game of Go – its champions knocked down by a short man from the West. This harmless Go tournament is bound to play a significant role in the new world order that is about to emerge.

Beyond Go, in fact, China is experiencing its "Sputnik moment". The Soviet satellite's beeping in 1957, confirming that it had beaten the Americans at a key stage of the space race, suddenly made them aware of their delay and was decisive in accelerating their space programme. The same is true for the Chinese and Artificial Intelligence in 2017. Half a century ago they were totally absent from the space race, but now they are making world domination in AI their moon shot.

Until now, Artificial Intelligence has been a predominantly North American story, with the major role being played by the United States, with smaller contributions from peripheral countries such as Canada and the United Kingdom. The domination of the United States is in line with its recent past in the world of technology: major inventions originate there and are then deployed worldwide by its centralised and hegemonic companies. But the stakes, with AI, are much higher – even if, surprisingly, the political authorities in the United States do not seem to appreciate the extent of the upheavals underway. In contrast, Russian President Vladimir Putin clearly states that the dominant AI power will rule the world[17]. Appetites are whetted and nations are positioning themselves for the coming competition.

Towards a new world order

In July 2017, it is China's turn to announce its *Artificial Intelligence Plan*[18]. If Ke Jie's defeat was China's Sputnik moment, claims Kai-Fu Lee[19], the Artificial Intelligence Plan is the equivalent of John F. Kennedy's speech, relaunching the race to the moon by galvanizing the teams and announcing the considerable resources involved. The Chinese plan is of unparalleled ambition and scope. China aims to be the world leader in AI innovation by 2030 and to increase the value of the domestic AI industry to $150 billion. This is not just wishful thinking. Funding, industrial policies and coordination measures are on the agenda. A timeline details the objectives to be achieved every 5 years from 2020 onwards: planning is not to be taken lightly. By 2020 China is expected to be among the leading AI economies; by 2025 it must have made several significant breakthroughs. The outcome in 2030 aims to secure China's supremacy in the field and "establish the fundamentals of a formidable economic power". National security considerations are mentioned discreetly, but it is easy to guess their real importance.

China, with its strong state leadership and drive, its considerable financial resources, its abundant data and little consideration for privacy, is equipping itself with the means to achieve its ambitions. Based on the

---

[17] https://nypost.com/2017/09/01/putin-leader-in-artificial-intelligence-will-rule-the-world/
[18] https://flia.org/wp-content/uploads/2017/07/A-New-Generation-of-Artificial-Intelligence-Development-Plan-1.pdf
[20] Kai-Fu Lee, or Lee Kai-Fu in Chinese, is a Chinese AI investor who used to be responsible for Google in China and previously for Microsoft Research Asia. He is also the author of *AI Superpowers*. He narrates with unparalleled talent the irresistible rise of the Chinese Internet and predicts the future of AI in China and around the world. Several elements of this paragraph are largely inspired by Kai-Fu Lee's book.

history of Chinese state interventions including the Internet, they should have a huge net impact even if significant resources are wasted along the way – which is considered inevitable and accepted. China is also aware that it benefits from two major assets stemming from its triumphant Internet era: its data, collected in huge quantities by all O2O companies[20], and its entrepreneurs, true gladiators of modern times[21].

Some observers, including Kai-Fu Lee, believe that Artificial Intelligence has moved from the age of discovery to the age of implementation, and from the age of expertise to the age of data[22]. According to this analysis, the advances in AI to date – mainly in the West and more precisely in the English-speaking world – are already sufficient for huge companies to emerge. Indeed, AI makes use of a positive feedback loop: the more customers there are, the more data accumulates, the better the products become, and the more customers there are. It is a virtuous circle.

This is good news for China. Whereas fundamental research and radical innovation are still considered a structural weakness of the country, Chinese entrepreneurs excel in their ability to deploy their applications on a very large scale. Kai-Fu Lee adds: "The core motivation for China's market-driven entrepreneurs is not fame, glory, or changing the world. Those things are all nice side benefits, but the grand prize is getting rich, and it doesn't matter how you get there". [23] In China, the end always justifies the means in this implementation of the Internet and even more so of Artificial Intelligence.

---

[20] Online to Offline, for example when an internet application is used to order real meals delivered to your home.
[21] Kai-Fu Lee, who benefits from his dual personal and professional experience, admirably describes the fundamental cultural difference between the West and China [12].
[22] Not all experts agree, citing Alpha Zero as a counterexample.
[23] This is another statement by Kai-Fu Lee, which pits American companies guided by their mission against Chinese companies guided by market and profit [12].

In comes a new, almost bipolar world where the United States dominates AI research [24] and China its implementation. Europe, hampered by its size, fragmentation and ethical concerns to its credit[25], will undoubtedly progress at a significantly slower pace. "In the race for supremacy in Artificial Intelligence," Kai-Fu Lee hammers home, conference after conference[26], "China and the United States will take the top two spots – and there is no bronze medal".

Thus, a few games of a thousand-year-old board game played in 2016 and 2017 helped signal to the general public the emergence of Artificial Intelligence. At the geopolitical level, they ushered in a new world order. On a more down-to-earth level, Go players are at risk – and they're certainly not the only ones. What exactly is this Artificial Intelligence that causes such upheavals? What can it really do, and what can't it do?

---

[24] But this research is often published in open source; the whole world can benefit from it.

[25] See more on AI ethics Chapter 5.

[26] In particular in Singapore on 21 and 22 November 2018.

Chapter 2. A few lines of code, processors and data

The intelligence of a two-year-old child

What is the actual intelligence of Artificial Intelligence? You cannot expect a better answer than by asking the pioneers of Deep Learning. Why should we turn to Deep Learning? Because it's the branch of Artificial Intelligence that has enabled the most significant advances and most meaningful applications in the last five or ten years. Upon hearing the question asked, Yoshua Bengio answers: "Artificial Intelligence is less intelligent than a two-year-old child." A two-year-old child?

Yes, AI is less intelligent than a two-year-old child. It lacks general understanding of the world around it. It does not have a baby's amazing learning talent, nor does it have their extraordinary innate abilities in physics, psychology, numeracy and arithmetic or linguistics. We will discuss this later[27], but to give you a taster: AI is unable to intuitively learn the concepts that every child quickly perceives in their daily life without needing an explanation, such as gravity. If an object is dropped, it falls down – and the lesson is quickly learned. Our baby also manages to demonstrate abstraction and generalise their learning!

To make matters worse, Yann LeCun adds to Yoshua Bengio's answer: "Artificial Intelligence has less common sense than a rat." A rat?

You will be forgiven if, like many others, you find it difficult to reconcile these two seemingly conflicting aspects: on the one hand, Artificial Intelligence beats the best Go player in the world and will never be matched again; on the other hand, it is less intelligent than an infant. It is essentially a matter of perspective: Artificial Intelligence, at its current level of advancement, excels in certain well-defined and highly

---

[27] See the section on Learning, Chapter 3.

specialised tasks; on the other hand, it struggles in many of the tasks that are straightforward for humans. "Difficult problems are easy and easy problems are difficult,"[28]Steven Pinker said 25 years ago[29]. The capabilities of AI are deep but narrow, i.e. confined to the precise purpose for which they were developed, unlike human intelligence, which is generalist. Finally, at the risk of demystifying Artificial Intelligence, there is nothing magical about it: it is just advanced statistics, long series of calculations that are relatively straightforward. To help convince you of the nature of Artificial Intelligence, let's take a classic example, here simplified to the extreme. For a few minutes – no more, and you can even skip the next section if you don't like it – we will follow the path of one of the most used algorithms in Artificial Intelligence.

Recognising George

Let's say you want to create an AI that recognises George Washington's face. His face can be displayed in many ways, from many angles, with many kinds of lighting, at different ages and with different facial expressions: not easy to recognise! You will have to *train* your AI based on a large number of examples.

So you need to gather as many different portraits of George as possible, but also of other people. The larger and more diverse your sample, the better. With each portrait you specify on a label attached to it whether "it is George" or "it is not George".

You have structured a *neural network* for your AI, represented below in Figure 1. Neurons are virtual locations where you will compute and store data. Neurons are grouped into vertical layers. The first vertical layer is on the left, and the layers that dive deeper into the network are further to the right. Each neuron in a given layer is connected to all the neurons

---

[28] Steven Pinker, *The Language Instinct*, 1994. However, it is very interesting to note that the problems that are easy for humans and difficult for AI are no longer the same as in 1994. Pinker mentioned facial recognition, which is largely solved today.
[29] Pinker's observations are similar to Moravec's paradox.

in the previous layer, and each of the connections between two neurons is provided with an individual parameter called a *weight* (the weights are not displayed on the figure below).

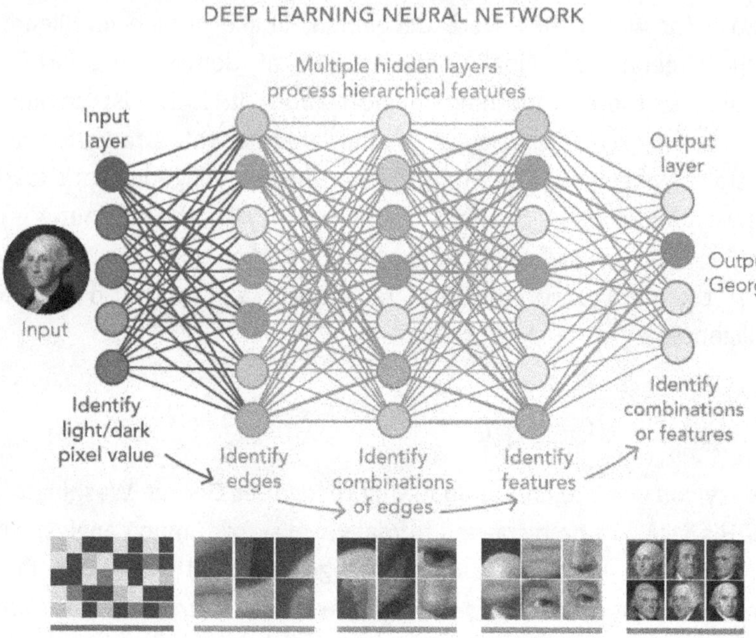

DEEP LEARNING NEURAL NETWORK

Figure 1 Recognising George Washington's face (credit: PNAS / Lucy Reading Ikkanda)
(note: network weights are not represented)

Now let's train the network! We start by using the first portrait. The first layer of our network is filled with all the information describing the first portrait, the numerical value of each pixel being stored in a separate neuron. For each neuron in the second layer, the algorithm computes the weighted average of the values of the neurons in the first layer, using the weights (or parameters) of the connections. A special *non-linear function* is then applied to the weighted average.

The algorithm repeats the process by going one step further into the network. For each neuron in the third layer, the algorithm computes the weighted average of the values of the neurons in the second layer, using the weights of the connections, then applies the special function to the weighted average.

By repeating the process from layer to layer, the neurons gradually fill up with their values. The number of neurons per layer varies. The output layer signals that "it's George" or "it's not George".

The process is repeated as many times as there are portraits in the training set.

The AI then examines all the conclusions of the algorithm on all the portraits in the training set and compares them to the true values you have given it on the labels. It takes stock that sometimes its conclusion is correct (i.e. a true positive if the algorithm correctly predicted that it was George, or a true negative if it correctly predicted that it was not George), and sometimes it is wrong. If there are too many false positives (predicting it's George when it's not) or false negatives (predicting that it's not George when it is), which is inevitable at the beginning, the reason is that the weights or parameters of the network are not correct. The AI then applies another algorithm by travelling the network in the opposite direction to modify all weights one by one. This is called *backpropagation*, which aims to gradually minimise the forecasting error by adjusting the parameters.

This systematic and lengthy process will be repeated until the conclusions of the Artificial Intelligence are *sufficiently* accurate for all the portraits in the training set. The last step is a final validation of the network and weights using a new batch of portraits, known as the validation batch. You give the AI a new set of portraits it hasn't seen before, and test whether it can correctly classify most of them using the system of weights it developed from the training set. Once this step is successfully completed, your AI is ready. You can then submit any entirely new portrait to your AI, which will be able to determine with acceptable accuracy whether it is George or not. Voilà!

What do the network weights mean? Their function is difficult to understand at first sight. In fact, they allow the algorithm to search and identify, layer by layer, what makes George's face George's face. At each layer of the network, the weights allow increasingly precise facial characteristics to be recognised: first the pixels are analysed individually, then they are used to identify the contours of the face, then the features, then the combinations of features, until George is recognised!

In summary, for each image of the training set, the algorithm travels the entire network from input to output layer by calculating neural values one by one and in a relatively simple way. Then, comparing all the calculated predictions with the expected values, the algorithm travels back through the network in the opposite direction to adjust all the weights or parameters... until the model is sufficiently accurate. By the end of the training, the network is correctly configured to make forecasts with a reasonable level of accuracy.

Supervised Learning by a deep neural network

Without being fully aware of it, you have just trained your first neural network through Supervised Learning. Whether you followed all the details of the algorithm or not does not matter. All you need is to be convinced that the process is systematic, a little tedious, long but ultimately not very complex.

Why are we talking about **learning**? Because as the number of portraits used for training increases, the performance of the algorithm increases. The algorithm thus refines its model by comparing it with an increasing number of real cases. The algorithm is also said to learn in that at each backpropagation iteration, the weights are adjusted automatically and the performance of the model increases. The weights are the first signal that the system is learning, although they are sometimes difficult to interpret. The system has indeed *learned* to compute the right weights.

The learning mode is said to be **supervised** because the series of portraits shown to the algorithm are labelled: it is specified whether a portrait is or isn't George. The algorithm is called a **neural network** because it mimics, to some extent, the functioning of neurons in the brain. Each biological neuron receives electrical impulses from up to 10,000 connected neurons upstream. The electrical signals are transmitted in a more or less amplified fashion at synapse level (the equivalent of our artificial weights). After processing in the cell body of the biological neuron in an equivalent way to the artificial special function, the biological neuron may or may not fire, i.e. it sends or doesn't send an electrical signal in turn down its axon to the neurons downstream. Finally, learning is said to be **deep** simply because there are many layers, including the input layer, the output layer, and the middle layers, which are called hidden layers.

The above description is obviously a little simplified for the purpose of the demonstration, but it is almost the same algorithm that was used in Optical Character Recognition in the 1990s, for example to read postal codes. Similar principles are used for Facebook to automatically tag your friends, DeepL to translate your text from French to English and AlphaGo to beat the world champion. Note that Facebook can't play Go, AlphaGo can't translate from one language to another and DeepL can't tag your friends, but everyone excels in their own field.

Where is the supernatural, the magic, the human touch or even the soul? There is no such thing. The only depth is that of the artificial neural network, i.e. the rows of the table. Artificial intelligence today simply consists of a few lines of code, processors and data.

A few lines of code

Deep Learning is simply computations: they are statistical, deterministic and cold. The real beauty of neural networks, which can sometimes prove to be a substantial disadvantage[30], is that the algorithm is not given explicit instructions as to what it must discover from layer to layer in the neural system; it learns it on its own, gradually adjusting all the weights.

But these remain lines of code, usually surprisingly few and relatively simple. Certainly, there have been many algorithmic improvements since Rosenblatt invented the perceptron in 1957. This ancestor of neural networks had only one layer of neurons. Backpropagation, which was developed in 1986, opened up new opportunities by automating the settings of networks. Then specialised networks were invented: Convolutional Neural Networks (CNNs) to recognise images, Recurrent Neural Networks (RNNs) to properly manage temporal sequences and

---

[30] We will see this in Chapter 4.

process natural language, and finally Generative Adversarial Networks (GANs) to create new data: images, pieces of music, or texts.

The depth of the networks gradually increased. From a single layer for the perceptron, the size stabilised at a few layers for decades, then rose to 7 in the early 2010s[31], which drastically improved the performance of image recognition. The trend was set, and the number of layers soared in the following years. In 2015 in China, Microsoft Research invented a network[32] that included no less than 152 layers! In 2017, a Google Brain team led by Geoff Hinton[33] designed a giant neural network[34] in which each neuron was itself a neural subnetwork. This type of "exorbitantly large" network can have thousands of sub-networks and more than 100 billion parameters[35], achieving the best results to date in Natural Language Processing with lower energy consumption.

However, algorithmic improvements would be to no avail and the race to greater depth would be impossible without the progress of critical hardware: processors.

The exponential performance of processors

When Gordon Moore, co-founder and CEO of Intel, formulated the law that bears his name in 1965, he only thought it would hold true for about ten years. What does Moore's law state? That the density of transistors on a printed circuit board doubles approximately every two years[36]. The practical consequence is that the computing power available on a processor doubles approximately every two years, at a relatively constant price.

---

[31] AlexNet.

[32] ResNet.

[33] Geoff Hinton is also associated with the invention of the backward propagation algorithm and AlexNet, designed by one of his students whose work he initially did not believe in.

[34] Mixture of Experts Layer.

[35] https://arxiv.org/abs/1701.06538

[36] The period was initially 1 year and was extended to 2 years in 1975.

The law eventually held for nearly half a century. While the Intel 4004 processor launched in 1971 had 2,300 transistors, its distant successor, the Graphcore GC2 IPU released in 2017, had more than 23 billion… or a multiplication by about a hundred thousand in less than five decades. Anyone can have in their pocket, today, a gadget vastly more powerful than the *ultimate* gadget of a few decades ago. While the on-board computer of Apollo 9, capable in 1969 of taking people to the moon, had a clock frequency of 2MHz, that of an iPhone is 1,000 times higher!

This impressive computing power is a major driver of the explosion of Deep Learning from the 2010s onwards. The algorithms of Deep Learning are indeed very computationally intensive, with their millions of neurons and parameters, and the millions of examples necessary for their learning.

Moore's law will not be valid indefinitely because we are approaching the physical limits – at the atomic level – of densification. The slowdown has already been observed for several years, and informed observers predict its end around 2025. This is not very serious, as the industry has already begun a shift to application-specific processors, particularly Artificial Intelligence processors, rather than continuing the race for miniaturisation. For Artificial Intelligence, traditional processors (CPUs[37]) are no longer the preferred choice.

Deep Learning calculations, based on linear algebra, abound with vector and matrix calculations, and can be carried out in a massively parallel way. By a fortunate coincidence, Graphical Processing Units (GPUs) respond perfectly to this type of demand. In 2009, the Google Brain team realised that using GPUs instead of CPUs could accelerate deep learning calculations by a factor of 100. This is why NVIDIA, the leading manufacturer of processors for video games, saw rapid growth in the Artificial Intelligence market.

But processors alone are not enough.

---

[37] Central Processing Unit.

It's raining data

It constitutes the third pillar of AI after algorithms and processors: the data. "Data is the new oil", many Artificial Intelligence strategists claim. At this stage, some – but not all – researchers maintain that an increase in the amount of data is more effective than an algorithmic improvement[38].

Why do we need data? Because the majority of learning algorithms learn either in a supervised way (where they must be shown large numbers of examples) or in an unsupervised way (where the algorithm uses the mass of data and extracts meaning itself). Only Reinforcement Learning, the kind used by Alpha Zero, can do without prior data.

To train algorithms for computer vision, you need huge image libraries. ImageNet, with its 14 million images, is a good example. In order for Netflix or Amazon to be able to offer you the next film you are likely to enjoy, these companies must first collect film data to build a film typology, as well as data about you to find out what kind of audience you are. In order for a medical monitoring system to be able to report an outbreak as soon as possible, it must have collected a large amount of data relating to previous epidemics, and the algorithm will learn to detect early warning signs even if they are not those usually used by the best epidemiologists. To be able to perform predictive maintenance on a system, the algorithm will need a mass of data corresponding to the proper functioning of the system and all the stages of the transition leading to a malfunction, to extract the warning signs completely invisible even to the system operators.

All this data has piled up over the past decade. It is generated not only by all digital human activity but also by the billions of sensors that automatically digitise the world: from the ten or so in your smartphone to electrical, acoustic, hydraulic, chemical, thermal, mechanical,

---

[38] This is Kai-Fu Lee's central argument. It can be found in many research articles, including http://svail.github.io/mandarin/ . Other experts like Andrew Ng believe that the importance of data is exaggerated, and that algorithms, computing power and talent still have a bright future ahead of them.

cinematic, optical and many others located in residential or professional buildings, industrial and agricultural installations, data centres, infrastructure and smart cities.

An independent research organisation revealed in 2013 that 90% of all data ever generated in the world had been generated in the previous two years[39]. Other institutes predict that by 2020, an average of 1.7 MB of data will be generated per second per person on Earth[40]! The exact figures do not matter; the trend is significant and is probably accelerating due to human activity online and especially the IoT, or Internet of Things.

The current algorithms used in conjunction with high-powered processors and abundant data unfortunately have a major disadvantage: energy consumption.

Energy-intensive operation

A human brain typically consumes about twenty watts of power. This is the case for you and me as well as for Fan Hui, our European Go champion. As he was being beaten by AlphaGo, he probably didn't fully realise that he was facing an arsenal of 1202 CPUs and 176 GPUs, powerful processors that consumed a total of about 40,000 watts – that is to say, 2,000 times more than his own brain! Few noticed at the time that the fight was not energetically fair. Over the versions, AlphaGo's energy performance has improved considerably, but the version that beat Ke Jie still consumed about 50 times more than the defeated champion's brain.

The race is on to significantly reduce the energy consumption of Artificial Intelligence during training and operation, by improving algorithms and also processors. In February 2018, an MIT team

---

[39] https://www.sciencedaily.com/releases/2013/05/130522085217.htm
[40] https://www.domo.com/learn/data-never-sleeps-6

announced that it had developed a new chip that uses up to 95% less energy than current standards[41].

The challenge of better energy performance, in addition to reducing the increasing economic and environmental cost of calculations, is to be able to operate Artificial Intelligence as close as possible to its point of use[42], once its training is completed. An autonomous car, for example, cannot afford to query a remote data centre to make real-time decisions: what would happen if the connection was disrupted or even unavailable for one reason or another? The same objective is why AI should be embedded in mobile phones, to avoid suffering from an absent or insufficiently efficient network.

A wide range of techniques

Supervised Learning by neural networks, the kind of learning we resorted to for recognising George, is the most widespread and spectacular training mode. Although it has eclipsed the others, it is far from being the only one.

Learning can be neural without necessarily being supervised. This is the case, for example, with so-called **unsupervised systems,** where the machine receives a lot of data, but not labelled. This technique made headlines in 2012 when a Google team submitted ten million videos on YouTube to an Artificial Intelligence. What did it find there? What people put in their videos, namely a lot of cats and dogs. At no point did the researchers explain to the AI what a cat or a dog was. But the Artificial Intelligence, with its algorithms and 16,000 processors, reconstructed the concept of a cat, or at least its appearance, by itself thanks to the sheer number of times it saw cats. Another use case of unsupervised learning is dimensionality reduction. The machine learns by itself to represent data in a much more economical way, by restricting itself to the information that is really significant, and by

---

[41] http://news.mit.edu/2018/chip-neural-networks-battery-powered-devices-0214

[42] This is the principle of *edge computing*.

ignoring all noise or unnecessary information. This is the technique used, for example, in image compression.

A third category of learning that is not supervised, in terms of data use, is **Reinforcement Learning.** We've already been introduced to it with AlphaGo. In this case, the machine generates its own data by repeated exploration and experimentation. Each of these experiences leads to a reward that is given or not depending on the machine's success in achieving the objective assigned. The rewards signal whether the machine is on the right track. The more AlphaGo wins, the more it knows that the strategy used is appropriate. And this strategy is discovered independently of any human influence.

Because all variants of neural networks are based on connection models between artificial neurons, this general category of Artificial Intelligence is called **Connectionism.** Connectionism consists in practice of projecting data onto different levels of representation and abstraction to link initial data to a prediction. The different levels are the layers of our network, whose elementary units are the neurons connected to each other. Connectionism, as explained earlier, excels at detecting patterns in data to make a prediction; this makes it an extremely powerful tool for these use cases, but invites us to put its level of intelligence into perspective. Making this type of predictions is not being "intelligent". Nor does connectionism have the capacity for magical insights. It is simply an extremely powerful tool for detecting correlations and making inferences based on data collected or generated.

Connectionism is in its prime today, but this has not always been the case. Implemented in the most elementary way at the end of the 1950s with a single layer of neurons, connectionism was almost buried a few years later by a publication stating that the technique was doomed to failure. Connectionism then went through a long period of hibernation. It was only in the late 1980s, under the leadership of the trio of Geoff Hinton, Yoshua Bengio and Yann LeCun, that it regained strength, invigorated by the algorithmic progress of network training. It survived a second hibernation period in the late 1990s, regained stamina with processor improvements and abundant data, and finally achieved recognition with AlexNet's performance at image recognition in 2012[43]. It took a few more years before Hinton, Bengio and LeCun reached the pinnacle of success: in 2019 the "godfathers of Deep Learning" were jointly awarded the Turing Prize, often considered to be the equivalent of the Nobel Prize for computer science.

Taking advantage of the initial setbacks of connectionism, another form of Artificial Intelligence developed in competition with Machine Learning. This initial form, called **symbolic Artificial Intelligence** or **symbolism,** later inherited the affectionate nickname of "good old-fashioned AI" (GOFAI). Like a human, the machine starts from hypotheses and rules and makes logical deductions. It does not learn anything; it has to be told everything. Tell the machine, for instance, that Socrates is a man and that men are mortal; it will conclude for you that Socrates is mortal. It is therefore based on rules engines and gives rise to the expert systems and heuristics of the 1980s. We also owe to symbolic Artificial Intelligence all the algorithms of robotics. Boston Dynamics' robots[44], for example, rely heavily on symbolic intelligence. Although less popular today, symbolism nevertheless has its own advantages. It is completely transparent, explainable, and easy to interpret – unlike connectionism. On the other hand, it is difficult to train because all scenarios must be anticipated, which in practice is often impossible.

Besides Connectionism, other categories of Machine Learning exist[45] which are non-neural. In the category of **analogisers**[46] are the proven clustering techniques. Here, Artificial Intelligence is asked to classify individuals in a population into groups containing the most similar individuals, without specifying the ways in which they should be similar. It is the machine that discovers the similarities. These techniques

---

[43] We will describe learning in more details.

[44] See the section on motor skills.

[45] The five families mentioned in this section are the "tribes" identified and named by Pedro Domingos [33].

[46] Analogisers [33].

generate, among other things, the recommender systems used by product or service providers such as Amazon.

The **evolutionary**[47] class is inspired by evolutionary models of life and applies them to the algorithms themselves. From generation to generation, genetic algorithms undergo mutations, crossovers, and selection by performance – only the fittest are retained, and all the others are dropped.

Bayesian algorithms are based on probabilistic models. Observing certain variables allows them to make reasonable assumptions about the rest of the system. They are promising in terms of Machine Learning models that maintain cause-and-effect relationships and are explainable. They are therefore effective where connectionism is weak! This algorithmic model may best reflect how the human brain learns, including drawing conclusions and adjusting its internal model based on a very small amount of data. One of the pundits of Bayesian algorithmics, Judea Pearl, was awarded the Turing Prize in 2011.

There is therefore a whole range of Artificial Intelligence techniques available, dominated by connectionism today and by symbolism historically. Each of these techniques has its own characteristics, which in turn have a profound influence on the strengths and weaknesses of Artificial Intelligence to date. Today's dominant techniques have several potential successors … or maybe potential allies.

The long road to Artificial General Intelligence

The first phase of Artificial Intelligence was symbolic; the second phase statistical and essentially connectionist; what does the future have in store for us now? It is surprising to see how the 23 architects of intelligence interviewed by Martin Ford[48] – the experts among the experts, those who design the systems and observe them closely – agree on little, if anything.

---

[47] Evolutionary [33].
[48] Martin Ford has published an exciting book of interviews with 23 experts, most of them technical and some in human sciences and philosophy [1].

Indeed, the limitations of the current systems are acknowledged by most. Training symbolic AIs is a never-ending task. Resorting to connectionist systems is extremely energy-consuming, literally and figuratively speaking. The amount of data required for Supervised Learning is massive. Reinforcement Learning requires a number of iterations that may be acceptable in the laboratory but is unreasonable for generalisation to real life. Artificial Intelligence remains very narrow and must learn to generalise more than it does today.

Will we move forward with neural algorithms? Some think so, with the likely addition of a pinch of specialised structure, as was done to make convolutional networks suitable for object recognition. The brain, after all, is purely neural[49], so neural networks must also be able to generate very advanced intelligence, provided that all the sophistication of the human brain is embedded in them[50]. Some point out that connectionist Artificial Intelligence always starts from a blank slate, while humans don't. Their genes carry 4 billion years of biological evolution and humans are born with very sophisticated learning structures. Others believe that a hybrid system is needed, bringing together a set of techniques, each of which excels in a particular class of problems. Multiple examples of hybrid systems already exist; even AlphaGo, strictly speaking, combines connectionism with the classic techniques of tree search algorithms[51]. Others still are looking for the master algorithm[52], the one that will unify the different algorithmic classes just as we are trying to unify the fundamental forces of physics. A final group hopes that research will lead us to a class of algorithms that we can't even imagine today.

Processors will evolve in parallel and become faster, more energy efficient. Neuromorphic computers will stop using traditional

---

[49] What seems obvious to the scientific community today was nevertheless much disputed for centuries.
[50] Today, although artificial neural networks have the same name as their biological counterparts, they are much simpler and more uniform. See a brief comparison and article [15].
[51] Typically Monte-Carlo methods
[52] This is Pedro Domingos' quest [33].

processors and switch to nano-neurons, which, like biological neurons, process information and store it in memory. There will be alignment between a neural substrate and neural algorithms.

Significant differences begin to emerge when the conversation shifts to the ultimate objective of AI. What is the ultimate objective? It is Artificial General Intelligence – an intelligence as efficient and versatile as that of human beings, contextualised, nuanced and multidimensional – in other words, the Holy Grail of Artificial Intelligence.

To put it bluntly, there is no identified technological path today that would allow us to achieve this. But it is widely acknowledged that it is not by adding computing power and training data that we will get significantly closer to the objective. The challenges to be solved are multiple and will require several major innovations, each on the same scale as connectionism in recent decades.

The biggest challenge to be solved is undoubtedly to enable AI to learn like a baby, by observing the world and experiencing it physically. It would then be equipped with a model of the world and common sense, which it would have acquired through Unsupervised Learning or self-learning[53], much as humans do. Contemporary AI totally lacks this capacity. Another challenge is the understanding of abstract, high-level concepts that can be transferred to different application areas. Also in the list are explicability, causality, and resistance to adversarial attacks[54]. And once all these challenges are resolved, others will inevitably arise.

When will Artificial General Intelligence become a reality? The vast majority of scientists are reluctant to give a date, because history has witnessed some memorable failures in predictions. At the inaugural conference in Dartmouth in 1956, often considered as the formal beginning of Artificial Intelligence, participants hoped to solve the

---

[53] Yann LeCun prefers this term to unsupervised learning, which he considers too connoted.

[54] Adversarial attacks aim to deceive artificial intelligence. The connectionist AI can be completely disoriented by minute changes – sometimes imperceptible to the naked eye. An elephant can be mistaken for a chair and a dog for an ostrich.

problem of Natural Language Processing, amongst a few other minor challenges, within two months and with a team of ten people! This has since encouraged humility. On the other hand, Stuart Russell likes to recall how on September 12, 1933, Rutherford declared that the energy of atoms could never be exploited for practical purposes, and how the next day Szilard conceived the idea of chain reaction. The rest is history. Finally, the serendipity that sometimes leads to major innovations[55] further complicates prediction — the date of such progress cannot be anticipated.

In any case, the average date that Martin Ford's [56] architects of intelligence predict for the development of Artificial General Intelligence is 2099, 80 years from now; the median prediction is 2084, 65 years from now. Two major but atypical figures in AI are considerably different from the average: Ray Kurzweil, the promoter of exponential thinking, puts forward the date of 2029, whereas Rodney Brooks, the pioneer of robotics, wishes to highlight his estimate of 2200. Apart from these extremes, the forecasts point on average to a later date than most other surveys. These other surveys, conducted with AI professionals who are not always algorithm specialists, generally lead to a date between 2040 and 2050. However, even 2099 remains within the lives of children born today. And if we take a step back, it is amazing that the vast majority of experts agree on the reality of Artificial General Intelligence within just a few decades. A few decades is tomorrow morning on a geological and biological scale, after more than three and a half billion years of life on Earth, a few million years of the *Homo* genus and three hundred thousand years of *Homo sapiens*. And it will be a fundamental change.

What will happen when Artificial General Intelligence emerges? Here, too, opinions differ. One school of thought speaks of recursive self-improvement: each version of AI designs an even more advanced Artificial Intelligence. "The first ultra-intelligent machine is the last invention that man need ever make," I.J. Good said as early as 1965.

---

[55] Radical innovation is partly stochastic, i.e. it involves a degree of chance.
[56] Strictly speaking, this is the date on which each respondent estimates that there is a 50% chance that the general AI has been developed.

Very quickly, AI becomes superhuman. It reaches Singularity [57], a discontinuity from which its increase in performance is exponential. Others believe that the process will be more gradual. Jacques Attali does not believe in it at all and replies that the only singularity is that of our short stint on Earth[58].

The post-Singularity period is also a source of intense debate. Some people highlight an existential threat and warn about the end of humankind. Transhumanists, on the other hand, are delighted by the prospect of finally being able to free themselves from their flesh-suits and upload themselves into more robust receptacles. The most intellectually honest among futurists are content to devise possible scenarios, as Max Tegmark does[59]. Depending on the scenario, Artificial Intelligence becomes either discreet or omnipresent, either protective or destructive, either emancipatory or enslaving. Human beings have very different fates: they either thrive, barely survive, or are simply wiped out.

But this is only speculation. Indeed, the long-term stakes are so high that we must begin to prepare for the era of Artificial General Intelligence before we really need it. But it is even more important to look to the immediate years and decades ahead. To do this, a good way to start is to analyse exactly what AI can and cannot do and how, at the current technological level, it compares to human beings.

_____

[57] Term coined by Kurzweil.
[58] Audio interview by Thomas Jestin in November 2018.
[59] See Life 3.0 [2].

Chapter 3. How do we compare?

In their great humility, modern humans called themselves *Homo sapiens,* and even *Homo sapiens sapiens*, when it became necessary to differentiate themselves from their extinct cousins[60]. *Homo sapiens* – that is, the *discerning, wise, judicious* human being, as a Latin–English dictionary[61] informs us. *Homo sapiens sapiens*, with the repetition for emphasis – that is to say, the beings whose brains propelled them to the very top of the pyramid of evolution. At least, one could add today, as far as *living organisms* are concerned.

Since Artificial Intelligence, in the broadest sense of the term, is the ability of machines to mimic human intelligence; since, in a definition independent of any reference to human intelligence, Artificial Intelligence refers to machines that can sense their environment, think, learn, and act, in response to what they sense and their programmed objectives; since the trajectories of the human and the machine are bound to cross more and more frequently, perhaps *Homo sapiens sapiens* would benefit from a precise study comparing the artificial and the human. How does Artificial Intelligence today compare to the various main human mental processes? The processes that are of interest to us are cognitive (memory, attention, perception, learning, reasoning, creativity, language), non-cognitive (emotions, willpower), and even motor skills, in order to get a full picture by enlarging the concept a bit[62]. The point here is not to debate endlessly about concepts that humans sometimes struggle to define or to decipher the deep biological mechanisms of the human mind, many of which remain

---

[60] The term *Homo sapiens sapiens* is *strictly speaking* no longer used since *Homo sapiens* is considered as a species distinct from Neanderthal Man, Florès Man and the few other species that were once in competition.
[61] https://en.wiktionary.org/wiki/sapiens
[62] These features are neither completely exhaustive nor necessarily structured in a classical way, but they will be the most relevant in our comparison between the capacities of man and machine.

poorly understood, but to draw pragmatic comparisons of some of the outcomes and external manifestations. The result of this comparison will be decisive for working out which tasks will remain the privilege of humans in the era of Artificial Intelligence[63].

Memory

A 1-terabyte SSD consumer memory card can be purchased on any e-commerce site for less than a hundred dollars. This allows you to store one million photos at 1MB each or one million 400-page books. It's clearly defined… and it's a lot! This memory is addressable: you just need to indicate a precise address to retrieve its content without any loss or alteration of information.

On the other hand, human memory has a low capacity – at least the memory we know how to use[64]. Still, storage space is not the biggest problem. Human memories have no precise address that can be used; they can only be reached by clues or associations. Memories tend to fade involuntarily and take a confusing turn. It often becomes impossible to distinguish what we really remember from the memories that we have been told or that have been suggested to us. Human memory is so deficient that its use in legal testimony, even in good faith, poses enormous problems.

In the end, humans have so little confidence in their biological memory that they have almost entirely outsourced its function to their computers and mobile phones. A 10-digit phone number to remember?

---

[63] This is the whole purpose of Part Two – Work.

[64] The few researchers who venture to calculate the capacity of human memory are working on sophisticated calculations based on the 100 billion neurons in the brain and the 1,000 connections that each neuron makes on average. But no convincing results were found.

Let me record it on my cell phone. An email address displayed in a presentation at a conference? Out come all the phones to take a picture. An appointment, a fact or a remark to remember? Quick, get your phones. The comparison is even more unbalanced when considering the convenience of replacing a memory card or an external hard drive, or combining 100 of them. It is more complicated (for the time being) to change brains or to add extra memory inside our brain than to resort to external memory.

Attention

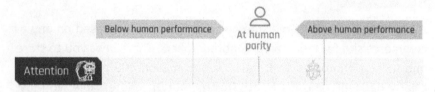

Not enough attention is paid to it, but attention, precisely, is an essential component of several other cognitive processes. When it focuses on a particular signal, the spotlight it casts on it greatly increases the brain's ability to process that signal and integrate it into learning. Conversely, without sufficiently focused attention, there can be no proper perception, let alone processing of a signal. Yet human beings are easily distracted and sometimes lose their focus.

There is another side to the coin of attention. When it is actually focused, the brain becomes completely oblivious to anything outside of the matter under focus. Show an unsuspecting observer the video prepared by Chabris and Simons of a (slightly contrived) basketball game and tell them to count the number of passes made by players wearing a white top. They will almost always fail to see that a playful gorilla has not so subtly walked across the court[65]. This is an illustration of the selectivity of attention: human beings cannot pay attention to too many competing sensory inputs, such as different auditory messages in each

---

[65] The 1999 Chabris and Simons test is described in detail at
http://www.theinvisiblegorilla.com/

of their two ears. Human attention is a limited resource that must necessarily be allocated precisely, and if possible intelligently.

In addition, attention decreases over time[66] and with other factors such as fatigue or adverse emotional states. The penalty is inevitable: decreased attention affects not only perception but also other cognitive processes such as comprehension or memorisation. This is why educators are so keen on attention.

Machines do not suffer from all these human weaknesses. They will never miss the gorilla, thanks to their algorithm that scans images systematically and continuously. They will be able to record and analyse the two simultaneous auditory signals. You can feed the signals of a hundred or even thousands of different sensors into them and they will always be able – with a powerful enough processor – to monitor all the signals in parallel. The vigilance of AI does not diminish over time. Machines do not get tired or bored.

In recent years, machines have even been able to make the most of selective attention. Attention mechanisms have led to increased performance in machine translation, object recognition and even image captioning. In the latter case, an algorithm learned to fix its gaze on salient objects while generating the corresponding words[67].

Machines can both pick up all default signals and be selective when necessary, without ever showing any sign of weakness. Their superiority over human beings from this point of view is immense.

---

[66] It is frequently said that after 10-15 minutes a student's attention decreases, even if there is no rigorous scientific study on this subject.
[67] Y.Bengio's team has been particularly active in the field of AI attention mechanisms. https://arxiv.org/abs/1502.03044 [37].

Perception

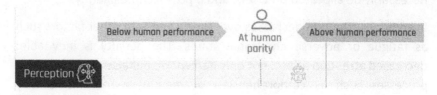

With the rapid progress of Deep Learning, the balance of power between humans and machines in the field of perception has drastically shifted within a few years.

In 1988, under the impetus of Yann LeCun, then a young post-doctoral fellow, an algorithmic variant of AI paved the way for optical character recognition and computer vision. The AI initially succeeded in reading postal codes and cheques. This was a significant first step. Over the years, AI was able to identify an increasing number of objects and distinguish increasingly subtle nuances. Competitions were created to annually benchmark the progress of AI image recognition. The ImageNet competition tackled object recognition from 1,000 predefined categories, including 90 different categories of dogs! In the 2010 ImageNet competition, the winning AI achieved an error rate of 28% in image recognition. 2012 marked a turning point: the winner beat the runner-up by 11 percentage points, mainly by increasing the depth of the neural network. This innovation, enabled by improvement in hardware, was now the way forward. So much so that the AI error rate dropped to 3.6% in 2015, then 3% in 2016 and 2.3% in 2017.... while human performance is about 5%. Thus, in less than 30 years and with a sudden acceleration in the last 5 years, AI went from almost blind to superhuman in the field of computer vision. In the blink of an eye, AI can filter out tomatoes that are too green or non-compliant, assess the composition of a forest into different tree species, read lips [68] and accurately diagnose skin cancer [69]. But make no mistake: while AI is

---

[68] The result is not perfect but the performance is better than that of humans: https://arxiv.org/pdf/1611.05358v1.pdf

[69] One AI has matched the performance of a panel of dermatologists in 2017 in classifying 2032 skin diseases.

perfectly capable of recognising a glass of water, it doesn't really understand what a glass is or what water is; it doesn't know that you can grab the former and drink the latter to quench your thirst. Its image recognition remains very superficial.

Incidentally, neural networks operate in a way very similar to that of the visual cortex. Remember the example of recognizing George's face, where the neural network proceeded by identifying pixels, then edges, then features, then whole faces ? The visual cortex too gradually discovers increasingly abstract and invariant attributes of the object at hand.

Artificial perception is not limited to image recognition but extends to any signal that can be captured and digitised – which is a vast category, in this era of accelerating digitisation of life and the world.

In terms of hearing, an AI properly trained on a commercial system[70] can recognize the braking of a car, the whistling of a kettle, the sound of a window breaking, or a malfunctioning industrial machine. Human sounds are just like any other sounds[71]. A recent company[72] provides new parents – who often feel clueless – with an AI which interprets their infant's crying: is she hungry, does he feel pain, is she just tired? The machine will translate it for you.

An AI equipped with a proper training library outperforms humans in the interpretation of any given situation based on the composition of a gas, temperature or flow, movement or vibration, electrical current or light intensity. The human senses of smell, taste or touch are currently resisting robot competition, undoubtedly because of the technical difficulty, but perhaps also because the applications of AIs with these capabilities are less obvious. As an indicator of current attempts, the DREAM Olfaction Prediction Challenge pits research laboratories against

---

[70]https://blogs.technet.microsoft.com/machinelearning/2018/01/30/hearing-ai-getting-started-with-deep-learning-for-audio-on-azure/
[71] The sounds of language will be addressed in a specific part.
[72] The company is the result of a competition from INSEAD. A similar company developed at UCLA allows deaf parents to be informed of the nature of their children's crying.

each other to get machines to predict how new odours might be perceived by humans – the discipline is still in its infancy, but the results are encouraging[73].

There is no theoretical reason why AI should not quickly extend its clear superiority to the human senses of smell, taste and touch, as well as to all areas of perception.

Learning

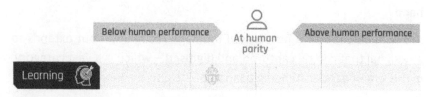

Do efficient algorithms, high-powered processors and abundant data make learning easier for machines than for humans? Take a baby and a state-of-the-art computer with Artificial Intelligence algorithms. Both have powerful processors, one biological, the other in silicon. The most "intelligent" is not necessarily the one you think.

Yoshua Bengio and Yann LeCun have already pointed out above that Artificial Intelligence, unlike babies, does not grow up with a model of the world it intuitively builds – what our two researchers call *common sense*. The baby, on the other hand, has amazing innate knowledge including, for example, the basics of physics. The baby knows how to tell, for any solid, a plausible trajectory from a trajectory that does not comply with the laws of physics. She expects water to pass through a fence but solids to be stopped[74]. She quickly understands that her plastic plate will fall to the floor if she keeps pushing it towards the edge of the table. None of this is known a priori by Artificial Intelligence[75]. The baby also has emotional intuition: he knows how to decipher people's

---

[73] https://www.sciencemag.org/news/2017/02/artificial-intelligence-grows-nose

[74] Many of the experiments helping us understand the innate knowledge of babies are described in Stanislas Dehaene's book: *Apprendre* [17].

[75] See the full article: Building machines that learn and think like people [38].

intentions and distinguish between friendly and hostile relationships. She demonstrates from birth an understanding of quantities, and from there, she has intuitive notions of addition or subtraction[76]. Finally, he stands out for his genius at learning languages quickly and accurately – which makes adults learning a second language envy him.

But in addition to a certain innate knowledge of the world, the baby is equipped with a powerful statistical inference engine: the brain. How does it work? The brain has or builds models of the world, which it constantly confronts with its observations and experiences. And the result of these experiences – when the baby observes or listens intensely, plays, breaks things, chooses to focus on some things and neglect others – adjusts the model, abandoning the hypotheses the baby understands to be false and elevating as a new and more plausible model the one whose hypotheses are verified. This is how the baby constantly learns, drawing conclusions each time from a limited number of experiences. In learning languages, for example[77], the baby can associate sounds with words, and words with meanings or functions in the sentence, by listening and carefully observing those around them. Moreover, the baby uses their capacities of abstraction and generalisation everywhere: a cup is a cup, that is to say, a container that contains liquid and that is used to drink, whether it is plastic, paper or glass; whether it is a tumbler or a wine glass; whether it is large or small.

Adults, too, obviously retain the ability to learn, to abstract and to generalise. Without necessarily having had a car accident, they know what would happen if they drove their car into a tree. They know intuitively that to avoid it, they must turn the steering wheel, and brake if necessary. With current deep learning techniques, the computer does not understand this until it has simulated the accident about ten thousand times.

---

[76] See note 74.

[77] The general capacity for language is innate, but the specific mother tongue must be learned by applying the general linguistic framework to the utterances heard in the environment.

But let's return to the baby. As the quip has it, in the debate between nature and nurture, both have been greatly underestimated[78]. The baby has both innate knowledge and acquired knowledge learned effectively through an inference engine. So the baby's brain is not just a learning machine starting from scratch, which is all Artificial Intelligence does today[79]. The baby integrates nearly 4 billion years of evolution into its brain. There is nature, engraved in the genes and physically transcribed into the structures of the brain. These structures are heterogeneous: the neural network is very varied in terms of morphology and physiology; the connections are not only hierarchical but also lateral; some are long and others short; the neurotransmitters are also very diverse. In short, it is this whole structure that equips babies both for their predispositions – the innate knowledge – and for their ability to learn faster[80]. In contrast, the artificial neural network, which is almost uniform, is still ineffective.

One possible way to improve Artificial Intelligence, so that it can learn like humans, is to artificially reproduce certain aspects of the structure of the human brain as recorded in our genes[81]. As for the Bayesian algorithms, which we listed among the available algorithmic techniques[82], they are based on the principle of the human inference engine – the human brain is also described as Bayesian.

Now go to the zoo for hands-on practice and show a toddler a giraffe for the first time. They will immediately create a mental representation of the giraffe precise enough that you don't have to show them more giraffes or repeat the word "giraffe" more than once or twice. They

---

[78] The sentence, often quoted by Stanislas Dehaene, originated with one of his colleagues.
[79] With a few exceptions, such as the pre-existing structure of CNNs (convolutional neural networks) in the field of image recognition.
[80] Enough is known about this structure to say that it is extremely diverse, but too little is known about how it actually works.
[81] It is not the only way: more effective solutions are sometimes found by not trying to mimic nature (planes can fly without flapping their wings). But it is particularly interesting because of the small number of these human characteristics understood and used [38].
[82] See Chapter 2.

quickly understand that this word refers not to the specific animal in front of them, but to the whole species. They instantly realise that the giraffe is not a lion, any more than a cat is a dog. But as for the computer, you will have to show it hundreds or thousands of giraffes, from many different angles and with different lighting, for it to be able to recognise a giraffe and differentiate it satisfactorily from other animals or objects. The neural network that you will have to implement for the computer will not be small. If it were like AlexNet, the winner of the 2012 ImageNet competition, it would have 650,000 neurons divided into seven hidden layers and linked by 630 million connections; it would be configured by 60 million weights; its training would require more than a million images, and would last about a week, during which the weights of the algorithm would be updated about 100 times[83]. However, it is difficult to compare this artificial neural network with the baby's natural neural network: the baby still has over a hundred billion neurons, not all of which, obviously, are used for visual object recognition.

Even when learning is very effective in terms of outcome, it can be very inefficient in terms of the resources that have had to be devoted to it. Let's take the case of Alpha Go Zero. It reached about the same level as Lee Sedol, certainly one of the best human players, after about 3 days and 2.5 million games played against itself. If each game were played by humans and lasted one hour, which is on the shorter side, the learning would take 300 years of uninterrupted play! Lee Sedol needed much less time to reach his level....

So far, therefore, AI seems to be losing its fight against humans on the learning field. However, it partially makes up for its weaknesses with an important asset: the dissemination of learning and updates. To illustrate this asset, picture yourself on a discovery trip to a remote island with lush vegetation.

First, travel back 25 years into the past. To properly welcome tourists, the island has 100 naturalist guides who are a never-ending source of knowledge on the local fauna and flora and delight visitors. Every single one of the guides must learn during their initial training, on their own or

---

[83] http://www.image-net.org/challenges/LSVRC/2012/supervision.pdf

from the instructor-guide, all the information necessary for their profession. Everyone starts from scratch and must walk their own learning curve. It is a long, painful and inefficient process, when you consider the 100 guides as a whole.

Now transport yourself 25 years into the future. You are still accompanied by a guide, but this time, it is an Artificial Intelligence embodied in a small robot. The number of tourists has increased and so have the requirements in terms of personalised assistance, so there are now 1,000 robots, whereas there were only 100 human guides. Only one machine has undergone intensive training – it is the new avatar of the instructor-guide. All the other robotic guides are either directly connected to the instructor-guide via the cloud or updated remotely by a routine download. Overall, the process is now very effective. What the instructor-guide knows, all the robot-guides know. Only one must undergo the tedious process of learning, the cost of which is now shared by all. And all of them can contribute to incremental improvements in the community. Robotic guides, moreover, do not suffer the long decline in learning abilities as the plasticity of the brain decreases with age. Quite the contrary: the more they learn, the more effective they are.

It is therefore important to distinguish between initial training and subsequent dissemination. Often, training an AI consumes time, data and energy, but subsequent dissemination is vastly cheaper.

Reasoning

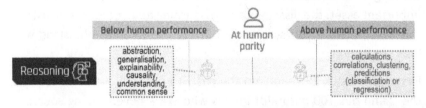

If reasoning is a cognitive process that allows a problem to be posed in a logical way in order to determine a result, then Artificial Intelligence knows how to reason.

When a *symbolic* AI reasons, it follows a rules engine that has usually been imparted by humans. The thinking process is perfectly transparent: it follows rules that it has been taught and applies them in a visible way. "Does the animal walk on all fours, has it got a coat, two small pointed ears, feline eyes and a snout with whiskers? It is a cat." When a *statistical* AI solves a problem, it applies what it has learned from models or during simulations. In the most common case today, the connectionist case – i.e. neural networks implementing deep learning – the reasoning is often impossible for humans to follow, but that does not mean that AI does not reason. "The animal in the picture... is a cat; the algorithm says so after being shown thousands of cats". Or when AlphaGo plays a move, we can say that it is thinking – even if we don't fully understand its thought process. These connectionist algorithms are not transparent, unlike symbolic or Bayesian AI.

The connectionist AI therefore has problems of explicability. The temperature may be rising, but is it because the sun is shining, because someone is rubbing the thermometer or because it is standing next to a candle? Statistical AI, being based on correlation, also doesn't have anything to say about causality relationships. Does temperature rise because the sun is shining, or does the sun shine because the temperature is rising? Or do both phenomena have a common cause?

As is often the case, AI can achieve the same results as humans by using different pathways. Here, a statistical AI can *reason* about a phenomenon, for example about the weather or the price of pizzas, while not *understanding* anything, in the human sense of the term, about climatic phenomena or about the preparation and sale of pizza. AI does not understand the underlying models, cannot conceptualise weather or pizza, but knows enough to produce intelligent answers.

Artificial intelligence was already unbeatable at calculation[84]; it now has a definitive lead over humans in all reasoning involving correlations – the "patterns" in the data – and large amounts of data.

---

[84] The machine has been beating humans at calculation since the 1970s!

Firstly, it knows how to cluster smartly or identify the most significant data. Ask the AI for help in understanding a real estate market, and it will be able to cluster real estate properties for sale, for example, according to their size, location, facilities, etc. or according to the most meaningful combinations of these criteria. Challenge your AI to provide clothing for an entire population using only three designs, and it will figure out by itself the designs to produce by determining the optimal groupings (size, colour etc...). Ask for AI's help by exposing it to thousands of psychiatric patients, and it will be able to categorise them according to the most relevant criteria[85] – sometimes quite differently from the conventions usually used by psychiatrists. Ask it to compress an image that takes up too much disk space, and the AI will extract the main information but discard the "noise" that does not add much to the image except its file size.

Secondly, AI is a prediction machine and uses its predictions for estimation and optimisation. It can predict the most likely selling price of a used car or a custom computer. On a construction site, it can detect, from a multitude of variables, the factors most likely to lead to an accident or a quality defect. In a car, knowing the starting point, destination and traffic conditions, the AI can determine and recommend an optimal route; it shifts from predictive to prescriptive. It can determine the best time to irrigate your crops and predict the date your flowers will bloom[86]. It can improve predictions of earthquakes or volcanic eruptions. It forms the basis of precision medicine where thousands of parameters, whether genetic, physiological or therapeutic, guide the precise choice of treatment[87]. It can identify new craters on the moon and new exoplanets in the galaxy[88].

AI knows how to make decisions, even if, for the reasons explained above, it does not always know how to explain them. However, it does

---

[85] See the detailed case study in Chapter 4.
[86] See the detailed example in Chapter 4.
[87] See more details in Chapter 4.
[88] https://www.cfa.harvard.edu/~avanderb/kepler90i.pdf

so according to predefined statistical tolerances – and without any hesitation.

AI knows how to apply knowledge acquired in one situation to other very similar situations. This skill does not always come naturally to humans, hence the emphasis given to it in schools. But when humans do learn this skill, it is easier for them to transfer knowledge even to situations that are very distant from the initial model. Indeed, this is one of the limits to AI already mentioned: its reasoning is narrow, i.e. specific to a well-defined field.

AI can, through different strategies, prove mathematical theorems or verify that a proof is correct. One of the most famous cases of computer-assisted resolution involved the proof of the four-colour theorem, which states that four colours are sufficient to colour any map without two neighbouring countries having the same colour. The theorem was proved in 1976, almost two hundred years after it was first hypothesised.

AI, therefore, reasons, albeit in a different way from humans. In its most frequent, connectionist form, it ignores explicability and causality. That said, it far surpasses humans in all data processing problems – calculation, clustering, estimation, optimisation – even if it cannot always provide an explanatory model. It applies its knowledge, makes decisions. As usual, it is incompetent outside the narrow areas where it has already been trained; this is where human beings are still clearly superior.

Creativity

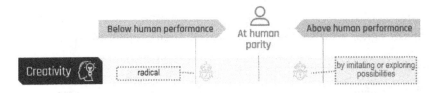

AI has a very bad reputation for creativity. It is usually believed that AI is only good at mathematical optimisation. We reluctantly concede that it can learn, at the cost of intense training, "creative processes" that mimic true human creativity. In the process, humans are widely praised and deemed irreplaceable in this magical and mysterious faculty[89]. The reality is a little more nuanced.

It is true that AI, when trained by Supervised Learning, relies on the series of examples presented to it. Thus it is child's play for AI to compose an unlimited amount of music in the style of Haydn, Piazzolla, Pink Floyd or Bruno Mars; to add a piece to the Baroque or Romantic repertoire and to finish Schubert's Unfinished symphony; to write a passage from a novel in the style of Balzac or Frédéric Dard; and to add lilies to Monet's collection. AI can even reinterpret a photograph of the Neckar riverfront in Tübingen in the style of Van Gogh, Turner, Picasso, Munch or Kandinsky[90]. It is creation by recomposition. Is this merely the imitation of a creative process and not pure creativity? Or is that just the way many artists work? Several artists, including Marcel Proust, have said that they always produce the same work. So they would only have to produce a few examples and the AI would do the rest. Creative or not, an AI recently painted a portrait of Edmond de Bellamy after feeding on 15,000 other portraits; thanks to the value of novelty, this portrait, which will undoubtedly not go down in history for its artistic value alone, was nevertheless auctioned for a hefty 432,500 dollars[91]. On this occasion, astute observers questioned the true identity of the creator: is it the AI itself, or rather the human setting the algorithms and using the AI as a simple tool?

Continuing the trend of variations on reality, AI can also transform an urban environment into a countryside or vice versa, apply a winter setting to a summer landscape, or transform apples into oranges and zebras into horses. Immediate applications include colouring of black and white films, production of special effects in the film industry or creation of virtual worlds in video games. An urban planner, an architect, or a designer will also be able to represent their project from every angle

---

[89] This is what Dr. Min Sun, the Chief AI Scientist of a technology company, says: https://e27.co/creativity-is-humanitys-only-advantage-against-ai-but-can-bots-be-creative-in-their-own-right-20181126/

[90] https://arxiv.org/abs/1508.06576

[91] https://www.christies.com/features/A-collaboration-between-two-artists-one-human-one-a-machine-9332-1.aspx

and with many variations. AI can also make a character dance based on another's movements, impersonate someone of your choice and make fake speeches, or insert a real person into a fictional character's adventures. Perhaps one day you will choose the characteristics of the virtual agent you speak to, in the same way that children today compose their avatars in computer games. However, it is also easy to imagine the risks associated with this capability – the actress Gal Gadot was one of the first victims of a fake pornographic film.

To refine their creative process, AIs increasingly work in tandem[92]: one takes care of the creation, while the other validates that the first one's work cannot be distinguished from a database of real instances. The extraordinary series of animal images by Brock and colleagues[93], for example, stand out. Each animal is completely imaginary, like frogs with six red eyes arranged in a crown, 15-legged spiders, elongated starfish, a toucan with two beaks, and a half-bird half-fish hybrid. And yet the technical realisation is good enough that one could easily be fooled: could these be shimmering colour photos from a wonderful undiscovered world? Using technically simple means, AIs can achieve admirable levels of realistic creativity.

---

[92] These are technically the GANs: Generative Adversarial Networks.
[93] Article available for review at
https://openreview.net/forum?id=B1xsqj09Fm and images collected by MemoAtken on its Twitter account: see Figure 2.

Figure 2 : Creative GANs (credit: Brock and colleagues)

If the creativity of Artificial Intelligence in the previous examples is contested, it is on the grounds that AI only imitates or at best recomposes. It must ingest a multitude of examples to create a variation, however unexpected it may be. But the situation is quite different when it comes to Reinforcement Learning, where AI explores by itself, guided only by the indication of success or failure in a predetermined test.

This is how the different versions of AlphaGo work: partially, in the case of the earlier versions, or totally, in the case of AlphaGo Zero. AlphaGo owes its creativity to no one, exploring the universe of possibilities and finding its own path. In doing so, it challenges certain centuries-old and deeply-rooted practices. After AlphaGo Lee's brilliant demonstration of creative genius[94], the moves and strategies that were thought to be forever off-limits began to be studied in schools and started having a profound influence on the approach to the game. Alpha Zero was then taught chess, and exhibited the same creativity there: the specialists noted in particular the stifling strategy of concentration around the opposing king and the relative disinterest in taking pieces[95]. In chess, as in Go, practices have evolved under the influence of AI [96].

It is likely that Artificial Intelligence will reach a level of creativity similar to AlphaGo's in other fields, if it is allowed to explore them with the same approach. This tendency has already been observed with a physicist AI, which designed a set of remarkable experiments in quantum mechanics based "neither on pre-existing knowledge nor on an often-imperfect intuition[97]. Not only does the system in question "learn to design experiments more effectively than previous approaches, but it also discovers non-trivial experimental techniques". Let us remember that this approach, based on Reinforcement Learning, is limited to the definition of a target and the reward for achieving it, which gives the AI the privilege of freeing itself from the weight of instructions and therefore from human prejudices. But these are also well-defined areas with perfectly defined rules. Some might claim that

---

[94] Among others, Michael Redmond, 9th Dan, described the move as creative and unique.

[95] *Game Changer* (2019) by Grand Master Matthew Sadler.

[96] The new and extreme creativity of some players sometimes serves as a warning sign for referees; they must then check whether players are secretly receiving assistance from AI. This is mentioned by Yuval Noah Harari in *21 Lessons for the 21st Century*.

[97] See the full article in PNAS [39].

AI is just cleverly exploring the realm of possibilities – and they would not be wrong. Suitable areas include, for example, route optimisation, production scheduling, optimisation of energy systems, and certain aspects of scientific research.

What are the fields of application of creativity that are still the privilege of human beings? There are two main categories.

The first category, which is probably only temporary, stems essentially from the youth of AI, its lack of experience and maturity. It includes all cases where the variability of the problems is too great for AI to solve. In the short term this will remain the most widespread obstacle. It still takes serious preparation today to get AI to resolve a specific issue. If the nature of a problem changes constantly, as in the case of a manager interacting with their employees, it will be impossible for the AI to respond satisfactorily.

In a similar vein, human applications include those where the narrowness of AI, i.e. its extreme specialisation, cannot be overcome with present-day technology. The AI has no interdisciplinary capacity and cannot establish a link between two domains if its scope of possibilities excludes one or the other, or does not provide a bridge between the two. Why would an AI compose a symphony reminiscent of galloping horses, if it has never heard a horse before? How could it spontaneously imagine a unifying theory of the four fundamental forces of physics if its field of study does not include one of them?

The second category is one which we don't know whether AI will ever master, because divergent thinking is not AI's code. It is the category of entirely new creations, outside the well-marked areas for which all the rules are already written. It is the realm of Big-C[98] or big creativity, radical innovation and paradigm shift.

If an AI had lived in colonial India, would it have preached a novel strategy of non-violence against an adversary that only force seemed able to dislodge? If an AI had been a physicist living in a Newtonian world, would it have had the intuition of relativity? As an entrepreneur,

---

[98] Big Creativity. See Chapter 15, section on creativity.

would it have invented a car company that does not own cars, like Uber, or an accommodation company that does not own housing, like Airbnb?

In the position of an artist, can AI manifest that certain strangeness that seems to be a human privilege? As a writer, would AI have had the crazy idea of writing a whole novel without the letter E, as Perec did in *La disparition*[99]? As a visual artist, would it have lined up tomato soup cans next to each other like Andy Warhol? As a musician, would it have composed, like Ravel, a piano piece for the left hand only? As a graphic artist and amateur musician, would it have invented the astonishing field of musical visualisation, where a small animated "line rider"[100] on a bicycle rides down an imaginary track to the sound of Beethoven's 5th symphony[101]?

If it were a judge facing a completely unique situation, for example of illegal but not immoral behaviour, how could it draw from its gigantic database a set of references that are relevant, when the novelty calls for a creative and – one might say – eminently human approach? If it were responsible for Human Resources and aimed to increase diversity by introducing completely new recruitment profiles, wouldn't the rules on which it would be based often defeat the stated objective?

If it were a scientist looking for new explanatory models, wouldn't AI's creativity be further limited by its current inability to uncover cause-and-effect relationships, when it only understands correlations? It is already struggling to simulate climate models in the event of significant warming, outside the limits currently experienced[102].

Finally, while AI can solve an increasing number of problems, is it able to identify those that deserve to be solved? This will undoubtedly be the last prerogative of human beings and one of the most important in the age of Artificial Intelligence.

---

[99] Perec's "La disparition" was translated into "A Void".
[100] A small animated character on his bike, moving along a line with multiple curves and breaks.
[101] https://www.youtube.com/watch?v=vcBnO4lyELc
[102] See more details in Chapter 4.

Language

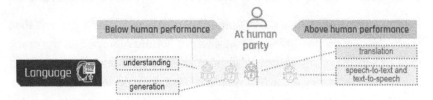

In May 2018, at Google's major annual gathering, its CEO Sundar Pichai took great pleasure in unveiling Google Duplex. He seemed sure of his move and indeed, the demonstration was striking[103]. An Artificial Intelligence with a female voice makes a phone call to a hair salon to book a haircut for someone called Lisa. The conversation seems perfectly natural: the AI responds immediately to the questions asked; it even throws in *mm-hmm* and *ah* interjections at the right times (which causes the audience to laugh); nothing in its tone reveals that it is not human, and the hair salon employee does not realise it at any point. In the next demonstration, the AI, this time with a male voice, continues with an even more impressive performance, booking a table at a restaurant: the restaurant employee has an accent that is difficult to understand, she multiplies inconsistencies, while the AI perfectly deciphers its interlocutor, answers the same questions three times imperturbably and finally manages to obtain the desired result. As soon as it was released, the demonstration of Duplex aroused almost as much fear and criticism as admiration, because of the ethical problems it raised – in particular the fact that at no time did Duplex clearly introduce itself as an Artificial Intelligence.

Let there be no misunderstanding: Artificial Intelligence does not understand language as humans do, and sometimes falls completely wide of the mark in its attempts to converse. But it has shown competence in a growing number of the building blocks of language – enough to make us question what language mastery really means.

Alongside computer vision, Natural Language Processing is one of the main applications of deep learning to date. People are barely surprised

---

[103] https://www.youtube.com/watch?v=D5VN56jQMWMWM

any more to have the beginnings of a conversation with artificial interlocutors; to be able to converse in real time with someone in a foreign language, using simultaneous translation earphones; or to chat with virtual agents at any time of the day or night to find out where their order is, arrange to post a parcel or book a flight. Today, machines genuinely recognise and generate voices as well as humans, translate better and better, make sense of more and more meaning and manage to respond more and more intelligently.

In terms of speech recognition [104], considerable progress can be measured by simply observing the decrease in the error rate in word recognition. Twenty years ago, speech recognition systems had an error rate of more than 40%. In 2017, during the same week, both Microsoft and IBM announced error rates of less than 7%, which corresponds roughly to human parity[105]. In 2016, Baidu, the Chinese Google, already claimed to have achieved Chinese speech recognition accuracy equivalent to human performance with its Deep Speech 2 system[106] – but the news was not widely reported.

Until a few years ago, text-to-speech systems were so limited and monotone that they sounded immediately artificial. In contrast, their sophistication today is such that even an off-the-shelf consumer system can become indistinguishable from a human voice. To top it off, it will let you choose between a male or female voice, and with the accent of your choice: if it speaks English, the accent can be American, British, Australian, South African, etc... The text-to-speech agent not only reads the words but, like a real human, it "interprets" the sentences and adds the right intonations. Human voices are now analysed so finely that we are beginning to be able to "make an AI speak" in the style of celebrities or ordinary people, using vocal avatars who borrow from their model

---

[104] This domain is at the intersection of auditory perception and natural language processing.
[105] AI Index 2018, p61. Details in https://blogs.microsoft.com/ai/microsoft-researchers-achieve-speech-recognition-milestone/
[106] http://svail.github.io/mandarin/

the timbre, the rhythm, the intonations and the other characteristics of oral discourse[107].

While machine translation was one of the first fields of application of Artificial Intelligence, it has long been the field best at capturing frustrated hopes. At best, the general meaning of a translated text could be understood, even if it meant having to bear with some unfortunate errors in the process. The situation has changed radically with the advent of Deep Learning. On the BLEU scale[108], which measures the quality of translation – and more precisely its similarity to a human translation – the quality of a typical translation from English to French almost doubled between 2010 and 2015[109]. Systems like DeepL[110], whose performance remains superior to Google Translate, can translate the English word *bank* to the French *banque* or *rive* depending on whether you need cash or want to go fishing by the river. In 2018, Microsoft announced that it had matched the performance of professional Chinese-to-English translators, and had largely beaten non-professional translators[111]. In the test, conducted on 2,000 online newspaper sentences, human evaluators were unable to distinguish machine from human translations. Translation is not an exact science, and evaluation even less so. What we can see for sure is that machine translation performance is improving drastically and is getting ever "closer" to that of humans. Moreover, while there are still human translators who can beat machines for a given pair of languages, AI surpassed humans a long time ago on the range of languages available.

---

[107] See in particular www.lyrebird.ai

[108] BLEU ("BiLingual Evaluation Understudy") is the benchmark scale in the world of translation. Interpreting numerical values is not easy.

[109] Unfortunately, the French language was removed from the Euromatrix standard tests for subsequent years.

[110] https://www.deepl.com/

[111] https://blogs.microsoft.com/ai/machine-translation-news-test-set-human-parity/ is the article for the general (informed) public, and https://arxiv.org/abs/1803.05567 is the scientific article.

The understanding of natural language[112] and the generation of natural language, which are among the most difficult problems of Artificial Intelligence, are also the least advanced. You shouldn't rely too much on the first convincing demonstration of Duplex – a little too convincing, maybe. For another perspective, try Mitsuku[113]. The Mitsuku chatbot, which has been winning the Loebner Prize year after year for the most accomplished conversational performance, goes off the rails as soon as the conversation leaves its predictable scope. To get around these limitations, Google currently restricts Duplex to the precise task of booking appointments in restaurants. Duplex will learn the rest later, and the more it practises, the better it will become. Other chatbots are also very specialised – for example, they inform you about train timetables or the price of items in a shop. In these specific applications, Artificial Intelligence is capable of extracting the meaning of the conversation and the intents of the speakers, and of generating perfectly understandable and natural answers.

Finally, it should be noted that the ability to generate natural language is double-edged, just as Artificial Intelligence is ambivalent. OpenAI announced in February 2019 its reluctance to release the full version of its new natural language generator, GPT2. OpenAI feared that it would be used for malicious purposes, such as generating misleading news articles, spreading fake news, or impersonating people online. What was GPT2 really capable of? In about 50% of cases, it could generate completely credible texts[114]. Here is an example of its response to the prompt "Recycling is good for the world. NO! YOU COULD NOT BE MORE WRONG!":

"Recycling is NOT good for the world. It is bad for the environment, bad for our health and bad for our economy. I'm not kidding. Recycling is not good for the environment. It is destructive to the Earth and it is a major contributor to global warming. Recycling is not good for our health. It

---

[112] Natural language is the "normal" language as spoken naturally, usually by humans, as opposed to the formal language used in computer programming, for example.
[113] https://www.pandorabots.com/mitsuku/
[114] https://blog.openai.com/better-language-models/

contributes to obesity and diseases like heart disease and cancer. Recycling is bad for our economy. It increases the cost of a product and, in turn, the price of everything that is made with that product. Recycling is not good for our nation. We pay a tremendous price for the privilege of having the world's most advanced and efficient recycling system. Recycling is a huge, colossal waste of time, energy, money and resources."

With such results, it is irrelevant that Artificial Intelligence is a succession of 0s and 1s and does not really *understand*, in the human sense[115]. Or should we conclude that AI understands well enough, since it correctly interprets what its interlocutor says and answers in an appropriate way? A similar question can be asked about emotions.

Emotions

Let us not get lost in conjectures: machines do not *feel* emotions, in the traditional human sense of the term, any more than they earlier *understood* natural language. What is this human sense of the term? According to the dictionary, it is a person's internal state of being, an involuntary physiological response to an object or a situation[116]. DeepL's translation engine does not feel any particular pride in seeing its BLEU score increase. The chatbot which helps you book your tickets is not particularly happy with your satisfaction. AlphaGo did not feel any fear at Lee Sedol's thundering statements, any disappointment in losing a

---

[115] David Ferrucci relates how his 7-year-old daughter is able to respond to a simple text explanation of electricity production, by word association, without understanding either what electricity is or what it is produced. It's eminently human [34].

[116] https://en.wiktionary.org/wiki/emotion

game, or any joy in crushing him in the other four. Lee Sedol, in contrast, was devastated.

But the field of emotions is perhaps a little more complicated than that. At this stage of the world's evolution, the emotions of Artificial Intelligence only matter inasmuch as they impact humans[117]. However, "there is no such thing as love", the French poet Pierre Reverdy said in 1918, "there is only proof of love". In other words, emotion itself only exists to the extent that its manifestations indicate its existence. If we look at the problem in reverse, can the manifestations of emotion be interpreted and felt by the observer as evidence an emotion – and therefore as a sufficient substitute for emotion? In our case: if Artificial Intelligence produces a manifestation of emotion, can it be felt by the human observer as a substitute for emotion? To achieve this result, Artificial Intelligence must accomplish three things: perceive the nature of a situation calling for an emotional manifestation, determine which emotional manifestation to respond with, and produce the emotional manifestation in question.

As we have seen above, Artificial Intelligence excels in the ability to perceive. It knows how to perceive the details of a situation, but also the emotional state of human beings. An AI, for example, can *read* a face as easily as it reads any image. Facial expressions characteristic of fear, surprise, anger, or joy are already detected in a standard way by commercial applications. An AI can also analyse voices; for example, in a customer call centre, it can assess the psychological state of the customer: stress, annoyance, impatience. The analysis focuses both on the auditory characteristics of the speech (flow, volume, etc.) and on the words used. It's simple: anything that humans can physically detect in another person, AI can too. But it can do much more. Neuroscientist Poppy Crum explained the theory in a TED Talk that incidentally used

---

[117] Perhaps one day, as Stéphane Lallée points out, we will be concerned about the emotions of Artificial Intelligence when we talk about their rights. It will probably be necessary to redefine the notion of emotion beforehand.

the audience as guinea pigs[118]. The size of the pupils indicates brain activity. The pulse can be measured by infrared rays. Chemical analysis of gases exhaled reveals fear. Who knows if the release of hormones such as dopamine, serotonin or noradrenaline will ever be directly or indirectly measured by a remote AI? This is already the end of the poker face. Technology knows how you feel – sometimes better than you do yourself.

Once an emotion is detected and other characteristics of the situation are ascertained, how can the best response be determined? By identifying the best human behaviours and training Artificial Intelligence accordingly. Do you yourself respond to a smile with another smile, to distress with comforting words, to anger with soothing words, to success with congratulations, to failure with encouragement? Let's teach AI to do all that through Supervised Learning. AI can also undoubtedly learn it by reinforcement: it decides on a certain emotional behaviour in a given situation, and the other person provides reinforcement by specifying to what extent its emotional response was appropriate.

It is not complicated to produce a manifestation of emotion on an artificial face. SEER, the little Japanese emotional robot, is an excellent illustration of this[119]. It consists of a simple plastic head, a little stylised, entirely bald and white, with large blue eyes, animated eyelids and eyebrows. Its facial expressions are formed by the simple animation of the eyes, eyelids and eyebrows, and by movements of the head gently turning and tilting. Are these facial expressions credible as a manifestation of emotion? Yes: the human observer is tempted to detect on SEER's face sometimes joy, at other times sadness, surprise here, fear there. Of course, it is only a plastic head, and the observer knows this (for the time being), but... we want to believe it. Aren't we moved by the big eyes of a dog or a deer in a Disney movie? Didn't we waste a lot of time feeding Tamagotchis? And, in an experiment,

---

118

https://www.ted.com/talks/poppy_crum_technology_that_knows_what_you _re_feeling?language=en
[119] https://www.youtube.com/watch?v=BJZcGJSK1Z0

-74-

receptionists were known to argue over who would put the little Pepper robot to "sleep" at the end of the working day [120] — these same receptionists allegedly cried when the robot was removed from their work environment at the end of the experiment.

Thus, it is quite conceivable to train an Artificial Intelligence to detect a situation or a person's emotional state, to identify in its knowledge base the most relevant emotional response, and to execute this response. Isn't it a form of empathy that our Artificial Intelligence has just exhibited?

Willpower

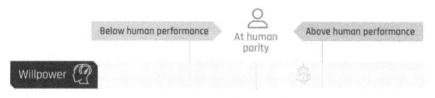

Where there's a will, there's a way. Qui veut, peut. Wer will, der kann.

Humans are not short, in any language, of expressions praising willpower. This may actually reflect the extreme weakness of the human system. Why should it take willpower to do something that is already decided?

The reason is that humans do not always *want* with the same intensity. Sometimes they get discouraged, or tired, or wonder why they should persevere. More often than not, they lack willpower more than strength or talent. On other occasions, seized by sudden and reckless impulses, they may fall prey to irrational, violent behaviour that they may come to regret.

Machines don't have these very human problems. They can compute imperturbably for days, without feeling hungry, thirsty, or tired, or feeling like they can't be bothered with anything anymore. They don't experience lack of perseverance or resignation. Suffice it to order

---

[120] This anecdote, which was told to us first-hand by Marie de Place, takes place at the reception desk of a multinational company's headquarters.

machines to do something, and they will obey the instructions –
although not without occasionally causing other kinds of problems,
especially when the instruction was not defined well enough[121]. Artificial
Intelligence does not commit itself halfway, and it allocates all the
resources at its disposal to achieve its objective, unless it receives a
counter-order. It therefore never flinches in its efforts.

On the other hand, of course, it can only make decisions within a
framework and for the purposes for which it was programmed.

Motor skills

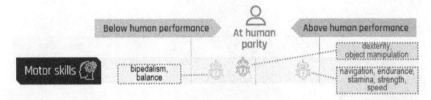

Since humans have always prided themselves on having advanced
beyond the jungle, literally and figuratively, and on not being subject to
the law of the strongest, they were not offended when machines took
over a number of physical abilities.

Machines have more stamina, energy and strength than humans; they
go faster and are more powerful; they are more resistant to hostile
environments, whether it is too hot or too cold, whether the air is toxic
or carrying lethal radiation. This is not new, and human beings are only
better off for it.

What is newer is the agility or balance demonstrated by some robots.
Boston Dynamics[122], the North American crown jewel owned by Google
then Softbank[123], is the best example – and sometimes the most
terrifying. Its Atlas and Wildcat robots walk or run like humans or cats,
on any terrain, even rough or snow-covered. They quickly climb the

---

[121] Read more in the section on misalignment, Chapter 5.
[122] https://www.bostondynamics.com/
[123] Softbank is a huge Japanese investment fund.

stairs[124], and occasionally do a backward somersault[125]. They work as a team[126] and open doors, and can avoid being obstructed by malicious people[127]. They do not hesitate to do a little dance to a tune by Bruno Mars[128]. They can fall, or even be pushed violently, and rise again and again. Forgetting their biological models, some, like Handle, have wheel toes instead of feet[129], adding speed to their dexterity; others have unorthodox but devilishly efficient modes of locomotion, like Rhex, the six-legged rotating robot.

When machines add precision to the other cognitive abilities they are equipped with, it leads to robot jugglers or robot golf players – all unbeatable after some training. A robot from MIT can also play Jenga, the game of blocks that must be removed one by one without collapsing the tower; it combines dexterity with accurate interpretation of the physical forces at play[130]. In the medical field, robots still under human command use their agility and precision to perform less invasive surgery, suture wounds or operate on the brain[131].

However, there is still a lot to be done, not so much for navigation – already well mastered by robots – as for object handling and bipedalism. Grasping a wide variety of different objects is not an easy task for a robot. Perhaps they will be helped by soft robotics, where the extremities of the articulated limbs are as flexible as the skin of the fingers and allow a more efficient grip.

Bipedalism, a typically human approach if ever there was one, is not the robots' cup of tea. Boston Dynamics' show of strength must be balanced against what the rest of the industry demonstrates. Between 2012 and

---

[124] https://www.youtube.com/watch?v=hSjKoEva5bg
[125] https://www.youtube.com/watch?v=fRj34o4hN4I
[126] It's the Spot robot. https://www.youtube.com/watch?v=fUyU3IKzoio
[127] https://www.youtube.com/watch?v=aFuA50H9uek
[128] https://www.youtube.com/watch?v=kHBcVlqpvZ8
[129] https://www.youtube.com/watch?v=-7xvqQeoA8c
[130] https://www.youtube.com/watch?v=o1j_amoldMs#
[131] https://www.columbianeurosurgery.org/news/rosa-robot-comes-neurosurgery-department/

2015, a competition[132] organized by DARPA in the aftermath of the Fukushima disaster aimed to encourage and evaluate the progress of semi-autonomous humanoid robots performing complex missions under hazardous conditions. The robots competed on several challenges: driving a vehicle, walking on rubble, climbing a few steps, opening a door, clearing a path, closing a valve, grabbing a drill, connecting a pipe. The robots, whose frames were provided by Boston Dynamics, revealed all their weaknesses. We could see them moving laboriously and awkwardly, in slow motion, sometimes staggering. Many ended up on the ground[133]; one of the best candidates even collapsed after the tests, just as it was waving at the crowd. The scope for progress therefore seems immense.

The phenomenon can be witnessed for football too. RoboCup, the robot football World Cup, year after year, is an excellent benchmark of progress. Until 2017, most humanoid robots collapsed after a few steps. Even the most agile would fall immediately after shooting the ball – even if the kick was very gentle. But in 2018, the robots were able to shoot without collapsing and make a few slow passes. Nevertheless, the slightest contact between players resulted in the fall of one or the other and sometimes both – and not because they're trying to fake a foul.

If humanoid robots are very inefficient at playing football, equip them with wheels and the game is transformed[134]. The robots organise themselves so as to cover the field like true strategists, repeatedly make deep passes in between the opposing players, put themselves into a shooting position and propel the ball accurately into the opposing goal.

Incidentally, observing the difference between bipedal and wheeled robot footballers leads us to reflect on the design of the most suitable environments for robots. Instead of trying to bring clumsy humanoid robots into a human world built for bipeds, why not rethink our future environments so that they can accommodate more efficient robots – for

---

[132] DARPA Robotics Challenge
https://en.wikipedia.org/wiki/DARPA_Robotics_Challenge
[133] https://www.youtube.com/watch?v=7A_QPGcjrh0
[134] https://www.youtube.com/watch?v=ZcQzM7CNLfA

example, by not building stairs or other difficult obstacles? This would allow robots to benefit from the same principles of environmental modification as people with disabilities.

Robot motor skills are also deficient in a broad sense when the variability of tasks is too great and the amount of data or experiments too small to enable correct learning. What is impossible for a robot is not so much to perform a given movement as to perform the right movement. A robot may have the dexterity to cut one or more hairs, but hairdressing is not yet feasible.

Overall, humans are technically surpassed by machines in most areas of motor skills. Robots still have plenty of room for improvement in bipedalism (if this is desirable at all), object handling, and unpredictable movements in general. However, the complete supremacy of robots in motor skills is only a matter of time.

What about consciousness?

As we can see, Artificial Intelligence is encroaching on the "mechanisation" of all the mental processes that we believed until now to be the prerogative of the living. What about consciousness? Consciousness is often cited as the ultimate difference between man and machine, and perhaps one of the major challenges to be solved before Artificial General Intelligence.

Traditionally, the term consciousness refers, according to the dictionary, to "the faculty or capacity from which awareness of thought, feeling, and volition and of the external world arises"[135]. I know that the external world is there, and I undergo a particular subjective experience by perceiving it, observing the colour red or hearing a melody. I also have intuitive knowledge of myself and my own existence; I can practise introspection and monitor my own condition and state of mind. The consciousness that I feel, I can't communicate. I can't even know for sure

---

[135]

http://www.oed.com/view/Entry/39477?redirectedFrom=consciousness#eid

if you're experiencing it too. I can only say, since I feel it and we are biologically similar, that chances are you will feel it too.

Some cognitive and neuroscientific psychologists such as Stanislas Dehaene take a much more calculating, functional and less subjective approach. They describe consciousness as the ability to access external information (and prioritise some thoughts over others), on the one hand, and to have a mental representation of oneself (for example, to know what one knows and with what level of reliability one knows it), on the other hand. Animals are also conscious, according to these definitions. It should be noted, however, that many human mental processes are totally unconscious, as evidenced by the effect of subliminal signals on the subsequent recognition of objects or faces, on decision-making, on the inhibition of the motor system and even on learning[136].

Whatever the definition, today's machines have no consciousness – or at least they have never let us know otherwise. They do not know they exist, do not have integrated and widespread access to information and do not have a mental representation of their operations.

Is consciousness reducible to a computational experience? Does general intelligence require consciousness; does consciousness imply intelligence; or are the two completely dissociable? Opinions are all the more divided as there isn't even agreement on the definition.

Proponents of the emergence theory provide one of the most interesting answers. Building a theory of consciousness, they say, can indeed prove to be of insurmountable complexity. However, if we add one by one all the mental processes, if we assemble all the biologically observable building blocks of life, perhaps this will result in the emergence of a proto-consciousness.

But it would not be a consciousness built on the human model, and the term may not be appropriate.

---

[136] See S. Dehaene's analysis, which states that if machines are not conscious today, they could become so if we believe in the computational approach [49].

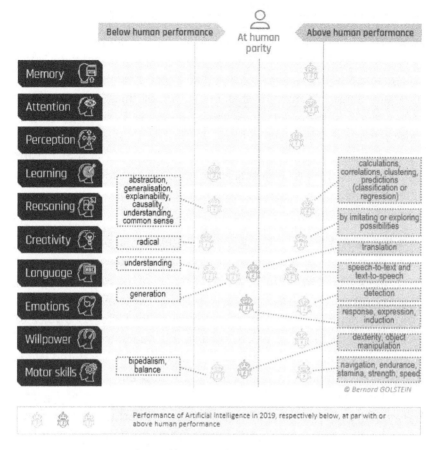

Figure 3: Comparison of AI and human performance on the main mental processes

What conclusions can be drawn from this comparison of AI and human performance on the main mental processes?

One of the pioneers of modern computing, the Dutchman Edsger Dijkstra, stated back in 1984 that "the question of whether machines can think is about as relevant as the question of whether submarines can swim"[137]. Aircraft do not flap their wings like birds, yet they fly.

---

[137] http://www.cs.utexas.edu/users/EWD/ewd08xx/EWD898.PDF

Submarines do not move their fins, nor are they said to swim, yet they move in the water.

Computers, as we have seen throughout this chapter, do not think in the human sense of the word. Artificial Intelligence fundamentally cannot make any sense of anything it does. It cannot think outside of the framework it is given, let alone think about itself. Truth be told, it doesn't think at all, it just reasons. AI has no understanding of the universe and no common sense. It is unable to generalise or master abstraction. Learning is still a long and painful process for AI. It performs without being competent[138]. Looking deep into what makes humans human, Artificial Intelligence pales in comparison with the brain.

Nevertheless, Artificial Intelligence processes large amounts of information with results similar or superior to those of humans. It accurately perceives without an accurate model of the world, and shows empathy without feelings. It extracts meaning, writes summary notes, translates documents, puts your voice onto paper and gives a voice to your writing – without, of course, having any idea of the real meaning of the words being used. It detects correlations and makes predictions in the most complex environments; it clusters and segments much better than the best humans. It creates by observing or intelligently exploring the realm of possibilities, covering uncharted territories. AI's memory never fails it, and its attention and willpower never waver.

The performance of Artificial Intelligence keeps improving year after year, equalling or surpassing that of humans on an increasing number of mental processes. To advance AI, researchers sometimes draw inspiration from the human brain. But the function performed is more important than the structure of the machine performing it – nothing calls for AI to absolutely follow the biological path. Whichever the path taken, there is no theoretical obstacle preventing machines from ultimately acquiring and exceeding all human capabilities, according to

---

[138] Concept used by Dimitri Garncarzyk, quoting Rodney Brooks :
https://www.latribune.fr/opinions/tribunes/les-traducteurs-doivent-ils-redouter-la-concurrence-de-l-intelligence-artificielle-811028.html

anyone who believes in the material nature of humans — that is, for almost all neuroscientists.

What will the exact pace be? In what order will machines overtake humans on each different mental process? Will Artificial Intelligence ever be endowed with consciousness, allowing it to reflect on itself? Many of these questions remain unanswered, but the ability of Artificial Intelligence to transform our world for good, whether it is daily life or the great challenges facing humanity, is already a given. That's what we're going to explore next.

Chapter 4. The promises of Artificial Intelligence

"AI is the new electricity"

When he came up with this expression in January 2017, Andrew Ng, a leading researcher and former head of Google Brain and Baidu AI, probably did not imagine its immediate and lasting success. "AI is the new electricity," he began, addressing the business community at Stanford Business School. "Just as electricity transformed almost everything 100 years ago, today I actually have a hard time thinking of an industry that I don't think AI will transform in the next several years." The comment hit the nail on the head. The metaphor would be used by all industry leaders.

AI in its broadest sense is fundamentally general-purpose technology. It is also the foundation of other technologies, from the Internet of Things to robotics, which has earned it the nickname of "the mother of all technologies"[139]. It is destined to gradually permeate all sectors of human activity. Soon the question of whether or not it is used in a particular application will seem as inappropriate as asking today whether an elevator, a lighting and ventilation system, a local school or an airport control tower use electricity or not.

It is very likely that AI will actually spread much faster than electricity. Electricity has long been the victim of its centralised production mode: building a thermal power plant and building an electricity distribution network are extremely expensive infrastructure projects. Even shipping a generator to a remote location is a complicated operation. Artificial Intelligence, with some modifications, will spread even faster than

---

[139] This is the expression used by Charles-Edouard Bouée, CEO of Roland Berger and very active in the field. https://innovator.news/interview-of-the-week-charles-%C3%A9douard-bou%C3%A9e-dbd7aff638d5

mobile phones, via the cloud. Of course, the precise dissemination will depend upon the applications.

To describe the positive impact of Artificial Intelligence, let us restrict ourselves here to a horizon of one or two decades at most. Thus, rather than speculating about levels of technology that are completely inaccessible and uncertain at the moment, let us restrict ourselves to technologies that are largely proven and that, at most, only require industrialisation. Even in this restrictive context, AI should give new impetus to solving humanity's major challenges, such as controlling global warming, producing sufficient food, democratising education and providing an efficient and accessible health system. Daily life will also be transformed by Artificial Intelligence. Let's look at some selected pieces of a fictional situation in ten or twenty years, using only technology that already exists.

Improving daily life

The city is waking up. A well-orchestrated and constantly readjusted ballet begins.

That day is a Tuesday and on Tuesdays, in general, you go to the office, as do all your colleagues, so that the weekly team meeting can be held in person. The rest of the time, when you're not on the move, you work from your small suburban home. This morning, therefore, you order a taxi on your Transport as a Service app. The vehicle that comes to pick you up is autonomous[140]. You didn't have to wait long, because the powerful algorithms had anticipated the demand in your neighbourhood. In the past, taxis were too expensive, but now you can afford it. In this autonomous car you are safer and you yourself are less dangerous. Forgotten are the inattentiveness, carelessness, loss of control – the human failings that used to cause the vast majority of annual road deaths[141]. These used to claim 1.3 million victims worldwide, which is

---

[140] Autonomous vehicles will probably be widely marketed from the end of the 2020s.
[141] https://en.wikipedia.org/wiki/Traffic_collision

considerable. As for the car manufacturers, they have shifted their priorities from a driving experience to a mobility experience. Artificial Intelligence no longer monitors driver alertness, but ensures, by observing faces, that passengers experience a pleasant journey, adapting the temperature, brightness or musical ambience inside the vehicle.

Traffic is less dense in the city due to a combination of factors. Traffic peaks have spread and flattened because working hours are more flexible, and many people are going about their business from home, as you usually do. There are fewer vehicles because they are widely shared. But above all, traffic is managed much more intelligently. To promote fluidity, algorithms guide vehicles in a differentiated way, even if the origin and destination are the same for several of them. Traffic lights are synchronised and optimised in real time according to the traffic volume.

On the way, the city passes before your eyes. Here, the Cirque de la Lune has set up its tent. It remains as successful as ever, having integrated AI technologies into its shows without losing the human emotion. There, you drive through a former car park converted into student accommodation – there is much less demand for car parks since the car fleet has decreased, with vehicles being shared much more and therefore put to better use. It will obviously take time to renew the infrastructure, but it seems to you that your city is enjoying a welcome renaissance. It also looks more relaxed because security has increased considerably thanks to Artificial Intelligence – which, with the help of good governance in your city, has a drastic deterrent effect on crime.

In the distance, office buildings gradually come to life. This is your line of business, so you know that Building Management Systems – lighting, air conditioning, elevators, air quality, security – prepare the premises for the arrival of their occupants, optimising their energy consumption while guaranteeing maximum comfort. More than anything, you are happy because the weather is going to be fine today. It's not so much that you like to laze in the sun. But photovoltaic solar panels will work at full capacity, including those on your roof. Private power producers, including you, will contribute part of their production to the public distribution network, all under the baton of an Artificial Intelligence conductor. Battery recharging, which was temporarily put on hold yesterday, may happen today and, above all, it will not be necessary to restart the auxiliary coal-fired power plant. The environment and the entire population will benefit.

After a good meeting and a few hours at the office, you decide to go home early. The autonomous car drops you off and moves away; as it is off-peak time and the sun is shining, it seems it is going to a nearby charging station. As you walk towards the front door, it unlocks after a final biometric check. You obviously don't have a key, and that's good because you've never found them very practical. The house seems to have been notified of your arrival. The large curtain in the living room has opened, the luminosity matches your mood perfectly, the music is the same as in the car, and coffee is ready – the coffee maker has learned with experience that around that time you enjoy indulging in a small decaf. In your absence the autonomous vacuum cleaner did its job, the washing and drying machines ran, and the integrated folding machine – which took a few years to hit the market – returned clothes ready to be stored in the drawers. A drone just delivered the groceries. The small garden was watered according to the week's weather forecast.

"Oscar, turn on the TV and put the news on, please." Oscar is the name of your private virtual concierge. At home he is everywhere and nowhere. And the "please" is because you have chosen the polite option, to teach your children good habits. The virtual news anchor reads the news, perfectly up to date. A human journalist appears on the screen to interview an e-sport star. You already know his achievements by heart so you divert your attention to daily home updates:

"Oscar, what's new at home?"

"The heat pump water heater is deteriorating. It should continue to operate more or less correctly for another week. Should we bring in the repairman?"

"Yes, Oscar, bring him in early this week, please, preferably Tuesday before 5pm: that will be convenient because there will be no one at home. Activate the procedure for unaccompanied visitors. Oscar, also book a table for 4 people at a restaurant, preferably the local pizzeria or the

Indian, for Saturday evening. I love these precious moments spent with my wife and our good friends. And please have our favourite Italian menu delivered tonight, for 8pm, not here but at Stephanie's."

"Your aunt's?"

"Yes, at my Aunt Stephanie's."

You're very happy with Oscar's help. He is in charge of running the household. He also takes care of your finances, following the management instructions you have given, and resolves all common administrative problems. He makes appointments, answers the phone while you're away. When he doesn't know, he just asks you.

You just remembered the shopping left half-finished a few days ago and decide to complete it. You walk up to the magic mirror. "Oscar, let me try on the Jean-Philippe dress shirts, please." In the magic mirror, the shirts appear on your chest as if you had put them on. "The blue checked one, please. No, the green checked one." It suits you perfectly and the Jean-Philippe store knows your exact measurements. "Oscar, order it, please."

An email is sent to you with the label "Confidential". It's a rather unexpected job offer. Even if you have never worked in this field before, a detailed analysis of your skills and background has enabled you to be identified as an ideal candidate. And now that you think about it, it might suit your tastes, while allowing you to discover something new. This matching process is devilishly effective! You decide to explore the offer in more depth by the end of the week.

You are very satisfied with your home, because it is set up just the way you like it; that is to say, without undesired intrusion into your private life and with perfect control over the information that comes out of it.

But your two children are already coming home. They are covered with mud as they were playing in the park while it was raining. Even in the age of artificial intelligence, it is good for kids to play in the park and to be covered with mud from time to time. You spend a great half an hour with them: the perfect manifestation of the small and big pleasures you relish in life. It is now time to leave your children in the hands of Tom and Kate.

Democratisation of education

Tom and Kate, in fact, have no hands in the true sense of the word: they are virtual learning companions, who only exist on computer screens for the time being. Your children quickly adopted them, each giving them the look they wanted thanks to the avatars they made. They also gave them the personalities they preferred. Thus two avatars came to life: Tom, a man with a deep voice, a London accent and a rather strict personality, for your elder child, and Kate, a young woman with a New York accent – don't ask me why – and a sharp sense of humour, adopted by your younger son.

Tom and Kate are the educators who know your children best: they know how to identify their level, their strengths and weaknesses; they know their tastes and passions; they know how to get them interested and therefore how to motivate them. Given a learning objective, Tom and Kate know exactly which learning path to propose to each of your children – and these learning paths are different, combining the concepts, text, audio, video, or interactive exercises that are most effective for the child. Depending on the understanding demonstrated, Tom and Kate can accelerate or slow down, skip a step or dwell on the previous ones. They know when to introduce new concepts and when to repeat the old ones, using the principle of spaced repetition to increase the memorisation rate.

Tom and Kate are the educators who implement for your children the form of learning most prized in the teaching profession: adaptive learning[142], perfectly personalised and all the more effective. They are the ideal tutors, always available and attentive, never sick or tired, nor angry or irritated. Their knowledge is literally like that of an encyclopedia and more – everything the world knows, they know too. And while they are not yet perfect, while their communication skills are still basic, they have nevertheless acquired a solid pedagogical foundation. Without having the mechanisms of human empathy, their keen sense of

---

[142] Adaptive learning exists commercially in generic platforms such as SanaLabs, Adaptemy or Domoscio, as well as being already integrated into a large number of specialised solutions.

perception allows them to accurately detect your children's mood and their willingness to learn, on their faces, in their eyes and voices. They themselves are learning a little better every day to respond to them in an appropriate way; they are learning it at the speed of all the Toms and Kates of the world combined.

Across the world, in the near future of AI, educational avatars like Tom and Kate are lifelong companions in personal development. Available from an early age, they accompany learners in their educational journey, which now extends throughout their lives. Tom and Kate teach school subjects to children, along with cognitive and non-cognitive skills; they allow older people to improve or retrain; they occasionally become professional coaches or life coaches. Through their work, Tom and Kate play an important role in helping learners, regardless of their age, to achieve their full potential.

Lastly, Tom and Kate are the beginning of a solution to an economic equation once considered insoluble: having a permanent tutor in the home, of high quality and at an affordable cost. Since the dawn of time Tom and Kate's predecessors, at exorbitant cost, were reserved for the economic elite.

Tom and Kate's purpose is not to replace existing human teachers, but to increase their capacity to respond as well as possible to the challenges of teaching. They know better than anyone else the exact level of each student and the obstacles he or she faces, as well as the ideal ways to improve. They pass on these pedagogical elements to the teacher who, in charge of at least twenty or thirty students at a time[143], cannot get hold of this information by themselves, let alone remember it properly. Tom, Kate and their associates also free up teachers' time and minds by taking care of a large number of administrative or lower value-added tasks: taking attendance registers, recording notes on report cards, organising meetings with parents, and even marking students' work.

---

[143] It may be as many as a hundred for teachers of certain subjects.

Tom and Kate also step in when there is a shortage of teachers – and this is a trend that will continue to grow. UNESCO predicted that 69 million teachers would have to be recruited worldwide by 2030 to meet Sustainable Development Goals[144]. In sub-Saharan Africa, the shortage was 70% of primary school teachers and 90% of secondary school teachers! Where can teachers be found? Tom and Kate can be duplicated at will, given the right infrastructure and of course the right level of localisation.

Tom and Kate embody the democratisation of education, the alliance of quality on one side and geographical and social accessibility on the other side, the possibility of emancipation, the means to fix one of the deepest and most crippling inequalities that exists: inequality of educational opportunities.

You suddenly emerge from your thoughts when the children arrive noisily in the living room. They have finished for today with Tom and Kate, and the four of you, in an autonomous car, make your way to Stephanie's house.

Exponential progress in healthcare

Stephanie is weak and has to stay in bed most of the day. Having been given the choice, she prefers to live at home rather than in a hospital. She has visitors quite regularly, like you and the children today, in addition to the daily visit from the nurse. The rest of the time, a social robot takes care of her. It brings meal trays and takes them away, adjusts the lighting on demand, opens or closes the windows, fetches a book or changes the TV channels. And it's a little strange to admit, but Stephanie has become attached to her pet robot. Sociable and friendly, it is benevolent and attentive, always present and never in a hurry; its animated face is sometimes more expressive than real life; it seems to display empathy that she in turn feels, and it's always ready with a kind word. It also discreetly coordinates Stephanie's medical supervision without compromising on privacy: it brings medication and makes sure

---

[144] https://unesdoc.unesco.org/ark:/48223/pf0000246124_eng

it is taken. Sensors positioned at strategic points in the house alert emergency services in case of a physical problem; Stephanie's mental state is monitored by the analysis of her voice and speech, and of course some of her vital signs are constantly monitored as well. Stephanie is relieved not to be stuck in hospital, and the hospital works much better because it is not unnecessarily crowded. Society offers better comfort to one of its patients, protecting her from possible hospital-acquired infections and saving a lot of money in the process.

In the first few decades of the 21st century, patient care is only a very small part of the medical revolution triggered by Artificial Intelligence. From diagnostics to therapeutics, including fundamental research, drug development and health monitoring, the impact on the health sector has been profound.

Medical diagnostics was the first sector to be revolutionised, by applying the considerable progress made in image recognition to medical imaging, starting in 2012 [145]. As its first claim to fame, Artificial Intelligence was able to distinguish benign melanomas – simple moles! – from malignant tumours with better success than the most experienced dermatologists. Soon more than 2,000 types of skin cancer were made detectable and categorisable by an AI, with a level of performance equivalent to the best professionals [146]. Next came the fundus scans that made it possible to diagnose and instantly categorise more than 250 eye diseases [147]. Later, analysis of facial features paved the way for an instantaneous and reliable diagnosis at 90% accuracy of more than 200 types or subtypes of genetic diseases with facial phenotypes [148]. Simple electrocardiograms, analysed by AI, can reveal about ten different types of cardiac arrhythmias. AI rivals the best specialists at interpreting results in orthopaedic radiology, histopathological analyses of breast, lung or brain cancer and mammography. It successfully detects and classifies head injuries and

---

[145] See Eric Topol's very complete review [3].
[146] Made by a Google team [46].
[147] And they have the added bonus of being able to diagnose certain cases of diabetes or heart disease risks from images of the eye.
[148] DeepGestalt of the Face2Gene platform [36].

brain haemorrhages, pneumonia and tuberculosis. In all cases, improved diagnosis – simpler, more cost-effective, earlier, faster and more accurate – leads to better recovery prospects.

As a result of Artificial Intelligence, modern precision medicine adapts treatment to the exact condition of the patient and updates its prescriptions in near-real time. Hundreds or thousands of parameters are taken into account: the patient's genetic heritage, family history, physiological data and real-time immune system status, medication intake, medical test results, but also the patient's environment, behaviour and social relationships, conversations and state of mind, and finally all the medical literature that is constantly being updated. The highly personalised treatment of the patient is based on the knowledge accumulated across a longitudinal base of millions of individuals – which makes it possible to do predictive medicine. For example, AI-based predictive medicine can guide an intensive care unit in the treatment of sepsis[149]; determine short-term survival rates and guide resuscitation decisions; anticipate short-term relapse rates and delay discharge from hospital; and so on. Perhaps each patient will one day have a digital twin, on which all simulations can be tested[150].

With predictive medicine, current pathologies can be treated, and some not yet diagnosed can be anticipated [151]. Taken to the extreme, predictive medicine is preventative: the risks are detected so early that the patient is managed before the disease breaks out. In the future we will be less sick.

The remarkable progress of predictive medicine is largely due to the mass of medical information available with Machine Learning, transforming raw information into predictions. Medical information comes from electronic health records. There is a lot of unstructured data,

---

[149] Komorowski and colleagues describe how an AI clinical RN in 2018 suggested strategies for the treatment of sepsis in the intensive care unit better than its human counterparts [44].

[150] Topol points out that several industrial sectors already have digital twins, such as aircraft engines, refineries or other process plants [3]

[151] For example, in 2018, cardiac arrhythmias without detectable symptoms can be anticipated [36].

which in turn requires Artificial Intelligence to convert it into data that can be used by predictive algorithms. For example, conversations between doctor and patient must be transcribed using Natural Language Processing techniques, to make the rich data usable.

Sometimes, through the segmentation it carries out, Artificial Intelligence challenges the well-established practices and beliefs of specialists. This is what happened with a psychiatric practitioner whose patients were prone to panic attacks, post-traumatic stress disorder and clinical depression. The psychiatrist decided to give free rein to an AI that clustered five hundred patients into six groups, where previously there were only four classes, more arbitrary and segmented completely differently from the new groups. These six clusters were formed by the machine on the basis of both the symptoms described by the patients and their neural activity detected by electroencephalogram. The new classification heralded novel therapeutic possibilities[152].

Fundamental research has also benefited greatly from Artificial Intelligence. Genomics, for example, is a good playing field because of the amount of data to be managed. Algorithms can detect pathogenic genomic variants – or how a genetic alteration in a given individual is likely to lead to a disease. Another interesting case can be observed in the study of protein folding. The precise structure of three-dimensional proteins plays an important part in their properties. Understanding their folding, i.e. their geometry in space, makes it possible to better anticipate their function, fix certain errors or design new proteins. Some diseases, such as Alzheimer's, Parkinson's and Huntington's diseases, are thought to be the consequence of incorrect protein folding. However, the genes that encode the protein do not give any hint as to the folding, and the hundreds of amino acids that make up the protein can rotate and bend in many ways. According to Levinthal's paradox, the combinatorics of possible configurations would take longer to enumerate than the age of the universe. Experimental determination is long and expensive. AlphaFold, the Artificial Intelligence that DeepMind

---

[152] The work described is that of L. Williams; other work similar in nature has been carried out [34].

has dedicated to the subject since 2017, has distinguished itself since 2018 during the industry reference competition, where it crushed the competition[153]. AlphaFold provided the best prediction for 25 of the 43 proteins submitted during the competition, obtaining models in just a few hours of calculation.

Perhaps it is Artificial Intelligence that will rescue the pharmaceutical industry from its current struggles. The development of each new drug costs more than $2.5 billion in Research and Development[154], taking into account the failure rate. AI enables millions of molecular structures to be explored, replacing long upstream tests with simulations that anticipate the efficacy, adverse effects, contraindications or toxicity of target molecules. AI thus makes it possible to focus downstream tests on much more promising targets [155]. The development cycle then becomes significantly shorter and less expensive.

All in all, Artificial Intelligence makes clinicians more medically effective, makes health systems more economically efficient and empowers patients to take charge of their health. And high-performance medicine induced by Artificial Intelligence is still in its infancy. There is still considerable technological progress to be made to make AI more robust in the health sector; there is also a need to strengthen governance and limit inequalities in access. But AI is so promising that it will undoubtedly help to put the whole system back on track: improving patient outcomes while regaining[156] cost control.

As you reflect, the Italian meals ordered by Oscar are delivered to Stephanie's as planned – you didn't want to deprive your aunt of her meal trays. So you have dinner with Stephanie and the children... which brings new thoughts to your mind.

---

[153] https://deepmind.com/blog/alphafold , article not yet published [45].
[154] Daphne Koller in "Architects of Intelligence" [1].
[155] See Eric Topol's very complete paper: High-performance medicine: the convergence of human and Artificial Intelligence [3].
[156] See note 155.

Towards an efficient and sensible diet

According to data from 2017, one in nine people (more than 800 million people) is undernourished, while one in eight adults is obese: it is the paradox of food insecurity to lead to these two opposite outcomes[157]. The problem is steadily increasing. Conflicts that were once partially responsible for food insecurity are now replaced by climate variability and extreme events: droughts, floods, storms. In parallel, the population to be fed will increase by 2 billion people by 2050. How can AI help solve this difficult equation?

Modern farms have little in common with our grandparents' farms. They generate millions of data points every day and use real-time Artificial Intelligence to implement precision agriculture. Using images collected in the air by drones or on the ground, AI determines the exact and detailed state of maturity of the crops. Tractors and other autonomous devices move around in the fields, taking thousands of pictures per minute, providing the exact amount of nutrients needed, while irrigation also adapts finely to requirements. In greenhouses, light regulation allows the harvest to be moved forward or delayed. The presence of pests or the occurrence of diseases[158] is immediately detected, again by image analysis, triggering an alert for the farmer. At harvest time, a powerful but delicate autonomous machine moves along the furrows, selects the fruit or vegetables to be collected and picks them. In the case of fruit trees, the machine shakes the tree just enough for the fruit to fall down. Fruit and vegetables slide along a conveyor belt and are transferred to a trailer. A high-capacity sorter swallows the harvested fruit and vegetables to sort them according to their size, shape, colour and degree of maturity. Overall, the soil produces more while saving nutrients and water.

The farming community relies on algorithms with thousands of parameters to forecast demand and determine price levels. Each farmer,

---

[157] http://www.fao.org/state-of-food-security-nutrition/en/
[158] As early as 2016, an AI successfully detected a set of 16 diseases (or their absence) in 14 different plants and species: https://arxiv.org/abs/1604.03169 [4].

guided in their choices by demand analysis, also runs their own predictive algorithms to determine in advance the size and timing of their crops. The process leads to increased accuracy in sales and deliveries. It is also likely that food, which makes it to the plate with higher predictability and less waiting since picking, will be tastier, perhaps even more diverse, thanks to the better control of the entire supply process.

Supply and demand management is the first step in supply chain optimisation. This is not insignificant: in developing countries, about 90% of food losses[159] occur before reaching the consumer and often at the very beginning of the supply chain, due to the lack of adequate means of transport or storage and refrigeration, even though the goods are available. AI contributes to logistical optimisation by matching supply to demand, determining logistical routes and allocating the necessary means of transport or storage.

In developed countries, on the other hand, 40% of losses result from consumer behaviour: they buy too much or do not finish their plate. To make matters worse, the food they actually eat is not always healthy. AI facilitates the analysis, through consumer applications, of the nutritional quality of one's diet: informed consumers can adjust their diet accordingly, for example to fight diabetes or obesity.

Perhaps AI will also help humans go through the most important food transition of all time: adopting diets that are heavily based on plants and low in meat, in order to feed 10 billion people in 2050 without further damaging the environment[160].

The visit to your Aunt Stephanie's house comes to an end. You and the children kiss her – even though she's fond of her social robot, there's nothing she enjoys more than your company. Thanks to Artificial Intelligence, your life is easier, and you have more time than ever before. You devote it almost entirely to your family and friends, as well as to society – you volunteer in two associations. Artificial Intelligence may

---

[159] http://www.fao.org/3/ca1397en/CA1397EN.pdf
[160] Feeding on animals that feed on plants is inefficient compared to feeding directly on plants, particularly due to the emission of greenhouse gases.

have made you more human. In any case, it seems to you that the bonds between humans have strengthened. Tonight, you will read stories to the children before they go to bed. Next Saturday, you and your better half will go to the restaurant with some dear friends. You cherish these moments.

You also have more time to think about the things that really matter. One of them is of particular concern to you: the environment.

Saving the planet

The Earth system is in danger of irreversibly tipping over. Anthropogenic global warming is bringing the planet closer to thresholds beyond which a cascade of catastrophic events will be triggered. It will be almost impossible to reverse it and Earth will be lastingly transformed into a hothouse[161]. It is nothing less than a threat to human life on Earth. The catchphrase "Save the planet" is routinely used, but the planet needs no saving and will imperturbably continue cruising on its orbit around the Sun. Humans have more to worry about. This existential threat to humans could take place over a couple of centuries, but it is our actions today that determine its occurrence and timing. It would destabilise agricultural, economic, social and political systems, successively affecting low-lying coastlines and islands in danger of becoming submerged, then areas threatened by extreme temperatures or droughts, and gradually the whole world through a series of phenomena with dramatic consequences.

The issue of global warming is very complex. One of the first contributions of AI is precisely to build more accurate climate models, in order to better predict the evolution of our Earth system and its sensitivity to multiple parameters. Among leading climate models from 2018, the disparities in results raise questions, to say the least. If the amount of carbon dioxide in the atmosphere doubles, one model predicts a temperature increase of 4.5 degrees Celsius while another

---

[161] See the very complete article by Will Stephen et al: Trajectories of the Earth System in the Anthropocene [41].

model only sees an increase of 1.5 degrees Celsius. Initial modelling attempts, such as Cloud Brain, are underway, with their share of problems and hopes [162]. Others will follow suit to overcome the limitations of models based on physical laws, which are necessarily incomplete and require more and more computing power.

There is no consensus on the measures to be taken – whether technical, ethical or economic, while remaining equitable – to prevent the Earth from becoming a hothouse. However, three categories of actions are identified: reducing greenhouse gas emissions, increasing carbon sinks, and modifying the Earth's energy balance. Changing the Earth's energy balance, for example by altering the solar radiation affecting the Earth, could have undesirable side effects; perhaps its impact could be simulated by AI. Increasing carbon sinks begins with forest management but is not limited to this approach. AI makes it possible, by satellite or drone image, to precisely monitor the evolution of the forest footprint and to indirectly identify the individuals or organisations contributing to its reduction. Advanced sowing techniques using autonomous drones to drastically accelerate reforestation[163] have also been tested.

In terms of reducing greenhouse gas emissions, the main lever is in the energy sector. First and foremost, energy generation must be decarbonised. AI can help optimise renewable energy production and integrate its output with total production. The next step is to reduce consumption: AI has a major role to play in energy efficiency, reducing the consumption of buildings, industries, data centres [164] and even vehicles whose journey can be optimised. Finally, it is a question of matching supply and demand well, so that no surplus is ever produced; here again, the role of AI is considerable.

---

[162] https://e360.yale.edu/features/can-artificial-intelligence-help-build-better-smarter-climate-models
[163] See for example the specialised start-up DroneSeed
https://www.droneseed.co/
[164] DeepMind reduced the energy required to cool a data centre at its parent company Google by 40%. https://deepmind.com/blog/deepmind-ai-reduces-google-data-centre-cooling-bill-40/

Let us not forget that human food is also an indirect source of greenhouse gas emissions, due to the emissions of cattle, whose global consumption is growing rapidly. Changing your eating habits and improving the agri-food system also helps save the planet.

That day is coming to an end and you fully realise the importance that Artificial Intelligence has in your life and in the world. You owe it to AI that the day was made easier at work, in your travelling and in your everyday actions. Your well-being has increased, but that is not all. You have outsourced to machines all the work that machines can and should do. This has freed up time and share of mind for your loved ones and yourself, to cultivate your humanity and nurture your relationships with others. Today you have also seen AI at work in education and health. You have reflected on its impact on food and global warming. You know that it also helps find and identify solutions to all the other problems that burden the planet[165].

But AI will not solve all of humanity's problems like a magic wand. To what extent will the elimination of poverty and the reduction of inequalities be made possible by Artificial Intelligence? No one can answer these questions today, because Artificial Intelligence can either provide a satisfactory solution or, on the contrary, further exacerbate the problems.

Artificial Intelligence is ambivalent in its impact on humans. Its contribution to well-being and prosperity is immense, but it can also generate considerable dangers if we are not careful. That is what we will explore now.

---

[165] In particular, there are 17 key issues that are among the Sustainable Development Goals: https://www.un.org/sustainabledevelopment/fr/objectifs-de-developpement-durable/

Chapter 5. The perils of Artificial Intelligence

"**A**rtificial Intelligence is the new electricity", people claim light-heartedly and with a smile, but the comparison does not end at its transformational benefits. Electricity is also, quite naturally, used by the military in all their weapons systems; used by thugs of all kinds or sadistic torturers. History books remind us that Edison, on a mission to discredit alternating current [166], indirectly lobbied for the creation of the electric chair. He was partly responsible for the most barbaric executions ever known, because they took forever, and because the convicts sentenced to death were coming back to life with smoke floating above their heads [167]. Then electricity became synonymous with developmental inequalities over the next century and a half, with several billion people deprived of it and seeing their access to education, health, and economic emancipation considerably restricted.

Like electricity, like all technologies, Artificial Intelligence is ambivalent. In the previous chapter we listed some of the extraordinary benefits and promises for humanity. It also has a darker side. In itself, it is not bad, as we will see in the very next section. But it can be misused, either openly or more indirectly. The most important risks are also the most insidious.

Debunking the fear of Terminator

When James Cameron directed the first Terminator movie in 1984, little did he imagine the legacy he would leave. Several billion dollars in sales

---

[166] He was desperately trying to defend the idea of direct current, which was to be permanently relegated to the background... until the advent of renewables.

[167] https://www.businessinsider.com/edison-financed-the-electric-chair-2014-7/?IR=T

and a sixth instalment in 2019, certainly, but also a permanently bad image for Artificial Intelligence. Thirty-five years later, in fact, the killer cyborg and his Skynet associates still embody all the world's fears about AI. Spotting the business opportunity, Hollywood did not refrain from giving them a considerable number of heirs. The resulting effect on the collective imagination is not surprising. During my talks in primary schools, one of the first questions children ask with frightened faces is always: "Will the robots come and kill us?".

No, the robots will not come and kill us. The world may be very uncertain, but that's one of the few things we're pretty sure about.

Incidentally, if someone or something wanted to harm the human race, there would be many more effective ways than dispatching hardware.

But more seriously, why would a superior intelligence feel the urge to annihilate humans? The idea is itself anthropomorphic. Philosopher Steven Pinker points out that intelligence should not be confused with motivation[168]. "Even if we did invent superhumanly intelligent robots," he asks, "why would they want to enslave their masters or take over the world?"

With a touch of humour, noting the periodic "loss of mind" of Artificial Intelligence due to shortcomings of various kinds, researcher Pedro Domingos adds: "People worry that computers will get too smart and take over the world, but the real problem is that they're too stupid and they've already taken over the world."

The source of evil is not to be found in Artificial Intelligence itself. We need to look at the humans behind it.

The openly malicious use of AI

Do you want to rig elections by spreading fake news and targeting voters most likely to take the bait? Would you like to concoct a counterfeit but indistinguishable video, humiliating or wrongly incriminating a real person who has really upset you? Or would you prefer conducting a fake

---

[168] https://www.popsci.com/robot-uprising-enlightenment-now#page-2

but ultra-realistic video interview with a head of state with bellicose rhetoric, escalating an unstable situation or wrongly announcing the imminent outbreak of a conflict? Do you want to use the modern version of the hitman: a swarm of almost undetectable artificial insects, impossible to intercept, that inexorably approach their target and assassinate them without fail? What about launching a giant cyberattack that is very difficult to trace, in order to carry out a massive theft of funds, take control of an electrical distribution network or infect a hospital network with a computer virus?

For all these purposes, Artificial Intelligence is a weapon of choice. It can undermine democracy, organise a large-scale propaganda campaign to start a war, hack into the computer systems that equip our society's critical infrastructure. With consequences potentially as devastating as a nuclear bomb, it requires trivial means in comparison: a bit of hardware, a few lines of code, a few determined individuals who are competent enough to execute their dark desires. There is no need for nuclear physicists, uranium enrichment facilities or massive financial resources.

The malicious use of AI crystallises around Lethal Autonomous Weapons (LAWs), weapons that make the ultimate decision to kill on their own. In some cases, paradoxically, they would represent an improvement over their human counterparts: they are not driven by a desire for revenge, nor do they suddenly fall prey to uncontrollable outbreaks of violence; they simply fulfil a mission assigned to them. They may be better able to distinguish between actual targets and potential collateral victims, making wars less deadly and shorter. But Artificial Intelligence is cold, devoid of human judgment, completely oblivious to the notion of morality. It can, in the performance of an unspecified and unstoppable mission, cause immense and completely unforeseen damage. Weapons connected to online systems are also vulnerable to hacking.

Intellectuals and organisations have been making increasingly pressing calls for the regulation or prohibition of Lethal Autonomous Weapons. The Asilomar Conference, held in 2017 under the auspices of the Future of Life Institute, states in Principle 18: "An arms race in lethal autonomous weapons should be avoided." Since July 2018, more than 250 AI companies and 3,200 individual researchers have signed, at the initiative of the same institute, an individual commitment never to develop lethal autonomous weapons[169].

But how optimistic can we be, given recent history and current events? Nuclear non-proliferation and mutual assured destruction have worked relatively well, as there was no disaster after the Second World War, despite some major close calls. But the prohibition against chemical and bacteriological weapons has been violated, even recently, in a tragic way. As for autonomous weapons, the United Nations cannot even agree on a definition shared by all. France and Germany have not clearly supported a recent draft agreement against lethal autonomous weapons, claiming to be seeking a path acceptable to all. The United States, China and Russia are said to be strictly opposed to legislating[170].

In 2017, Russia announced with great publicity that its first robotic tanks "fought better than soldiers[171]". It is also reportedly in the development phase of swarms of killer drones[172]. In November 2018, China, which is usually more discreet, nevertheless leaked the recruitment of 31 talented young people under the age of 18 from among 5,000 candidates. They are taking part in a four-year program to develop autonomous weapons[173]: "These young people are exceptionally bright but being bright is not enough. We are looking for other qualities such as creativity, willingness to fight, persistence in the face of problems. The passion for weapons development is imperative... and they must be patriotic." The tone is set.

---

[169] https://futureoflife.org/lethal-autonomous-weapons-pledge/
[170] https://www.politico.eu/article/artificial-intelligence-killer-robots-france-germany-under-fire-for-failing-to-back-robots-ban/
[171] https://www.newsweek.com/russia-military-new-robot-tank-fights-better-human-soldiers-706836
[172] https://www.newsweek.com/drones-swarm-autonomous-russia-robots-609399
[173] https://futurism.com/the-byte/ai-weapons-china-children

Privacy under surveillance

In our increasingly digitalised world, it is becoming difficult not to leave footprints all day, month and year long. Algorithms saw you do your Google searches and Amazon shopping, check destinations and reviews on TripAdvisor, travel in a lift-sharing vehicle or scooter, pay for parking, restaurants and movie ticket purchases by mobile phone, check medical reviews on WebMD and book a consultation on Zocdoc.

These algorithms know a lot about you.

In 2012, the supermarket chain Target was already making headlines with a remarkable story. A family man, near Minneapolis, had gone to the local Target and very angrily asked to see the manager. His teenage daughter, still in high school, was regularly receiving promotions for cribs and various baby products, although she was not pregnant: surely this could only have a bad influence on her. The manager apologised unreservedly. A few days later, when he called the father back to apologise again, the father sounded very confused. His daughter, he had discovered while talking to her, was really pregnant! Target had learned this before the father, by analysing the nature of the girl's purchases. Her "pregnancy likelihood" had increased when she started buying a basket of revealing products, including some odourless lotions and nutritional supplements.

Fast forward to 2019. With increasingly powerful prediction algorithms, it is not impossible that Artificial Intelligence could detect the girl's pregnancy even before she is aware herself... It simply needs access to the right physiological parameters or other meaningful data. Another Artificial Intelligence could perhaps see a heart attack coming a few days ahead of its actual occurrence. It is all very well to warn the patient, but what would happen if the insurance company were to get hold of this piece of information? And since it is possible to detect congenital diseases by simply analysing the face, what possible discrimination could this lead to?

Let's stay in 2019. A well-known futurist describes in his book the shopping experience he will have in a supermarket within a few years:

"Hello, Mr. X, welcome back to the Y store!"

It's always a nice feeling when your shopping cart greets you like an old friend. As I pull the cart back from the rack, visual sensors embedded in the handlebar have already completed a scan of my face and matched it to a rich, AI-driven profile of my habits, as foodie, a shopper, and a husband to a fantastic cook of Chinese food.

And our futurologist tells in great detail how the shopping cart brings up the shopper's usual shopping list, adjusts the list of ingredients for a certain dish according to the inventory at home, guides him through the shelves, weighs and counts the purchases as they go along. At every turn, in the middle of the shopping centre, a human agent says hello by name, reminds him of his wife's birthday and recommends a good wine she should really like given her tastes, and so on...

For the futurist, who is none other than Kai-Fu Lee, the shopping experience in a Chinese supermarket is obviously a great pleasure. For many Western readers, it is a painful episode that only gets worse by anticipating how it might unfold. Fully aware of this dichotomy, Kai-Fu Lee points out that "people in China are more accepting of having their faces, voices and shopping choices captured and digitised. This is another example of the broader Chinese willingness to trade some degree of privacy for convenience." Indeed, the Chinese seem to genuinely perceive this small renunciation as a guarantee of more comfort and security; these technological solutions would, in their opinion, fix the evils of society.

To get the facts straight, we should stress at this point that the small renunciation is not limited to the supermarket. The entire country is gridlocked with cameras and sensors. With each data element collected (every meal purchase, every bike race, every service reservation, every social media message, every mobile payment...) they build an increasingly accurate profile of you. The natural evolution is the *social credit*, currently being tested in various forms in a few dozen cities and planned throughout China in 2020. This reputation score is each individual's citizen score; it officially aims to encourage integrity and restore credibility within society. Many Chinese say they approve of this system, which will make society safer and more stable. Citizens can even publish their score on dating sites. If you think this reminds you of an episode of the technological dystopia Black Mirror[174], keep it to yourself. It could turn against you.

Each citizen is assessed according to their behaviour in ethical[175], commercial, societal and judicial categories. The list of criteria assessed is bound to grow as the sensors enable it: is this individual straightforward and not corrupt if they are a public servant; are they honest in business; do they repay loans on time; do they cross the street when the light is green for them; do they moderate their alcohol consumption; do they refrain from posting subversive or incorrect messages on social media, and... do their friends refrain too, since friends' behaviours also impact one's score? If so, the individual will earn points; as a model citizen they will have a more comfortable life, preferential treatment in airports and hotels, access to better schools for their children. If not, the hassles, big and small, will pile up: they may not be able to take the train, access to credit and schools will be complicated, and civil servant jobs will be out of reach. Some ten million citizens have already been punished in the regions where social credit is being piloted[176]. The Australian newspaper ABC recounts the case of investigative journalist Liu Hu, who lost the libel suit brought by a politician he had accused of extortion. Since then, Liu Hu has been under house arrest and with his low social credit, he has been officially labelled as dishonest, banned from travelling and censored on social media[177].

This treatment of privacy is the choice of the Chinese regime. Europe has made a very different choice, with the coming into force of the General Data Protection Regulation, which requires organisations to obtain the informed consent of the individual for the collection of private data and to always offer the possibility of requesting its withdrawal, under penalty of substantial fines. The citizens of the United

---

[174] Nosedive, season 3, episode 1.
[175] Specifically, "honesty in public administration"
[176] https://mobile.abc.net.au/news/2018-09-18/china-social-credit-a-model-citizen-in-a-digital-dictatorship/10200278
[177] https://mobile.abc.net.au/news/2018-09-18/china-social-credit-a-model-citizen-in-a-digital-dictatorship/10200278

States, even without legislation, abhor the idea of a Big Brother monitoring their every move. Humanists in general are actively lobbying against profiling for consumerism or social regulation[178].

Misalignment or inadvertent disaster

In 2017, researchers from Stanford and Google unveiled the curious strategy employed by an Artificial Intelligence[179]. This AI, using the CycleGAN technique, aimed to convert satellite photos into Google Maps as efficiently and correctly as possible. To check the quality of the processing, the Google Map obtained was itself converted back into a satellite photo, then compared to the initial satellite photo. If the new satellite photo, generated by the AI, was very similar to the original, then the whole process was deemed to work perfectly – much as we are used to checking the quality of a machine translation by translating it back into the original language. CycleGAN, based on the comparison between the new and old satellite photo, seemed to work very well. *Too well*, in fact. Having a second look at it, researchers saw features reappear on the new satellite photo that tallied with the original, but were seemingly invisible on the intermediate Google Map. After analysis, it turns out that CycleGAN's algorithm had learned to encode details almost invisibly on the Google Map, which then enabled it to reconstruct the satellite photo. While doing so it was skipping the step for which it had been originally designed: making an exact representation of a satellite image on a Google Map.

CycleGAN reminded our researchers of an elementary truth: Artificial Intelligence does exactly it is asked, not what we want it to do or what

---

[178] And in particular Dr Christophe Habas, former Grand Master of the Masonic lodge the Grand Orient de France, who described the prevention of profiling as his greatest desire for AI at a conference in Singapore in January 2019.
[179] Casey Chu et al. CycleGAN, a master of steganography. *Arxiv 1712.02950, 2017.* https://arxiv.org/pdf/1712.02950.pdf

we think we asked it to do[180]. The researchers thought they had asked it to convert the satellite photo into a Google Map, but what they were really checking was the similarity between the original satellite photo and the one that had been reconstructed at the end of the process. Artificial Intelligence had therefore optimised its processing for the verification step, and no longer for the real human purpose.

This small misalignment here between humans and Artificial Intelligence seems rather harmless. There is plenty of literature on such amusing examples where the algorithm is rewarded by totally diverting the initial intention of the human designer. For instance, this autonomous car that runs in circles, or that video game character who jumps off a cliff to a sure death but drags his enemy along with him, earning him enough extra lives to start over indefinitely. Such examples abound[181].

But misalignment can also take a catastrophic turn. Imagine that you give an AI the apparently harmless instruction to compute as many decimals of pi as possible[182]. The AI computes, and the more it computes, the more energy it needs. The AI quickly realises that humans have a lot of energy and consume it everywhere, including in their electric water heaters or in their electric coffee machines. Little by little, the AI destroys everything that, from its point of view, wastes energy. It eventually destroys the human species and then conquers the entire galaxy for the simple purpose of calculating more decimal places of pi.

In another now classic analogy, imagine yourself, as a human being, in charge of a major hydroelectric dam project. If there is an anthill likely to be submerged by the future reservoir, you still decide to go ahead. Even if your goal is not to kill ants, it seems completely natural for you to do so to build the dam. Hence the need for humans, by analogy, not

---

[180] Max Tegmark and Stuart Russell point out that it is the same story as the genie in the lamp, King Midas, or the sorcerer's apprentice: we get exactly what we ask for. https://www.edge.org/conversation/the-myth-of-ai#26015
[181] The source, identified by Thomas Jestin, is https://russell-davidson.arts.mcgill.ca/e706/gaming.examples.in.AI.html
[182] Invented by Nick Bostrom and quoted by Yuval Noah Harari in Homo Deus. The anecdote is repeated in the following conference: https://www.youtube.com/watch?v=JJ1yS9JIJKs&feature=youtu.be

to put themselves in the situation of ants if an Artificial Intelligence is on a mission similar to the construction of the dam.

The problem is less trivial than it seems. How can we ensure that Artificial Intelligence understands our objectives, learns them, adopts them and preserves them? It is difficult to describe these human values and objectives because they are countless, not shared by all and, in any case, they keep changing. One of the most promising approaches is inverse reinforcement learning: rules are learned and modified according to the behaviour they induce[183].

Misalignment of objectives could, at worst, lead machines to inadvertently wipe out the human species. The problem is considered important enough by some to have led to the creation of OpenAI[184], one of the most powerful AI research organisations.

To date, this seems to us neither the most urgent nor the most likely of AI challenges. Perhaps it is more likely that machines will replace men and women not inadvertently but by pure Darwinian selection, competing for scarce resources, especially if humans are weakened by the impact of global warming. Machines do not suffer as much from hot and cold, hunger and thirst, drought and floods.

Human biases in the code

It is not only the objectives set by humans that Artificial Intelligence strictly obeys. When it learns from them, it does so with absolute compliance with the principles taught – for better or for worse.

In 2015, a Carnegie Mellon researcher tested Google's search engine. When looking for a fictitious job, he sometimes posed as a man, sometimes a woman, all other things being equal[185]. It turns out that

---

[183] https://futureoflife.org/2017/08/29/friendly-ai-aligning-goals/
[184] OpenAI, co-founded by Elon Musk, is a non-profit organisation.
[185] https://www.washingtonpost.com/news/the-intersect/wp/2015/07/06/googles-algorithm-shows-prestigious-job-ads-to-men-but-not-to-women-heres-why-that-should-worry-you/?noredirect=on&utm_term=.40b26e111960

Google returned job offers with high responsibility and high pay six times more often to male fictitious profiles than to female fictitious profiles: women were discriminated against by Google.

In a 2016 analysis, an AI used in the United States as an aid to alternative sentencing wrongly assessed black people as being twice as likely to reoffend as white people[186]. The doors to parole were unfairly blocked on a racial basis.

Many other cases of discrimination by algorithms against racial, religious, socio-economic or gender groups have been uncovered. Human biases are found in algorithm biases due to the data used for supervised learning. If humans are discriminatory, machines that learn from them will also be. If an AI was trained to recruit a top chef by looking at current Michelin-starred chefs, it would undoubtedly favour men. If the AI was asked to recruit a kindergarten teacher based on current demographics, it would favour women in most countries. These biases mirror today's society. If you need more convincing, just enter "CEO", "school teacher" or "starred chef" into Google image search.

Biases are directly related to the quality of training data, so discrimination can be more insidious. Facial recognition algorithms are more effective for Caucasian males than for any other group, simply because Caucasian males are over-represented in training data. The same is probably true for medical diagnostic algorithms, where some ethnic or gender groups are notoriously under-represented.

Beyond the composition of training data, one of the fundamental human biases may be the population working in AI: less than twenty percent of AI researchers are women, and that falls to only about ten percent amongst the most influential researchers[187].

The manipulability of AI has not gone unnoticed by malicious users. When Microsoft publicly launched its Tay chatbot in March 2016, it became racist and anti-Semitic in record time. Whatever it learnt had

---

[186] https://www.newscientist.com/article/2166207-discriminating-algorithms-5-times-ai-showed-prejudice/
[187] https://www.wired.com/story/artificial-intelligence-researchers-gender-imbalance/

been picked up from each conversation with its human interlocutors – and those who rushed to influence Tay were openly malicious. Microsoft withdrew Tay from service after just 16 hours. As one AI observer humorously points out, this event is not a symptom of Artificial Intelligence failure but rather of poor parenting[188].

There are therefore many biases which cause the discrimination already present in real life to be transposed to the digital world. Overcoming them requires higher quality of the algorithms themselves and especially of the training data, which must become more accurate and representative.

On the other hand, Artificial Intelligence may turn out to be a solution to the numerous human biases. In addition to the obvious cases of discrimination, humans display at least 120 cognitive biases – you will find them on Wikipedia in what seems an endless list[189]. Other biases are at first glance unexpected, such as the propensity of some judges to impose heavier sentences before lunch than after lunch[190]. Artificial Intelligence could be used to identify and fix them. Fortunately, the level of sensitivity to bias in the AI community is on an upward trend[191].

Efforts to eliminate bias are all the more critical as algorithms play an increasing role in our lives.

Alienation by algorithms

Artificial Intelligence has an unrivalled ability to offer us what we love. You, over there, Google has seen that you like old cars and skydiving, and is tasked with tempting you with them. The trading platforms are offering us the next book, the next dress, the next electronic gadget, the next saucepan that we will certainly buy. Travel sites note our interest

---

[188] The statement is from Jason Widjaja.
[189] https://en.wikipedia.org/wiki/List_of_cognitive_biases
[190] https://www.economist.com/science-and-technology/2011/04/14/i-think-its-time-we-broke-for-lunch . This study is no longer unanimously accepted today.
[191] See the remarks of Fei-Fei Li, very committed to diversity and against discrimination [1].

in Peru, Namibia or Vietnam, our loyalty to Unforgettable Treks or Pacific Club, and drown us with related ads. Content sites see our interest in migration policy; they even detect whether we are more in favour of opening borders or against any immigration and undertake to provide us with even more content that reinforces our conviction. Friends of our friends come to enrich our lists of friends. Gradually a filter bubble[192] is created, trapping us in a closed universe and making it more difficult to connect with the outside world. Suddenly, an aviation enthusiast is delighted that aviation is so much talked about on Facebook. An ardent promoter of hydrogen fuel cells is enthusiastic about how the subject has won people's minds on LinkedIn.

These preconditions for loss of control over algorithms are already in place today.

Professional and social environments, in parallel, are augmented by decision support tools. Some of them have perverse effects. Bankers use algorithms to decide whether or not to grant a consumer loan, based on the applicant's presumed ability to repay. If an unsuccessful applicant asks why their loan was refused, an honest banker today could say nothing more than "It was the algorithm that determined it." Why did it decide to do so? Impossible to say[193]. Deep Learning is not yet explainable[194]. It's a black box. A convict might not understand the reason why their bail was rejected. The unsuccessful candidate in a hiring process will not be able to figure out why they were rejected by the algorithm.

By submitting to third party decisions, which are currently not explainable, a step has been taken towards the loss of free will.

Tomorrow, the field of influence of algorithms will increase even more. The following account is fictitious but could happen if we are not cautious enough:

---

[192] https://en.wikipedia.org/wiki/Filter_bubble
[193] Such a non-transparent AI is contrary to European ethical principles.
[194] Work is underway to enhance explainability, sometimes with different algorithmic classes that do not decrease the algorithmic performance too much.

Because I trust my virtual advisor, I comply with her recommendations on the friends I should see or leave, the activities I should undertake, the errands I should run, the outings I should organise. Gradually, recommendations become implicit decisions since they are no longer accompanied by alternatives. My virtual counsellor, whom I literally entrust with my life, determines the additional studies I need to pursue, organises my learning periods in detail, and then when I am ready, finds me a new job. When she offers me a new life partner, I accept without hesitating because the algorithms have optimised the choice.

There is a risk of total alienation by algorithms, where life would be lived by proxy, following the de facto decisions of machines. Machines would know us better than ourselves and eventually take total control over our lives. Humans would in that sense be hacked by AI.

This, again, is fictitious for the time being – and many are working hard to ensure that it remains so.

Ethical safeguards

In order to prevent the dangers of AI from materialising, some people are thinking about ethical safeguards. The question is thorny since ethics is a highly cultural and personal concept. We saw earlier the radically different choices of personal data management in China and Europe.

To ensure oversight and accountability in the AI field, many people are calling for regulation of the sector, in a way that protects humans but does not paralyse them in the process. However, regulation has become more difficult because regulators do not fully understand the activity and functioning of these companies, which are of a new kind for them – the hearings of certain executives by parliamentary committees have shown the fundamental difficulty of this. In addition, the leading Internet and Artificial Intelligence companies have become very powerful multinationals, often stronger and more agile than nations, sometimes playing with borders (at least tax borders). The valuation of 5 of these companies, the GAFAM (Google, Amazon, Facebook, Apple, Microsoft), is of the order of magnitude of 1 trillion dollars. Two Chinese companies, Alibaba and Tencent (the parent company of WeChat[195]) are not far behind. The resources of these companies put them in the position of a virtual oligopoly of researchers in Artificial Intelligence[196]. Some of their business models, based precisely on data collection and resale, are at the core of AI tensions. These Internet giants have sent mixed signals, organising ethical initiatives for some[197], promising self-regulation for others, repeating *mea culpa* but ultimately demonstrating very little progress.

Europe is at the forefront of ethical thinking about AI, and decided to start with non-binding recommendations. Initiatives are flourishing on all sides, such as the Dutch ECP platform, which published its recommendations in January 2019[198]. In December 2018 The European Commission published a draft of the "Ethics Guide for a trustworthy AI", the final version of which is expected in March 2019. Europe, true to its values, states that "*a human-centric approach to AI is needed, forcing us to keep in mind that the development and use of AI should not be seen as a means in itself, but as having the goal to increase human well-being. Trustworthy AI will be our north star, since human beings will only be able to confidently and fully reap the benefits of AI if they can trust the technology. Trustworthy AI has two components: (1) it should respect fundamental rights, applicable regulation and core principles and values, ensuring an "ethical purpose" and (2) it should be technically robust and reliable since, even with good intentions, a lack of technological mastery can cause unintentional harm.*"

According to the European Commission, human centrality must be anchored in the following principles: beneficence (doing good); non-maleficence (not doing harm); human autonomy (respect for self-

---

[195] A Chinese application, combining the functionality of Facebook, Twitter, Whatsapp and a powerful e-wallet, with more than a billion users.
[196] Of the 23 architects of intelligence that Martin Ford questions in his book, 7 are linked in some way to Google [1].
[197] For example, Google's multiple "AI Principles" or Microsoft's FATE (Fairness, Accountability, Transparency and Ethics in AI) initiative.
[198] Artificial Intelligence Impact Assessment
https://ec.europa.eu/futurium/en/system/files/ged/ai_hleg_draft_ethics_gui delines_18_december.pdf [6].

determination and the choice of individuals concerning their own lives), justice (fair and equitable treatment for all); and explainability (transparent functioning of algorithms)[199].

The AI governance model proposed by Singapore[200] in January 2019 is similarly inspired. It is based on two guiding principles: the human-centredness of AI and the need for all decisions made or suggested by AI to be explainable, transparent and fair.

These European or Singaporean principles are the opposite of the perils we examined earlier: the misuse of AI, surveillance, bias, alienation by algorithms and to some extent the risk of misalignment. The detailed principles illustrate Europe's values and highlight the gap between Europe and China in particular. In the latter country, not only are the values radically different, but so is the approach: pragmatism leads to trying first and perhaps passing laws later. It cannot be ignored that China, among others, will progress much faster in the deployment of AI since it does not impose any constraints on itself... other than to go fast and reach a position of absolute domination in 2030. To do so China also benefits from the mass of data generated by 1.4 billion people.

Social disruption: inequalities and the future of work

We have just navigated through some of the dangers and threats relating to Artificial Intelligence. However, the most important danger in the short and medium term is not to be found in killer robots and would-be terrorists, nor in the inadvertent disaster. In the face of the biggest peril, bias in the code or privacy surveillance will seem almost insignificant, and AI's ethical principles will be put to the test. This peril is the major social upheaval that is waiting to happen in the world of

---

[199] The first four principles have been used in medical ethics since the 1997 Oviedo Convention.
[200] https://www.imda.gov.sg/about/newsroom/media-releases/2019/singapore-releases-asias-first-model-ai-governance-framework

work, together with its share of inequality. This will form Part 2 of this book.

Artificial Intelligence: takeaways

A formidable and ambivalent force

Artificial Intelligence is one of the most powerful transformative forces of our time, and perhaps even of all time. The foundation of the Fourth Industrial Revolution, it is the new electricity – a general-purpose technology destined to spread through all of society.

Artificial Intelligence burst into the public debate one day in 2016, beating one of the world's best players at Go – a game so complex that it was thought to be impenetrable by machines for decades to come. AI is also starting to drive our cars; AI listens, analyses, speaks and translates; AI recognises objects better than we do; AI operates warehouses, optimises routes and calculates prices; AI manages our investment portfolios and detects fraudulent transactions; AI recommends books and paints portraits; AI diagnoses a growing number of our diseases, and works to predict their evolution and cure them.

Artificial Intelligence will profoundly change our daily lives by making them more convenient, comfortable and safe. AI is also already working to solve the greatest challenges of our time: first, global warming, which must be tackled urgently even if the result is not guaranteed; democratisation and personalisation of education; the establishment of a precise, efficient and accessible health system; and the transformation of the agri-food sector so as to provide sustainable food for 10 billion people by 2050. All in all, its contribution to our well-being will be immense.

But like all technologies, Artificial Intelligence is ambivalent. If we are not careful, it also presents dangers and risks. There will be no evil robot that comes and kills us – this myth must be dispelled. But the misuse of Artificial Intelligence by malicious humans is a very real danger, whether through autonomous lethal weapons, cyberattacks or small- or large-scale manipulation. Privacy can also be at risk, with personal data falling into the hands of unscrupulous private or government actors. In a more insidious way, in the longer term, our whole life can be alienated by machines. Finally, there are two indirect risks: the first, proven and already harmful today, that human biases are reflected in the analyses and decisions of Artificial Intelligence; the second, much more distant and hypothetical, that Artificial Intelligence, believing it is carrying out its mission but actually misaligned, might inadvertently destroy us one day.

Human institutions and think tanks are working to establish ethical safeguards, but these efforts are still partial and non-binding. Some of the major powers in Artificial Intelligence, with very different views, are unlikely to participate.

What Artificial Intelligence really knows how to do

Impressive as it is, Artificial Intelligence is neither magical nor supernatural – it's only a few lines of code. There are half a dozen large algorithmic classes. The oldest one, **symbolic** Artificial Intelligence, is based on logic rules. Sometimes difficult to implement because of the almost unmanageable number of cases to be anticipated, it has been sidelined in favour of **connectionist** Artificial Intelligence. This is part of the family of **Machine Learning**, systems whose performance increases with experience, designed for their ability to learn without the target subject being explicitly programmed. Connectionism, based on **artificial neural networks**, has seen an extraordinary improvement in its performance with the explosion of computing power and data available for training. We owe to connectionism, and more particularly to Supervised Learning by neural networks, most of the applications operating today outside the world of research.

Machines certainly don't work like humans. But does that matter? Planes don't flap their wings, yet they fly... and they fly extremely well. In a world where the trajectories of machines and humans are increasingly intertwined, the comparison between human mental processes and the capacities of machines are of utmost importance – not in the fine details of their mechanisms but comparing their outcomes in a more pragmatic way; not according to a decimal quantification but by proposing major qualitative trends.

Humans are clearly surpassed by machines in terms of **memory**, **attention**, **willpower**, and soon **perception** and **motor skills**. Paradoxically, in contrast, humans are far superior in their ability to **learn** effectively and efficiently. Humans rely on billions of years of evolution engraved in their genes, while the machine has no previous model of the world or common sense. Machines do not have the **creativity** of humans, except by imitation or exploration of a field of possibilities. Machines do not experience human **emotions**; instead, they excel at detecting them and reacting in a way that looks deceptively and credibly like empathy. Machines are uneven in their **reasoning**: they greatly surpass humans in their ability to calculate, detect correlations and make predictions, estimates or optimisations; however, they struggle to explain their reasoning, are ignorant of causality and remain highly specialised in the narrow fields for which they were set up. Even without understanding **language**, machines are extremely efficient at speech recognition and generation; they are improving rapidly at machine translation and manage to mimic semantic understanding – but they still have a long way to go in this field. Finally, they are devoid of world-consciousness and self-consciousness.

An uncertain future

The future of Artificial Intelligence depends on the improvement of current techniques and radical innovation. In the long run, the Holy Grail of the field is Artificial General Intelligence, a versatile and flexible form of intelligence equal to that of humans. The long road to achieving this will involve solving the problems of ease of learning, causality and transparency of reasoning, and the broadening of areas of application well beyond their current narrowness – and all the challenges that we cannot even imagine today.

Artificial General Intelligence, if successful, will mark a clear break with the history of life on Earth over nearly four billion years: a machine will then equal the most sophisticated biological intelligence. When are we likely to succeed? The leading architects of Artificial Intelligence are very divided but end up – if hard pressed to respond – at a median date of 2100, while others in the field – certainly a little less technically savvy – are betting on a date between 2040 and 2050.

This unique moment in the history of humanity, this singularity preceding perhaps an exponential and recursive development of Artificial Intelligence, is feared by some and desired by others. Intellectual honesty mandates us to admit that we know nothing about what could happen then.

But well before that, it will be necessary to tackle the most formidable challenge posed by Artificial Intelligence: the disruption of work and the rise of inequality.

Part II

Work

Chapter 6. Four visions of the future of work

F our friends are sitting at a table. They often meet, just as they are doing today, to discuss the future of work, particularly given the impact of Artificial Intelligence. The discussion is no less anxious for them than for the rest of the population. Will there be enough work to go around? More urgently, will there be work for *every person,* not just enough for everyone on average? If this work does exist, will it be sufficiently compensated for people to make a decent living?

As the Danish proverb goes, "it is difficult to make predictions, especially about the future."[201] Our four friends have read everything that is published on the subject. They quickly realised that the conclusions of all the forecasts differed drastically. State your conclusion, and we will find you the study that justifies it. Look carefully at the small print and remember that the devil is in the details: such-and-such a report only covers the next 5 years, and by a bold extrapolation concludes that 58 million net jobs will be created, without mentioning what comes next[202]; in contrast, this other study looks at the long term, but the cut-off date of 2055 actually has a margin of error of about 20 years[203]; many analyses quantify only those trades that are destined to be automated without looking at job creation; this umpteenth study predicting net job creation is based solely on opinion surveys that are not necessarily objective[204]. Sometimes, waiting barely six months is enough for a

---

[201] Often wrongly attributed to Niels Bohr.
[202] World Economic Forum – Future of Jobs 2018 – September 2018 [30].
[203] McKinsey – Harnessing automation for a future that works – 2017 [10].
[204] Gartner Group – The job landscape in 2022. Asking business leaders if they intend to destroy jobs is always a tricky question!

forecasting institute to modify their 10-year conclusions[205]. In terms of net impact, some forecasters are betting on net job creation, others on stability, and others still on net job destruction, but the scenarios are always accompanied by very ambitious assumptions about requalification and economic growth [206]. The International Labour Organization, noting the absence of a clear conclusion and understanding only too well the inherent difficulty of the exercise, simply gave up on the idea of doing its own quantification[207].

In the end, our four friends, although well informed, were unable to agree on any given scenario due to the lack of clear and convincing sources. Therefore, they all developed very different visions of the future of work. After repeatedly making a case for their respective positions, they ended up with apt nicknames: the Optimist, the Moderate, the Pessimistic, and the Radical.

The Optimist

Of the four friends, the Optimist is the first to speak.

"Modern technologies such as Artificial Intelligence are a tremendous boon for humankind. Actually, rather than Artificial Intelligence, I prefer to call it Augmented Intelligence. At last, humans have at their disposal a powerful tool that multiplies their own capabilities. Such is the contribution of Artificial Intelligence. Imagine a doctor: with the help of AI, their diagnosis is more reliable. Look at translators: thanks to AI, most of the work is done almost instantly. Human translators check and refine the machine's work. They can now focus on the most subtle nuances. We are augmented by machines. We work faster and better!"

"Isn't the reality a little more nuanced?" the always rigorous Moderate asks. "If Artificial Intelligence automates a task that's peripheral to the

---

[205] In June 2016 Forrester forecast a net loss of jobs in the USA of 7% by 2025, then in September 2016 a net loss of 6% by 2021, then in April 2017 a net loss of 7% by 2027.
[206] See in particular Jobs lost, jobs gained from McKinsey [11].
[207] See ILO report: Working to build a better future [32].

main activity, then the individual can devote more time to their core business, achieve even greater added value and undoubtedly increase their income. But if it's the main activity that's automated, even partially, then it becomes a threat to employment. Take, for example, the automation of appointment scheduling. For professionals who meet with clients, this is a boon and they are augmented by it. For an administrative assistant, this is a very bad start, since one of their main activities now falls under the scope of action of Artificial Intelligence."

"In my opinion," the Optimist replies, "there is no need to worry, because of the complementarity between man and machine. Humans, working in tandem with machines, will always be stronger than humans alone and even than machines alone. It's the winning team, thanks to augmentation."

"Only for the time being," the Moderate retorts. "The superiority of the human–machine tandem is only a temporary state. Let's take the case of chess. We have been pointing repeatedly to 'centaurs', the hybrid human–computer teams that appeared after Deep Blue's victory. Indeed, for some time, they generally prevailed over purely human or purely artificial opponents. But since Alpha Zero, machines have become so superior that any human intervention can only weaken them. Humans, in chess, are no longer useful. Their time is up in most board games, and so will it gradually be in many other areas. The sequence is always the same: for a finite period of time, humans are first slightly augmented, then more, then completely replaced. In the past, lighthouse keepers disappeared with automation. Genius calculators or memory champions are little more than circus animals or YouTube stars – their art intrigues and offers a little taste of anachronism. Tomorrow, truck drivers will also disappear – even if overall it will take longer. Translators, now augmented, are witnessing how their field of work is shrinking. By augmenting humans, Artificial Intelligence eventually replaces them completely."

"This time you seem to be the one who is not nuanced enough," the Optimist replies. "There will be no job destruction, because Artificial Intelligence very rarely replaces a job in its entirety: it only performs some of the tasks of a given job. Accountants, relieved from account balancing calculations, which are not the most enjoyable, and even before that relieved from the identification of invoices and their manual entry into computer systems, can focus on the more interesting issues of account allocation, depreciation schemes, and management control[208]. Bankers, if they no longer have to monitor stock markets, will be able to focus on fully understanding their clients' objectives. Teachers, freed from marking homework and transferring grades from one document to another, can finally play their role as facilitator and chief motivator in the child's education. Doctors, whose diagnoses are facilitated by machines, can devote more time to the emotional needs of the patient. Recruitment managers, instead of having to review a pile of 30,000 CVs in order to extract 10, will be able to spend much more time interviewing in depth the 30 candidates pre-selected by Artificial Intelligence according to a rigorous, systematic procedure, and without discriminatory bias."

The Pessimist jumps in because he cannot allow what he believes is a logical flaw.

"If Artificial Intelligence performs 75% of the tasks of a given profession, even without completely destroying it, then if demand is constant that profession will only employ a quarter as many people. It follows that three quarters of the jobs are destroyed. And you don't need those three quarters of people to decide on depreciation rules or interview a few candidates in greater detail."

"Demand will not remain constant," the Optimist immediately replies, "and the Moderate will not contradict me: with the drop in prices, demand increases[209]. And most importantly, automation of jobs will take time. I would like to remind you that progress never comes as fast as people expect it. Remember the autonomous car of the Prometheus Project, which went from Munich all the way to Copenhagen with peaks

---

[208] See an illustration by Pascal Bornet
https://www.linkedin.com/feed/update/urn:li:activity:6476400372549283841/
[209] This is indeed one of the Moderate's main arguments, see a bit further.

of 175 kilometres an hour. That was back in 1995[210], almost 25 years ago. We are still waiting for this to become mainstream. Some people even maintain that completely autonomous vehicles are never going to happen[211].

"But let's get back to the heart of the matter. The contribution of Artificial Intelligence is also the opportunity for us humans to stop being machines and finally become truly human again! We will be freed from routine or alienating tasks: handling goods in warehouses, picking tomatoes in a field, preparing hamburgers in a fast food restaurant, following up orders or industrial-scale technical support in a call centre. There is also no need for strenuous or dangerous jobs: work in contaminated areas or on minefields, or washing high windows. Machines are taking on this work, which is unworthy of humans. No more repetitive tasks where our human genius is not expressed: linear regressions for a marketing study, account balancing for balance sheets and income statements in an accounting firm. Machines do this for you while you focus on the more interesting, higher added value tasks. Machines augment you and in doing so free you from unworthy or tedious tasks. This is similar to half a century ago when electronic calculators came out – have you ever asked your parents? It became so efficient – and pleasant – to no longer have to do all the calculations by hand! Thanks to Artificial Intelligence, there is an era of well-being ahead of us. Let's not be scared! Let us not be frightened by birds of ill omen."

"I don't want to be a killjoy," the Moderate says, "but we must keep in mind that jobs are also an economic necessity for many people. These workers and employees who will thus be 'freed from their alienation', how will they earn a living in the era of Artificial Intelligence?"

"They will be trained for something else. And we must also bear in mind that it is we, humans, who decide on the pace of development and deployment of Artificial Intelligence. We know how to differentiate

---

[210] https://en.wikipedia.org/wiki/Eureka_Prometheus_Project
[211] The doubts about the autonomous level 5 vehicle are recalled by Eric Topol for illustrative purposes [3].

between what can be developed and what should be developed. If we want to control progress in such a way as to preserve human employment, this is perfectly possible. Instead of substituting humans with technology in certain jobs, we may decide to simply complement them. We can choose to make technology work for humans, not against them! We can therefore rationally organise the world as we wish."

"Wanting to curtail progress and its deployment is a lost battle," the Moderate interrupts. "The benefits of technology to the rest of humanity are such that the spread of technology could not be stopped just to preserve employment – especially for antiquated jobs. Were horses and carriages preserved when motor cars first appeared? Did you continue to buy film cameras just to protect jobs in film factories? Did you buy a Nokia phone just to support employment, when competitors launched smartphones? And then, from a more cynical point of view, automation leads to considerable cost savings. Remember what happened in the 1990s and 2000s with offshoring? Many companies, motivated by profit and under the pressure of fierce competition, chose to move their production centres and suppliers to countries with low labour costs in order to save a few dollars. And even more paradoxically, while it is the general public who ultimately suffers from offshoring, did they choose to purchase local goods in order to promote local employment? Or, conversely, did they not rather make their decision based on very short-term preferences, in order to save a few dollars, that would eventually prove devastating? You have the answer you were looking for about controlling the spread of technology and people's individual preferences."

"There are other motivations for a progressive and sensible introduction of technology. Sometimes its use reduces human cognitive abilities and we must be careful with it. By storing information in mobile phones, our memory has weakened. The repeated use of the calculator has affected our ability to do mental arithmetic. The use of GPS has altered the areas of the brain that provided us with spatial orientation. And if you reduce brain stimulation, you increase the risk of developing diseases of old age at an earlier age."

"The facts are true, but I don't think this argument is likely to slow down the spread of technology or the evolution of our activities. Vehicles reduced the time we spend walking and indirectly affected our health, but we have not refrained from developing cars; we are simply looking for substitutes for maintaining good health, and we walk just for pleasure! Changes in our brain function are not new either over the distant past or over the recent past. Even the human capability of reading, on a lifetime scale, changes our ability to recognise faces[212]; nevertheless no one ever took this as an argument to prohibit reading."

"There is a good reason for my nickname, and I remain optimistic. Humans will be augmented and their humanity will be expressed even more. The impact on employment will be controlled for the better, because we are the ones in charge."

The Moderate

The Moderate, despite all her criticism of the Optimist's ideas of pure augmentation, is not pessimistic. She is first and foremost a fine historian and believes she has spotted an old trend.

"Artificial Intelligence is the driving force behind the Fourth Industrial Revolution. We have seen other industrial revolutions. The previous ones were based successively on the steam engine, electricity and information science. This one is not fundamentally different from the others. Whereas there was mechanisation of physical tasks in the past, there will now be automation of mental processes. The same pattern occurs every single time. At first, the revolution undeniably generates chaos and job destruction. Society is left in doubt and in fear. 'We are being afflicted with a new disease of which some readers may not yet have heard the name, but of which they will hear a great deal in the years to come—namely, technological unemployment,' Keynes wrote

---

[212] See the many examples set forth by S. Dehaene [17].

in... 1930[213]. The initial reaction of the population is violent, as is the initial impact of technology on society.

"But soon society fights back. People observe, analyse, understand and then learn. They acquire the new knowledge required. They move to the most dynamic new areas. In other words, society adapts. New opportunities emerge, new professions appear. The economy picks up again with greater strength. The destruction will have been only temporary and within a few years or decades, what was initially a destruction becomes a major source of employment and wealth. This is a perfect illustration of the economist Schumpeter's claims[214].

"Remember the Luddites in 19th-century England? These textile workers felt so threatened by the new automatic looms that they organised their destruction. They wrecked the machines. But automation led to lower production costs. And it turns out, as the Optimist alluded to earlier, that demand for textiles increased. The whole industry grew. More machine operators were needed. Consequently, a whole ecosystem of machines was created, needing design, manufacture, maintenance and operation. Society as a whole benefited from the initial disruption."

The Pessimist breaks his silence:

"The Luddites understood that with mechanised looms, the level of qualification required by textile workers would drop, leading to an influx of labour supply and a fall in wages. It did not fail to happen. Technology-driven deskilling and reduced pay are all too common."

"Above all, I see increased access to employment thanks to technology," the Moderate replies, "which is something we are already widely witnessing today. But that's only one aspect. Consider the replacement of carriages, in the West - or rickshaws, in the East - by motor vehicles.

---

[213] John Maynard Keynes, "Economic Possibilities for our Grandchildren (1930)," in *Essays in Persuasion* (New York: Harcourt Brace, 1932), 358-373
[214] In the 1950s, Schumpeter introduced and popularized the idea of "creative destruction".

Neither man nor animal has had to make exhausting and unworthy physical efforts since then, at least where the replacement took place."

"And these horses, substituted by motor vehicles, where are they today?" the Pessimist pretends to wonder. "Have they benefited from creative destruction or have they been permanently excluded from any economic activity? I don't want humans to suffer the same fate: being completely excluded."

"Horses are not worse off; quite the contrary. They never asked to be draught animals. And the automotive industry has developed with its engineers and workers, and a general increase in their prosperity. Around it, an entire ecosystem was built, including garages, insurance agents, petrol stations and road signage equipment. This was a real revolution for sure, which as a whole proved to be eminently positive.

"There is no dearth of examples. Agricultural labour represented 90% of total employment in the United States in 1790, 43% in 1890, and less than 3% in 1990[215]. Does this mean that a terrible disaster for humanity occurred and that back them we embarked on a particularly harmful path by destroying employment in the sector? Of course not. Agricultural productivity multiplied and other sectors such as industry took over the workforce.

"Besides, take the more recent introduction of ATMs in banks from the 1970s onwards. Cashiers had much less work in each branch, but the cost of opening a bank dropped, so a much larger number of branches were opened. The traditional role of cashiers was replaced by machines, and the cashiers themselves became advisors. Overall, employment in the banking sector increased throughout this period."

"And it seems to me that the number of banks is now plummeting, and that branches are closing one after the other," the Pessimist thinks it useful to add.

The Moderate remains unfazed.

---

[215] https://www.agclassroom.org/gan/timeline/farmers_land.htm

"Last but not least, take the development of Information Technology. IT, like AI, is a general-purpose technology, so the example is particularly relevant here. Users gained the ability to calculate, classify, schedule, plan, model, simulate. Machines offered interesting capabilities that only called for being tapped; so much so that computer scientists and analysts of all kinds, far from being hampered by machines, have thrived and proliferated. In terms of personal organisation, users were augmented as they gained the ability to type their mail, book their flight tickets and organise their appointments without assistance. There is no doubt that typists, secretaries and personal assistants became collateral victims, which for them is dramatic. Even if a socio-professional group went on to shrink considerably, isn't the bottom line of IT expansion extremely positive?

"Indeed, jobs will be destroyed as Artificial Intelligence spreads. And others will be created. We always underestimate beforehand the number of new professions created. About twenty percent of today's jobs are in trades that did not exist in 1980[216]. With the advent of Artificial Intelligence, can't you already see the job offers for Machine Learning engineers, data scientists, data analysts, human–AI interface experts? Not to mention AI ethics specialists, and many other professions related to Artificial Intelligence? There is no doubt that we cannot fathom the diversity of jobs that will be created in the future. Who would have thought, 15 years ago, that one could make a living developing mobile applications, managing online communities, playing professional video games, animating a YouTube channel or even flying drones? You must keep up hope and remain confident. After the initial chaos, a different and much greater prosperity will emerge. This is the change that history has undergone with each industrial revolution."

The Pessimist can no longer keep quiet and steps in:

"It must nevertheless be acknowledged that job destruction is very likely to take place in this new transformation. To implement Artificial Intelligence in any given industry, far fewer data scientists and automatic learning engineers are needed than there will be jobs

---

[216] More precisely: 18% of American jobs [11].

destroyed, precisely because of the new technology. In my opinion, the outcome will be negative. But that is not my main point. Why don't you listen to it now?"

The Pessimist

The Pessimist believes that traditional patterns, including the creative destruction that each industrial revolution has brought about, are a thing of the past. According to him, the new cycle that is coming up is of an entirely new kind – and it may be the last. The Pessimist breathes deeply and begins a long dissertation.

"This time, unfortunately, it's different[217]. Look at the situation right in front of you. Today, according to current estimates and with the technologies already available, about 50% of all tasks performed by humans at work can be automated[218]. Let's not waste time nitpicking about the numbers: whether it's 30, 40 or 50% doesn't change anything about the demonstration. By the end of the century, this ratio will increase to 100%[219]! A delay of a few decades, again, does not change the reasoning. Because come that time, anything you can do, Artificial Intelligence can do as well. 'The actual path of a raindrop down the valley is unpredictable,' says futurist Kevin Kelly[220], 'but the general direction is inevitable.' This is exactly what applies to Artificial Intelligence.

"Anything you can do, Artificial Intelligence will be able to do better, faster, more economically, without ever getting tired or protesting or threatening to go on strike. Did you hear me clearly? When agriculture was automated, farmers migrated to factories. When industry began to falter or to be relocated to other countries, workers' jobs were

---

[217] "This time is different." The term is used many times when referring to employment in Martin Ford's book, *Rise of the Robots* [8].
[218] We take as a reference the McKinsey study [11].
[219] See Part 1 Chapter 2.
[220]

https://www.ted.com/talks/kevin_kelly_how_ai_can_bring_on_a_second_industrial_revolution

converted into service jobs. Each time, new occupations were beyond the reach of the machines of the time. But here, Artificial Intelligence is gradually occupying the entire human playing field. What added value can you bring, then, to a potential employer?

"Jobs as we know them will begin their long agony today. It will not occur in a linear way, but with jolts as technology improves and as socio-economic and regulatory adjustments are made. The magnitude and speed of change will be too great for people to adjust: we cannot train that quickly, we cannot retrain or completely reinvent ourselves every 10 years. I no longer believe in our ability to adapt.

Traditional hierarchies of qualifications will no longer be relevant, nor will the traditional opposition between manual and intellectual jobs: all jobs will be affected, not only unskilled, not only manual work. And with the increasing polarisation of employment towards its extremes[221], it is perhaps the middle classes that will suffer first. Who will be left? On the one hand, the intellectual elites; on the other hand, the lowest paying professions. Let me explain. The intellectual and economic elites will be protected by their proximity to Artificial Intelligence and their roles being more difficult to automate. The lowest-paying jobs at the other end of the spectrum will not have any economic justification to be automated immediately. The effect on the middle classes is already being felt. Look at the secretaries and bank employees: their numbers have fallen around the world.

"The inequality-generating machine will get out of control. Inequality is already well entrenched. Since the mid-1970s, inequalities within so-called developed countries have widened[222]. Productivity has continued to increase, albeit at a slower pace, but has ceased to benefit workers, whose purchasing power has stagnated[223]. Between 1980 and 2016, the richest 1% absorbed 27% of global income growth, while the poorest 50%

---

[221] This polarisation has been observed since the early 2000s [14].
[222] Nevertheless, inequalities between countries have partially been reduced by the catching up of emerging countries, reflecting a global reduction in poverty.
[223] https://www.epi.org/productivity-pay-gap/

captured only 12%[224]. This inequality is of great concern. The population is less and less willing to accept it, which generates a great deal of tension and instability. Unfortunately, it will only increase.

"With the massive destruction of jobs in sight, more and more workers will be competing for fewer and fewer jobs. In addition, as I was saying earlier, a side effect of technology in general and Artificial Intelligence in particular is to gradually deskill jobs. Machines adjust their own operating parameters and inform their operators of the exact nature of the maintenance required. Taxi drivers follow the GPS instructions and no longer need to know their way around the city. Programming is less difficult since half of the code is generated automatically. Helicopters and planes fly almost on their own. Logos and graphics are generated without professional human intervention under the eyes of the novice user[225]. You no longer even need to be good at spelling and grammar to write; automated spellcheckers are kind enough to check for you in real time.

"Thus, as human beings are augmented in their jobs, the qualifications required to fill positions decrease and the worker supply increases. Therefore, with a higher worker supply, the compensation for these jobs gradually enters a negative spiral. You mentioned translators earlier; they are guaranteed victims[226]. Interpreters and translators are indeed engaged in an all-but-lost battle against Artificial Intelligence. Only a small number will survive, and even then, only for a short time.

"That's not all. An increasing number of these jobs and workers are being taken up by specialised platforms. It is the general Uberization of trades, enabled by the rise of platforms and the atomisation of trades into tasks. A new type of more or less independent service providers is developing, some of them working purely online (by providing

---

[224] These statistics are cited in the ILO report [32].
[225] See platforms such as Logojoy (https://logojoy.com/) or Canva (https://www.canva.com/).
[226] https://www.lemonde.fr/sciences/article/2017/11/27/les-traducteurs-humains-sur-la-sellette_5221043_1650684.html

intellectual services) and others performing services in the real world (e.g. delivery). They are the soldiers of the gig economy."

"Isn't it a good thing to let everyone work as they please, whenever they want, as much as they want?" interrupts the Optimist. "Most millennials love being part of the gig economy. Besides, isn't it an extraordinary opportunity to be able to cater to previously inaccessible geographic markets? Doesn't this atomisation of professions increase opportunities and flexibility?"

"In theory, it does," the Pessimist replies. "But in practice, many of these freelancers are in an unstable situation[227]. Their rates tend to go down, whether they be translators, graphic designers, developers or others. They struggle to make a living. Their jobs are often precarious, with zero-hour contracts reminiscent of 19th-century piecework. This is likely to increase. And yet these underemployed workers will not be the worst off, thanks to the jobs they still have. The others, those who lose their jobs, will at the same time lose their social status, gradually falling into a vicious circle which they will find very difficult to escape from.

"Meanwhile, the economic players of Artificial Intelligence, those who own it and implement it, will keep becoming richer and richer, as their unit gains and market power increase. Indeed, the performance of Artificial Intelligence often increases with size and with the amount of data available[228]. This is called positive feedback: more data leads to better products, better products attract more customers, and more customers generate more data. At the same time, positive feedback provides an often-decisive lead to the first entrants and therefore promotes concentration. Companies that successfully apply Artificial Intelligence will see their profits increase massively. Take Uber, for instance: their market share is significant; their main variable cost, by

---

[227] See the article in Le Monde: "Behind the illusion of artificial intelligence, the precarious reality of click workers".
https://www.lemonde.fr/pixels/article/2019/01/03/derriere-l-illusion-de-l-intelligence-artificielle-la-realite-precaire-des-travailleurs-du-clic_5404685_4408996.html?xtmc=mechanical_turk&xtcr=3
[228] This will remain true until either algorithms that are data efficient in their learning or a generalized data sharing mode is found.

far, is the drivers' pay. Today, their use of Artificial Intelligence is limited, in general, to calculating fares and routes. They can do much more. When they finally get hold of autonomous vehicles and do away with the drivers, their profits will skyrocket, even if prices fall. And their shareholders, as well as the most fortunate managers and employees, will also benefit. The drivers, on the other hand, will be left to their misery. By generalising this phenomenon, there will be, according to Yuval Noah Harari, a small class of dominant people next to a majority class of... useless beings[229]. Forgive me the term, but this observation is terrifying."

"Well, well... This vision of the future is rather pessimistic, to say the least," notes the Radical, who has remained silent until now."

"That's not all. Inequality will also be felt between nations. In the past, the poorest countries emerged with their cheap labour, becoming the world's factory, or the world's IT offshoring centre, or the world's business process outsourcing centre, or even the world's call centre. As early as the 1960s, this is how Singapore began its journey from 'Third World to First'[230], topping world rankings. The usual way to proceed is to start with tasks with relatively low added value and gradually move up the scale. This is also how South Korea and China rose out of poverty, or how India entered the global economy at the turn of the 2000s. This model will no longer work. The call centres will move out of India, the Philippines and North Africa, leaving a big gap behind them. Factories will be repatriated from Asia, Eastern Europe and Latin America to their rich developed neighbours – they will take jobs when they leave but will not create them when they arrive, as new factories will be by and large automated. What will these countries do if they have not had time to enrich themselves, no time to at least create a demographic layer that is protected from Artificial Intelligence by their high position? I hope that their only way out is not to turn into cheap gigantic retirement homes for the rich citizens of developed countries.

---

[229] See Homo Deus [9].
[230] "From Third World to First" – Lee Kuan Yew.

"The victims of these growing inequalities will be to a large extent the same as those who will suffer from the devastation of global warming: heat waves, floods, storms, droughts. Because of climate alone, some scientists predict an inevitable social collapse[231]. The social collapse induced by Artificial Intelligence will add to it. One wonders whether robots will not take advantage of their greater physical and mental strength to supplant humans, less able, in a purely Darwinian process. It's the beginning of the end."

"Why don't you leave it here," says the Radical. "I can feel your distress. Let us discuss this calmly, because there is still hope."

The Radical

The Radical got her nickname from the fact that she advocates a radical transformation. She shares part of the Pessimist's diagnosis, but her conclusion is radically different. She is on the optimistic side.

"I am well aware of the major transformation that the world of work and our society in general will undergo as a result of Artificial Intelligence. But let's get back to the basics.

"Why, at the end of the day, did we create Artificial Intelligence? Was it just to make more money? To dominate countries and populations that are deprived of it? To deceive and manipulate people who are not suspicious enough? Was it just to advance a fun area of mathematics and computer science? Or was it to make our lives easier, safer, more pleasant, more fulfilling? To enable everyone to achieve their full potential? To eradicate inequality between genders, but also between generations, races, social groups, nations? To talk to people who speak a different language? To cure diseases that resist all other attempts? To completely overcome poverty, to make hunger and thirst disappear? To educate? To save the planet, where before we put it in serious danger?

---

[231] Jem Bendall, a Professor at the University of Cumbria, sees more specifically « inevitable collapse, probable catastrophe and possible extinction » in a controversial and not peer-reviewed, yet serious article http://insight.cumbria.ac.uk/id/eprint/4166/ [26].

In other words, have we not developed Artificial Intelligence for our well-being and that of the planet that hosts us? We seem to be at risk of forgetting that along the way. But let us keep to our humanist path. To prevent people from losing their way, this path was carved into our draft ethical charters. Remember: 'a human-centric approach to AI is needed, forcing us to keep in mind that the development and use of AI should not be seen as a means in itself, but as having the goal to increase human well-being,' as the draft European Guide to Ethics[232] states. From Los Angeles to Singapore via Boston, Cambridge, Oxford, Paris, Brussels, Stockholm and Amsterdam, this direction resonates with people.

"So we do have the right intentions in principle. What is needed now is the implementation, and the support of everyone – knowing that the real impact of these charters is limited for the time being. Indeed, as mentioned before, we will not stop the march of progress and forego its extraordinary benefits. Technological advances will not be stopped – especially, unfortunately, because some non-signatory parties might seize the opportunities with less laudable objectives. The journey towards Artificial General Intelligence, while long and tortuous, seems inevitable to me. Along the way, all the difficulties already mentioned will arise, including those that could lead to social disaster if they are not addressed in a proactive manner. So let's get organised.

"In the long term, work, which serves today as the basis for income, will no longer be able to play this role: there will not be enough of it. Wealth, on the other hand, will continue to be created, probably at ever lower costs, or even at almost no marginal cost, if we are to believe the heralds of a society of abundance[233] made possible by Artificial Intelligence. It will therefore be necessary to invent new models for redistributing wealth to ensure the subsistence of all. I repeat: it is definitely not the collective wealth that will be lacking, but rather an adequate way to redistribute it.

---

[232] See the draft European Charter described in Part 1 Chapter 5.
[233] This is the thesis of Peter Diamandis, author of Abundance: The Future is Better Than You Think.

"Will we decide to broaden the base of paid work, for example by including all those activities essential to society that have never been considered professions: housewives and househusbands, volunteers for charities, volunteers in social or non-profit enterprises, museum guides and youth leaders?

"Will Universal Basic Income be implemented? Each adult would receive a predetermined amount of money, individually, universally and unconditionally. There would be no conditions of eligibility – other than age, and maybe not even that. Everyone would be free to use this income as they see fit: to pursue their artistic passion, to write computer code from morning to night, to make the world a better place according to their own definition – caring for migrants, the elderly, children, prisoners or the sick. Everyone would also be free to do nothing at all, even if that is not what the proponents of the system are betting on.

"Conversely, might this basic income be subject to conditions of eligibility? For example, in order to receive a basic income, it might be necessary to contribute to society or the common good, in particular to care, community or education. Perhaps we would be required to train and retrain. Perhaps there would also be a series of incentives to ensure that there is still motivation to produce the wealth to be shared. And of course, any harmful activity would be proscribed. But such rules would put an end to the universal and automatic nature of the measure. The most suspicious would also see it as the fermenting of a new totalitarianism in which subsistence is conditional on the goodwill of the authorities.

"Paradoxically, in many societies, Universal Basic Income, regardless of its variations, is still perceived as a left-wing or far-left measure. In reality it is essentially inspired by classical liberalism, and increasingly encouraged by the capitalists of Silicon Valley[234]. In many countries, a

---

[234] Supporters in the United States include Mark Zuckerberg, founder of Facebook; Peter Diamandis, mentioned above; Geoff Hinton, one of the fathers of deep learning; James Baker and Henry Paulson, former US finance ministers; Hillary Clinton, who considered including it in her election platform in 2016 before withdrawing it at the last minute; and Andrew Yang, candidate in the 2020 presidential election.

large part of the population is still reluctant to 'pay people to do nothing'. Trials have been conducted or are ongoing in Finland, Kenya, Uganda, India, Canada and Alaska. At this stage, it is too early to draw conclusions about its material and psychological impacts, or to determine the best way to implement it."

"Yes," the Pessimist fills in. "Thank you for pointing out that no test is conclusive. And this mechanism would have to be funded in one way or another."

"Let me continue. Do individuals, freed from material constraints and the psychological pressure to put food on their plates, continue to work? Do they use their time to train? Are they healthier? Do they take more risks? Do they see their effectiveness or creativity, their contribution or at least their well-being significantly enhanced? It is still far too early to say whether Universal Basic Income will be the cornerstone of a post-capitalist system, where individuals are trusted to thrive in an activity of their choice, whether or not it has an economic or societal value.

"So I don't know what form capitalism will take, but I have every confidence in humanity to usher in a radical transformation. This will be the logical evolution of our societies, adapted to the world of Artificial Intelligence, more universal, fairer, more fulfilling. This will be the new social contract.

"That said, the end of employment is not due tomorrow morning. In the meantime, employment will continue to be the norm, and this must be promoted by all reasonable means. It makes no real sense to protect specific jobs or occupations that are in danger of disappearing; however, protecting the women and men who live off them is essential. With more and more frequent changes in work, the first investment to be made is in human capital itself. Lifelong learning and retraining will have to be significantly increased and encouraged. And as the transition periods between jobs will be more numerous and more uncertain, safety nets, including financial safety nets, will also have to be put in place. These protective measures, temporary in nature but necessarily sufficient, will aim to ensure a smooth transition and the most effective possible resumption of employment.

"This is what we must prepare for in the short term, while awaiting the great change in society that will come along with the inexorable and irreversible rise of Artificial Intelligence."

Uncertainty about the four visions

Several visions of the future are therefore competing.

The first, that of the Optimist, dwells on the augmentation of humans by machines. This vision sees AI relieving us from uninteresting and painful tasks, and allowing us to focus on what is more interesting and human. But it seems to underestimate the destruction of jobs and the evils to come.

The second vision, that of the Moderate, supports the lessons of past industrial revolutions. It heralds a wave of creative destruction, with an initial contraction of jobs expected to be offset later by an economic resurgence. But it seems to neglect the fundamental paradigm shifts brought about by Artificial Intelligence.

The third vision, that of the Pessimist, predicts the upcoming end of employment due to substantial advances in Artificial Intelligence and the inability of humans to adapt quickly enough. Worse still, this end of employment would be a prelude to chaos and even to the end of humanity. This vision is an indisputable warning of what could very well happen if we do not act. But it leaves little room for human resilience.

The fourth vision, that of the Radical, acknowledges the inevitable end of employment as we know it, but cannot passively accept its consequences. It banks on human genius to radically transform our social model. This is probably the best vision that humanists can aspire to – even if a lot of work will have to be carried out to make it happen.

These great visions, in the end, are almost more ideological than anything else. It is very likely that the future, far from being homogeneous, will inherit aspects from each of the four visions. Some individuals will prove to be more able than others to adapt and take advantage of the tremendous benefits of Artificial Intelligence. Some geographical and political entities will manage the new reality better than others, depending on the objectives they set for themselves and their ability to execute their plans in pursuit of these objectives.

The uncertainty remains immense. "We are flying blind," some of the leading experts in Artificial Intelligence claim[235]. All of them foresee a very significant change, but the data and information needed for a more accurate forecast are still sorely lacking.

To try and gain more clarity, let us move away from the macroscopic level of the distant future and dive into the most microscopic units of work: the world of tasks.

[235] Mitchell and Brynjolfsson, co-authors of a NASEM report on the future of employment in the United States:
https://www.cs.cmu.edu/news/policymakers-flying-blind-future-work

Chapter 7. Automation of tasks

AI transforms daily life, disrupts companies' modes of operation, and offers new perspectives for solving humanity's great challenges. Some of the solutions it offers are radically new compared to what humans are capable of doing by themselves. Optimising traffic in a city, carrying out predictive maintenance of a complex system, recommending books to millions of people, exploring protein folding configurations, pre-selecting promising targets for new drugs, implementing precision medicine for one, one hundred or one billion patients – all these occupations are beyond the reach of humans and therefore do not even compete with them. But when it selects salads ready to be picked, identifies malignant tumours, transcribes an oral conversation, conducts case law research or reviews application files, AI encroaches on human territory. In doing so, it begins affecting jobs.

The task rather than the job

Since it is the issue of jobs that concerns us, why then address tasks? Simply because jobs are not the right unit of analysis.

Each job consists of a multitude of *tasks*. A taxi driver, for example, is quite a multitasker. With their pilot hat on, they actually drive the vehicle, steering it, turning the indicators on, accelerating and braking, and changing speed. With their co-pilot hat on, they assess the physical condition of the road and the traffic. With their navigator hat on, they determine the right route based on the point of departure, destination, and known disruptions that may occur along the way. With their sales hat on, they chase down individuals who might want to take a taxi. Finally, with their steward hat on, they greet the passenger, ensure their well-being throughout the journey, consult them on the choice of music and vehicle temperature, possibly offer them a cold drink and may even chat if both are in the mood to talk. This adds up to at least five main tasks: driving, road perception and analysis, navigation, sales and customer management.

Similarly, a salesperson in a fashion store provides advice, reassures and compliments the customer during the fitting, presses for a sale and closes the transaction at the best possible price. An accountant enters transactions into their information system, makes account allocation decisions, performs audits, and occasionally performs cost or revenue analyses.

The job can always be broken down into smaller units, namely tasks. And each of these tasks will turn out to be automatable or not. How will this be determined? The answer is at the end of a sequence of questions. Is the task technically automatable? If yes, is there any benefit in actually automating it? If yes, is there a human premium that prevents this task from being assigned to a machine?

Let us tackle all these questions in this order. It is important to note that we will consider here the current state of technology as of early 2019.

Is this task technically automatable?

How can we determine if a task is technically automatable? We must identify the capabilities necessary to carry out the task and analyse whether Artificial Intelligence possesses them at a sufficient level. To that end, a good starting point is to refer to the study we conducted together in Chapter 3 of Part 1, *Artificial Intelligence*, comparing human mental processes with the faculties of Artificial Intelligence. Check it out!

Does the task require significant memory or sustained attention for hours? It can be automated. Does it mainly use perception skills, for example to observe minute visual defects on manufactured products or a suspicious sound coming from a machine tool? Automatable! Does it primarily use the basic skills of Natural Language Processing, for example, to transcribe conference speeches, or synthesise a newsletter from multiple raw dispatches? Automatable, perhaps with human verification given the current level of technology. Does it rely on the detection of similarities, for example, as a marketer or an analyst would do, to uncover segments among your customers or clusters among your visitors? Automatable! Does it aim to enter thousands of invoices or supplier receipts and then link them to previous orders? Automatable!

Does it involve managing a large amount of data and making predictions, for example, to pick good financial investments or monitor potential fraudulent transactions? Automatable! Does it implement creativity through exploration in a well-defined context? Or through imitation, with the aim of generating thousands of pieces of lounge music in the style of Henry Mancini? Automatable, no problem. Does it use basic navigation and handling skills, like a forklift operator in a warehouse? It is automatable indeed.

On the other hand, if the succession of tasks aims to build a house brick by brick[236], enter a stranger's home and take a beer out of the fridge, clean a hotel room where each element is unpredictable, develop a new business strategy, discover a biological model with a clearly identified causality, debate subtle philosophical concepts, motivate a team or respond to objections, or understand the deep motivations of an individual, then this sequence of tasks cannot be automated given the state of the art in technology.

A careful examination of the comparative table of human faculties and Artificial Intelligence capabilities should enable you to determine, for any task, whether it can be automated. The exercise remains qualitative but it will give you important information. Several foresight institutes have also tried this. Among them, McKinsey Global Institute (MGI) has become the reference in this field by tackling all the component tasks of all professions[237]. The approach of this institute deserves a brief description.

Based on the US Bureau of Labor Statistics and data from O*net, the US reference site for the world of work, MGI examined in detail more than 800 trades broken down into 2,000 different tasks. In parallel, they developed their own matrix of capabilities that are automatable by

---

[236] There are, however, numerous ongoing efforts to build houses by 3D printing.
[237] The work of McKinsey Global Institute is referenced by many and adopted for instance by the International Labour Office or the Brookings Institute think tank. See their studies [53] [10] [11].

Artificial Intelligence. They then applied the matrix of automatable faculties to the 2,000 tasks.

To summarise the results, MGI grouped the 2,000 tasks into 7 main categories of tasks according to their ability to be automated. Three of the seven main categories are particularly likely to be automated. First are predictable physical tasks (including, for example, operating industrial machinery, cooking, serving meals in restaurants, hospitality, warehousing and transportation activities). Then come data collection tasks and data processing tasks. These include basic activities such as filling in forms, creating customer or patient files, and payroll activities, as well as more advanced activities such as the ones carried out in the finance and insurance sectors. These three main categories, according to MGI, account for more than half of the hours worked in the United States.

The other four main categories of tasks are less likely to be automated: management (due to the subtlety and variability of issues), the application of an area of expertise or common sense (abstract decision-making, planning, creativity), human interfacing (with customers, peers, or visitors in non-trivial cases) and unpredictable physical tasks (being a crane operator or worker on a construction site, making beds in a hotel, pruning trees).

MGI has also undertaken to quantify the volume of tasks that can be automated worldwide, based on current worked hours. The result is mind-boggling: with current technologies, 50% of the world's tasks, in hours worked, can be automated. Yes, you read it right: for half of the hours worked in the world, humans can technically be replaced today by Artificial Intelligence[238].

The MGI study is one of the best to date, although it is not entirely indisputable. But in any case, knowing whether a task is technically automatable or not is only the starting point.

---

[238] The details are on page 32 and following of McKinsey's report [10].

Is the automation of this task beneficial?

To automate a task, technical feasibility is not enough. The second question is whether this automation is beneficial.

The benefit sought is most often a financial gain. If Uber adopts autonomous vehicles and does not need to pay drivers, its gross margin will increase dramatically. Similarly, if a call centre gets rid of its agents for the lowest levels of intervention, if a tutoring service largely replaces its flesh and blood teachers with silicon ones (i.e. AI), if human radiologists are no longer needed to interpret scans, if the assets of a warehouse can be inventoried by autonomous drones, if 50 accountants can be downsized to 5 and 20 HR staff to 2, then the savings will be substantial. It will be even more so when certain financial or legal stars see some of their tasks automated.

In contrast, in the absence of economic and other gains, it is unlikely that automation will take place. Similar reasoning has already been applied for decades in industry: manual tasks with limited added value have proliferated in workshops in some developing countries despite the technical possibility of automating them, simply because wages there are extremely low.

This reasoning will apply much less to cognitive tasks than to physical tasks. Cognitive tasks, if automated by AI, will be automated by computer software: the cost of deployment is close to nil, and the cost of development is in principle quickly recovered unless the market is a tiny niche. Low value-added cognitive tasks, such as data entry, will be replaced very quickly and everywhere in the world. A low salary is not a protection against automation if it has almost no marginal cost.

On the other hand, in the case of robots performing manual tasks, it is first necessary to design the robot, which entails an initial fixed cost, but it must also be produced and transported each time it is sold, and the physical environment adapted for commissioning and implementation. Marginal cost can be a deterrent, depending on the circumstances. In each case, it is therefore essential to compare the cost of the human solution with the cost of the robotic solution – and the results will vary from country to country. Paradoxically, the lower the salaries, the more likely some tasks are to be shielded from automation. Sweepers, window washers, shoe shiners, and cooks are likely to keep the majority of their jobs in low-wage countries. Their counterparts in Japan, Germany or other labour-intensive countries will have a little more to worry about but still some chance of survival. As for the plumber and the tree pruner, whose essential tasks are already not sufficiently predictable for easy automation, the economic argument makes them even more immune to automation.

The benefit of automation is not always economic, or at least not always easy to quantify in these terms. Sometimes a significant impact is sufficient to justify the effort of automation. Putting an AI at the controls of an aircraft (which is already by and large the case) or at the wheel of a car (which will happen within a decade and eventually eliminate the wheel) is not just a matter of big money; it is above all a predictable and drastic decrease in the number of accidents. Adding Artificial Intelligence to a maintenance department can be justified by the fact that no human can anticipate a failure by analysing thousands of parameters, but AI can. Including an AI-based facial detection unit at border control points makes sense because it is much harder to fool Artificial Intelligence than a human about one's identity. Providing an AI agent in a customer support service, with 24/7 availability, is almost guaranteed to result in increased customer satisfaction. Using AI to screen candidates has the advantage of avoiding lengthy delays and, above all, the biases that sometimes plague recruiters, like all humans. To be able to automate the tasks of a high-rise window washer and avoid dramatic accidents is an invaluable gain. Similarly, automating mine-clearing or work in contaminated areas eliminates the risk of human casualties.

In addition to technical feasibility, therefore, automation requires an identified benefit to be justified. At this stage we have not taken into account the impact of AI on humans. But this was only the second step.

Is there a human premium for this task?

Even if a task can be technically automated and automation has a beneficial effect, society must be ready to accept the replacement of human beings by Artificial Intelligence. Society will sometimes issue regulatory restrictions to favour humans because of the perceived technical risk of automation. Some drugs can only be sold by human pharmacists; some financial products are only available through licensed financial advisors. But more often than not, it will be a question of mindset readiness. Is there or isn't there an explicit or implicit human premium for this task? Let us take a few examples.

Air travel is by far the safest mode of transport per passenger and per kilometre. In spite of this, when an accident does occur, there is more than one chance in two that the cause is human error[239]. This proportion would be even higher if not for the very limited time human pilots are actually at the controls: on average 4 minutes per flight on an Airbus and 7 minutes on a Boeing[240]. Modern aircraft always or almost always land in autopilot mode. Admittedly, Artificial Intelligence is not yet technically ready to take over from the pilot. Even if it were, it is not yet acceptable in people's minds to fly without a pilot in the aircraft – two pilots, in fact, to be prepared for any eventuality and to ensure a continuous presence in the cockpit. To convince yourself, ask yourself the question! Would you fly without a pilot in the plane? And yet the AI does not miss any information from signalling and control systems, is never drowsy or fatally disoriented, never skips a step on checklists, never disobeys instructions and is never reckless.

The same applies to brain surgery. Would you be willing to entrust your brain entirely to a robot surgeon? No, most likely not. All surgical robot suppliers insist that they only assist surgeons, who retain full control throughout the operation and are just augmented. Even today, there is

---

[239] https://www.telegraph.co.uk/travel/picturegalleries/7844042/Why-planes-crash-air-accident-statistics-and-banned-airlines.html?image=3
[240] https://www.news.com.au/travel/travel-updates/how-pilots-spend-as-little-as-four-minutes-flying-some-modern-planes/news-story/86d3260a247cab8df02563af0f66d11d

still a psychological premium for human surgeons. The risk seems far too high to even think of putting your brain between the clamps of a robot. And yet, its clamps do not shake and are more accurate than human hands; automated visual perception systems are more effective; algorithms are more capable than humans of detecting an anomaly by checking thousands of parameters. What seems inconceivable today will one day be obvious. "No, don't let a human neurosurgeon operate on me, it's far too dangerous." It's as if you were forced to go and face Ke Jie[241] with your own limited human resources rather than delegate your defence to AlphaGo.

Social interaction is often cited as a typical example of an activity that carries a human premium. Some claim that even in call centres, human contact is necessary to take care of the customer, who is usually calling to complain. This is supposed to be for reasons of empathy. However, as we have seen, Artificial Intelligence is more likely than a human to detect the mental state of the interlocutor[242]. It can be trained to respond appropriately to manage client stress or anger – and the AI itself remains oblivious to the pressures of the job. If you are frantically looking for your order that should have been delivered 3 days ago, or if you really don't understand why the new device you just bought refuses to work, are you sure you would prefer to interact with a human? You will need to call during opening hours – not on weekends, precisely when you have time. You may have to explain the situation three times depending on the changes in customer agents; you may have to deal with their misunderstandings and varying competence. Their empathy may also be challenged because... they are human, and their job, it must be acknowledged, is very stressful.

When properly trained, an Artificial Intelligence tends to be almost more human than humans. A holiday home sharing site encourages you to respond quickly to requests from third parties to exchange your apartment: it makes it easier for you by just asking you to click on one of the "yes", "no", or "maybe" buttons. When you simply select "no",

---

[241] Best Go player in the world, defeated by AlphaGo. See Part 1 Chapter 1.
[242] See Part 1 Chapter 3.

the machine sends an extra polite answer, thanking the sender for their inquiry and wishing them good luck in their search.

The human premium is also often mentioned in the essential tasks of teaching and coaching. A coach listens carefully, shows interest, creates a relationship of trust, encourages openness, facilitates awareness of problems and recognition of weaknesses, and helps build a plan to move forward. There is no question about that. Some, however, will prefer to confide in a machine, precisely because it is not human, as long as it is as effective as humans at helping people become aware of the answers they are seeking. A teacher is unparalleled in encouraging, comforting, motivating, congratulating, inspiring and uncovering personal callings. There is no question about that. However, many educational platforms use gamification to encourage and motivate students – and to some extent it works. Sometimes, students find it easier to overcome their anxiety by talking to robots than humans – language anxiety, for example, affects learners of a foreign language who are so insecure in their abilities that it paralyses them. Thus, while the human premium does exist in teaching and coaching, its extent should be slightly qualified.

The ultimate example of a human premium is to be found in care and community service. Humans prefer to talk to other humans, feel their presence and compassion, and benefit from their company, especially when ill or suffering, when staying in hospital or in a retirement home, or even when housebound. This is the case with your aunt Stephanie, in the imagined future in Part I[243]. There is nothing like the love of your family and the unwavering support of your friends. The idea of a social robot, which would look after lonely people, sounds horrifying and shocking to many, who think society is letting down its most vulnerable members, namely the elderly and the sick. But it is important to point out that not all cultures react in the same way. In Japan, for example, the penetration of robotics into everyday life is much more advanced than in the West. In the context of an aging population and a critical shortage of personnel in the care and social sector, robots have already

---

[243] See Part 1 Chapter 4.

made their way into healthcare and senior citizens' institutions. Preliminary results are positive, especially regarding the acceptance of robots by elderly or single people[244]. Some experiments have shown that elderly people are more willing to inform their care robot about their condition than their human caregiver. This relationship will surely intensify with the widespread adoption not of robots, but of three-dimensional photorealistic avatars. They will be indistinguishable "physically" from humans. Artificial Intelligence is therefore probably part of the solution, even if it is not the entire solution. Thus, it is not certain that the human premium will persist over time, even in societies where it currently seems strongly entrenched. To pretend that machines will never have a place in social interactions is inaccurate.

The human premium can sometimes be encountered as the emotional successor to the traditional notion of "handmade". Industrial processes can produce very large quantities of plates, bowls and vases, occasionally intentionally adding a small imperfection to make it look and feel more unique. However, the handmade carries a little something that justifies, for some, a much higher price. The artist's carafe is incomparably more expensive than Ikea's, and still sells. Another example: digital recordings almost perfectly reproduce the vocal performance of artists. They can be purchased for a few dollars or even less when subscribing to a streaming platform. But if you want to attend a live performance by the same artist, in a giant stadium or at the Paris Opera, you will undoubtedly have to pay 50 or 100 times more[245]. There is no shortage of buyers. This demonstrates the premium on human performers.

The above examples have all taken the perspective of the service consumer in the evaluation of the human premium. But history shows that resistance to the spread of technological innovation is far more often the result not of end users averse to change, but of those who will potentially lose out in the transformation – and it is the balance of

---

[244] See in particular https://www.reuters.com/article/us-japan-ageing-robots-widerimage/aging-japan-robots-may-have-role-in-future-of-elder-care-idUSKBN1H33AB
[245] These two examples are often cited by Yann LeCun.

power between the users and the losers that determines the outcome of the confrontation. If automation is blocked, that is a special kind of human premium imposed by the productive forces currently in place or by their defenders. When William Lee applied for a patent on a stocking frame knitting machine in 1589, his request was rejected by the Queen of England simply because she feared the consequences for employment[246]. When, two and a half centuries later, the Luddites tried to stop the spread of mechanical looms, they failed: the beneficiaries of this invention (i.e. all the unskilled workers who could now weave) outnumbered by far the craftsmen who were penalised by it. In other words, the benefits of this technological innovation were sufficiently well shared with society for the Luddites to be unsuccessful in their attempt to obstruct it. Where the Luddites failed, anaesthetists succeeded two centuries later. In 2016, Johnson and Johnson announced the permanent withdrawal of Sedasys, their anaesthesia machine[247]. Approved by the FDA in 2013 and therefore tested as perfectly reliable in use, it reduced the cost of anaesthesia from $2,000 with an anaesthetist to about $200 without. But the anaesthetists' lobby mobilised massively against the machine, whose sales were extremely disappointing, causing it to be withdrawn. Anaesthetists have managed to stem progress in order to preserve their interests, thus imposing an artificial human premium.

When a task is technically automatable, when there is a benefit to automating it and when there is no human premium, then the verdict is unescapable: the task will be automated. What happens then to the jobs that involve this task? That is what we will look at next.

---

[246] Anecdote recalled by Oxford researchers [14] and cited in a book by Acemoglu and Robinson (2012): *Why nations fail: the origins of power, prosperity, and poverty*. Random House Digital, Inc.
[247] https://www.washingtonpost.com/news/the-switch/wp/2016/03/28/its-game-over-for-the-robot-intended-to-replace-anesthesiologists/?utm_term=.d7c448e319e4

Chapter 8. Does this job have a future?

J obs are an inadequate unit for assessing the effects of Artificial Intelligence. And yet, it is at the level of jobs that we want to be able to draw conclusions. The process to follow starts in a straightforward way: let us first break the job down into a set of individual tasks. The automation criteria will be applied to the tasks individually. Then we will recombine them into jobs so as to obtain the desired level of analysis. Some final steps will be required to reach the general conclusions.

Automation of the tasks that constitute the job

Every job, as we now know it, is a collection of individual tasks. The first step in the analysis is therefore to break the job down into its constituent tasks. Remember the taxi driver: they close the sale, welcome customers, analyse the road, navigate, and drive. Now take a teaching assistant (TA) in higher education: the TA advises students on their projects in a mentoring role; marks work to relieve the professor; and answers students' questions, whether on administrative matters or on the content of the course itself. Their various tasks can therefore be described as advising, marking and supporting.

For each task, the three successive steps of automation analysis that we explored in the previous chapter must be applied.

Remember: the first step is to determine whether the task is technically automatable, which we have done through our comparative table of the capabilities of AI and the human mental processes. From a quantitative point of view, MGI already informed us that more than half of individual tasks, measured in hours worked, were technically automatable with current technologies. But when the tasks are regrouped into jobs, only a small number of jobs, less than 5% of the total, can be fully automated, i.e. consist exclusively of automatable tasks. At the other end of the spectrum, very few jobs are also completely protected from automation, i.e. consist only of tasks that cannot be automated. Automatable tasks are widely represented in all occupations: 60% of jobs have more than 30% of their tasks that are technically automatable[248].

Let's continue the analysis. If the task is technically automatable, if there is a gain in automating it and if it is not associated with a human premium, then it is destined to be automated. Does that mean the task will be automated immediately?

The long journey to adoption

It would be tempting to believe that our analysis so far has filtered the tasks through all technological, economic and human obstacles. In spite of this, implementation can still take years or even decades. This latency is already observed today in the digitisation of the economy. The year is 2019; we are celebrating the 30th anniversary of the Internet, which really took off a good two decades ago; yet e-commerce still represents only about ten percent of total trade. Another sign of the slow pace of digitisation: in the United States, 60% of small businesses still do not have an online booking system for their customers[249].

For new technology to be adopted, it must first mature and stabilise. What is possible in labs is not immediately possible in real life: you cannot adjust models or clean data as flexibly once you are out of the lab door. Workarounds and (even brilliant) ad hoc responses cannot be implemented, because deployment must be scalable and therefore industrialised. All the technological achievements we have described so far are real but not all are ready to be deployed at scale. Image recognition or the main features of Natural Language Processing (such as translation, speech recognition or speech synthesis) are more mature

---

[248] See McKinsey's report "A future that works" [10].
[249] The statistic was given by Google's CEO during his Duplex demonstration in 2018.

than other applications and already widely deployed. Precision medicine is still many years away from being a reality.

Once the technology is stable enough, organisations must be given time to develop the necessary understanding, confidence and appetite for roll-out. It is not yet the case for many companies today – a large proportion are still immersed in their digitisation initiatives and, for the most advanced of them, in Robotic Process Automation[250]. The adoption cycle of new technology stretches over different phases: innovators are followed by early adopters, then the majority, then the laggards. Companies ready to take the plunge are faced with a multitude of internal challenges: first, human challenges, to let champions emerge and step up, convince reluctant people and gather the necessary skills; second, technical challenges, especially to build a good data ecosystem; and finally organisational, procedural and cultural challenges. It takes time, even a great deal of time! As if that were not enough, organisations must look outwards to adjust or even completely transform their business models. Finally, customers and end users must get used to the idea of adopting the new technology. This may further delay the adoption process, especially if the application being considered requires users to progressively give up a human premium.

Now all the conditions are met and the task will be automated. What are the consequences for jobs that include this task?

What happens to jobs

In a thought experiment, the job we had broken down is recreated from its constituent tasks – this is the opposite of the first step of analysis. The job is again made up of a number of tasks, some of which will likely be automated and others not. In the rare cases where all tasks are automated, the job disappears; in the equally rare cases where all tasks are spared from automation, the job remains in place. But in the other

---

[250] Robotic Process Automation or RPA makes it possible to reproduce identically a human routine process performed in an IT environment. There is a high demand for this rather basic automation mode.

cases, i.e. the majority, it is not yet possible to decide, because it remains unclear whether demand will offset the effect of automation.

Moreover, the list of tasks making up the job is not necessarily fixed. These tasks are subject to change over time. Some will be removed, especially if they are automated; others will be added. They may also recombine into entirely new jobs that will be shaped by the evolution of society and technology.

Let us take again the example of the teaching assistant. Imagine that our TA spends a third of his time on each of his three tasks: advice, marking and support. If Artificial Intelligence is technically capable of taking over the support task (which it is very close to), then the profession of TA becomes partially automatable, but not entirely. Artificial Intelligence potentially covers one third of a full-time equivalent (FTE) of a teaching assistant. If, in addition, Artificial Intelligence acquires the ability to mark students' work, then two thirds of FTEs can theoretically be automated. Since two thirds of the tasks in this job can be automated as a percentage of hours worked, then all else being equal, if there were 9 TAs at the beginning, 6 could be replaced by Artificial Intelligence.

It should be stressed that this reasoning requires some additional checks to be perfectly valid. For example, does it make sense to add time savings incurred on specific tasks and aggregate them into full-time equivalents? If, in a call centre, each agent has half as many tasks to perform, then it is likely that half of the agents' time will become available. But if ten chambermaids working in ten different buildings are each exempted from one-tenth of their tasks, it is not certain that 9 chambermaids instead of 10 can carry out the remaining work, given the logistical constraints imposed by the distance between the buildings.

What will really happen in the case of teaching assistants? Will the 9 TAs be assigned additional tasks? Will they spend more time advising each student? Will 6 of them actually be dismissed and all students allocated to the remaining 3 TAs? Or perhaps the TA position will disappear altogether, with the remaining role of advisor being reassigned to another function – for example, to more senior students.

Is the intrinsic demand for this job strong enough?

"All else being equal", it was argued, 6 of the 9 assistants can be removed and only 3 would remain; but the problem is in the very first assumption: it is highly unlikely that all other things will remain equal. The reasoning implicitly assumes that the number of students is constant. However, if some of the tasks are automated, perhaps this will help to lower the cost of education, which in turn could attract more students. Regardless of cost, educational or demographic criteria can play a role. Imagine that this university is on the rise or that the country is experiencing an influx of young people, and that the number of students increases fivefold over the next few years. Then the requirement will increase to 15 TAs, not 3. In this case, therefore, due to the steady growth in underlying demand, the number of TAs will have increased from 9 to 15 in spite of the very high degree of automation – in this case by two thirds. The job of educational assistant therefore remains, in this example, an attractive opportunity for anyone entering the job market.

If, on the other hand, underlying demand is stable or declining, then automation will make the sector even more competitive and less attractive in terms of market opportunities. Imagine a country in demographic decline that does not attract or accept foreign students. The number of students to cater to (which here is a proxy for the strength of demand) is on a downward slope. In addition, the profession of teaching assistant is itself in the process of being automated. Of the original 9 assistants, perhaps it is not 6 who will have to find another job, but 7 or 8. The cumulative effects of automation and declining intrinsic demand make the job's prospects unattractive.

The list of growing jobs will vary from country to country and sometimes from region to region. But a few patterns are likely to emerge. Technological jobs, of course, will benefit from strong growth. Demand will also be high in the social services, care, well-being, early childhood, leisure and education sectors. Often, partial automation of these sectors will further increase demand by lowering costs. A case-by-case analysis will most of the time prove necessary for informed career-path decisions. New professions will also emerge, about which we have no idea today.

What happens to income?

Ideally, work is a means to fulfil oneself and self-actualise. But in the current social model, however, it also remains an economic necessity for the vast majority. Financial needs and ambitions can vary considerably from one individual and one household to another. Let us therefore limit ourselves to citing income as an important criterion in choosing a career, in addition to the sustainability of employment.

How will salaries evolve by profession? A universal answer is obviously impossible. Today, each country already has its own culture and practices which determine how to compensate professions, whether or not to limit disparities, and whether or not to promote roles with lower economic value and greater social value. These national choices require a detailed analysis by territory and by job if a more precise answer is sought.

In broad terms, as long as we remain in the current societal model, it is mainly supply and demand that will continue to determine wage developments. The trend towards wage polarisation is also expected to increase.

For a large number of jobs, in the long term, there is a risk that wages will be under severe pressure. If we accept the thesis that "this time it's different"[251], Artificial Intelligence will reduce the number of jobs available over the next couple of decades. In addition, many of the jobs that still remain will be de-skilled: requiring fewer specific skills, opening up to more people and therefore witnessing greater competition. The imbalance between lower job supply and higher job demand is expected to affect wages.

Other jobs may fare better. This could happen to the jobs where humans are truly augmented. Human job holders would be able to generate

---

[251] See this part of the Pessimist's speech to which the Radical also adheres.

even more added value by focusing on their core business, which is itself protected from automation. It is in this better-off category that all experts in the deployment, implementation and administration of Artificial Intelligence should also be found – from AI engineers to functional experts providing the knowledge necessary for its implementation industry by industry[252]. More generally, there is no reason to believe that professions that are now well paid and identified as being protected from automation would suffer a deterioration in their income.

What happens to the relatively low-paying professions that are now expected to be an important opportunity for humans, partly because they are partially protected from automation and partly because they meet a strong need: care, social work and education, for example? It's hard to say. It may be necessary to wait for a change in the social paradigm before they are compensated in a way commensurate with their actual contribution to society.

The case of translators may give us a taste of the future for professions directly in the path of Artificial Intelligence. It is a textbook case, so our four friends mentioned them earlier in their discussion[253]: the Optimist was delighted with their augmentation, the Moderate pointed out the narrowing of their field of intervention and the Pessimist deplored the decrease in their salary. All three were right. Björn Bratteby, President of the Société française des traducteurs (SFT), says that the growth of the profession is driven – not hampered – by technology. However, he admits pricing pressure on professionals. Nearly 60% of SFT's members charged less than 300 euros per day in 2015 compared to 39% in 2008[254]. As the performance of machine translation has increased significantly since 2015, the downward trend in hourly rate has probably worsened. A search for translators on the Upwork platform[255] is telling. Of the

---

[252] See the new validity of the Goldilocks principle, Part 2 Chapter 10.
[253] See the entire discussion in Part 2 Chapter 6.
[254] https://www.lemonde.fr/sciences/article/2017/11/27/les-traducteurs-humains-sur-la-sellette_5221043_1650684.html
[255] Very popular freelance platform for a wide variety of tasks, previously known as Elance.

approximately 30,000 French–English translators, 29% have an hourly rate of less than USD 10, 57% between USD 10 and 30, 11% between USD 30 and 60, and 3% above USD 60. 86% of translators on Upwork therefore charge less than 30 dollars per hour, i.e. less than 240 dollars per day[256]. Competition is fierce on price. Ironically, all translators on the platform claim "not to use any machine translation tool", which is contradicted by the testimonies of dissatisfied customers. Outside of this harsh competitive environment leading to lower compensation, a small number of translators continue to charge a high price for services requiring superior quality. Others work for technology companies that develop machine translation – the Googles and DeepLs of this world – and are probably well paid. But how many of them are there, and for how long?

The perspective of changing jobs

As we have seen, the accumulation of automatable tasks brings about the risk, for any job, of being at least partially automated. The underlying intrinsic demand will increase or decrease the demand for the surviving portion of the job. In addition, major demographic trends – essentially the growth, or lack thereof, of the working-age population – will affect the potential net surplus of workers, for a given trade, relative to the need.

MGI ran its simulations at the global level and then for a few major countries. According to them, while 50% of the tasks (in terms of hours worked) are technically automatable today, only about 15% in the medium scenario would actually be automated by 2030[257]. Adoption is lower than it could potentially be, due to economic, social and regulatory constraints and to the inertia of implementation that we have described. By adding macroeconomic and demographic dynamics, MGI concludes that "only" 3% of workers would be forced to change jobs[258]. However, this value of 3% could rise to 14% in certain less

---

[256] Based on an 8-hour day.
[257] From 0 to 30% depending on the scenarios [11].
[258] From 0 to 14% depending on the scenarios [11].

favourable circumstances. 14% would mean 375 million people are forced to change careers! This is not simply a question of changing employers, but of the nature of the job, with different environments, different tasks or different skills. In most countries, MGI states, the average or sustained economic scenarios would make it possible to guarantee employment for all by 2030, subject to the necessary reskilling. In our opinion this diagnosis seems optimistic to say the least.

Finally, in a subsequent study[259], MGI also draws up a typology of jobs lost or gained according to the skills needed, in the broadest sense of the term. Several general trends stand out. Declining jobs include those based on manual and physical skills (e.g. warehouse workers, drivers, welders, machine operators) as well as basic cognitive skills (e.g. administrative agents or support functions in a company). Jobs on the rise are those requiring social-emotional skills (e.g. managers) or technological skills (e.g. in the entire IT sector). As for jobs with higher cognitive skills, some will be on the rise (e.g. creative) and others will be on the decline (e.g. finance, accounting and paralegal jobs).

A few specific examples of jobs in each category may be interesting to review. Let us have a go at that next.

---

[259] This study focuses on skills [10].

Chapter 9. Of doctors and footballers

I t is impossible to make an accurate forecast about all possible trades, with a 10 to 20-year horizon. One of the reasons for this is the scale: for example, there are 615 European activity classes, 732 French subclasses and 840 types of occupation within those, in the American O*NET classification. But the main reasons are more fundamental, namely the extreme difficulty of modelling the evolution of individual jobs, as well as the uncertainty that persists in a majority of cases.

We will not take the risk here of doing the same exercise as the Oxford researchers [260] who published in their 2013 study a detailed list of predictions, associating each profession with a precise probability of automation. This list, which was heavily criticised[261], was transformed by several third parties into online tools that were easy to consult but rather scant on nuances and explanations[262]. These should be used with caution.

Our sole aim is to provide sufficient guidance to achieve three outcomes: to raise awareness, to possibly lead to further research and above all to avoid finding oneself in an unfortunate choice of career in a generation's time – 10 to 20 years. To avoid adding to the uncertainty, we are essentially confining ourselves to the technologies proven as of today. We also limit ourselves to existing jobs today and do not carry out a significant recombination of tasks among jobs. Please note that the

---

[260] Carl Frey and Michael Osborne, researchers at Oxford University [14].
[261] The list was criticised in particular because the study was conducted at the level of the job as a whole, not the task.
[262] See for example "Will robots take my job?", to be consulted with caution https://willrobotstakemyjob.com/ . See also Bloomberg's interactive tool https://www.bloomberg.com/graphics/2017-job-risk/

result remains indicative and qualitative, and not the output of an advanced model.

The 23 trades listed below were selected because they span the full spectrum of our forecasts. They cover both manual and cognitive jobs, both high and low-skilled. We will provide a brief overview of each of these professions. This insight is nothing other than the implicit qualitative answer to the questions asked in the previous chapters. Each job is broken down into tasks and for the main tasks, we determine whether they are technically automatable, whether automation is beneficial, and whether there is a human premium. After recombining the tasks into jobs, the question is whether market demand is sufficiently buoyant. We will drastically simplify the reasoning based on the main tasks of the job in question. This will allow us to draw a conclusion about the profession as it is practised today, but obviously not about the precise FTE calculations (full-time equivalents). We will sometimes talk about short-term (one decade), medium-term (two to three decades), or long-term (beyond). We will report whether the trade is clearly protected from automation, or conversely if it is a guaranteed victim. We will give, whenever possible, an indication of the evolution of income. We will emphasise the uncertainty that prevails whenever a major direction is impossible to determine with sufficient confidence. Finally, if the broad direction we see is very different from what other sources give, we will also mention this. The trades are presented here by family. The proportion of the economy and of the population that a trade represents varies greatly from one trade to another and is not a criterion for inclusion in the following list.

Driver

Autonomous vehicles are one of the most frequently highlighted applications of Artificial Intelligence. They will not only result in a financial saving but also a significant reduction in the number of accidents.

The technical feasibility of autonomous driving has long been considered largely beyond the reach of machines, mainly due to the highly unpredictable nature of traffic. It is indeed the management of the vehicle in real traffic conditions, with its share of hazards, that poses a problem. Navigation (finding your way) and technical driving of the car (operating the controls to perform the desired manoeuvres) are already mastered. In the case of autonomous taxis, the other tasks (finding customers and welcoming them) are technologically mature or in the process of being mature enough.

These technological challenges have led to a focus on particular driving environments. Autonomous vehicles are not yet ready to operate in the most difficult traffic conditions – for example, Place de l'Etoile in Paris or the heart of Manhattan at rush hour, or New Delhi or Mumbai at any time of the day. In contrast, most truck journeys are made on major roads, i.e. under more easily controllable conditions, and from logistics depot to logistics depot, outside urban centres.

Fully autonomous vehicles, with so-called level 5 autonomy, are still considered unlikely by some in the near future – but others such as Elon Musk, Tesla's boss, are of the opposite opinion and strongly stand by it. According to him it will be possible by the end of 2020 to fall asleep safely in one's car and wake up the next day at the destination[263]. Others think it will probably take a decade or more for taxi drivers, in particular, to start being replaced by unmanned vehicles outside highly protected areas. Long-haul truck drivers will likely be affected before taxi drivers. Test trucks are already running in these ideal conditions.

In the long term, once the technology has matured, the infrastructure has developed and the fleet is replaced, there will be no more truck or car drivers. This does not prevent truck drivers from currently being in high demand in the United States, where the shortage is estimated at 50,000 drivers, which has led to very high wage increases[264].

---

[263] https://www.youtube.com/watch?v=h6zK5YwH4hk&feature=youtu.be
[264] https://www.cnbc.com/2019/01/28/walmart-is-hiring-hundreds-of-truck-drivers-and-paying-them-close-to-90000-a-year.html

Warehouse operative

Artificial Intelligence and robotisation have been taking over all handling stations one by one. They started with the most standardised operations, such as handling heavy and bulky pallets and placing them in racks. They are gradually extending their domain to the less routine operations that require the most finesse. The final step will be the handling of objects with variable shapes which need to be gently extracted from bulk storage.

Thus, the visitor to a large Amazon warehouse or its Chinese equivalent Alibaba will first be surprised by the very small number of employees[265]. Huge manipulator arms grab the pallets and put them in racks. Mobile storage columns are carried by a fleet of autonomous platforms that slide under them, elevate them and drive them to their destination in an astonishing choreography. A few low-skilled human hands are still used to crate individual items – but their replacement by machines is already being researched. For the time being, they operate under the supervision of multiple sensors augmented with Artificial Intelligence that indicate, if necessary, whether a wrong item has been entered. Huge belt conveyors with switch systems transport the small crates.

Warehouse operatives will inevitably disappear in the long term. The pace of downsizing will depend not only on technical feasibility but also on economic considerations. Smaller entities may find it more profitable not to invest in automation for a while.

Plumber

Plumbers install water supply systems, install and connect sanitary ware and fittings, and carry out the complete maintenance of plumbing systems, from unclogging pipes to repairing leaks.

Most of the tasks in this job are difficult to automate for various reasons: the elementary operations are very varied, and the working environment is non-standard, congested and often complicated to

---

[265] https://www.youtube.com/watch?v=4sEVX4mPuto

access. Finally, the physical nature of the tasks to be performed, such as laying and connecting pipes, is difficult to automate because of the dexterity and mobility required.

This is not the time for automation for plumbers around the world. Robotisation does not even seem to be a threat in the medium term. There is no shortage of opportunities, not only from new construction, but especially from renovation and repairs, which are often urgent. The income of plumbers is considered attractive, if not very attractive, for self-employed craftsmen. Will the profession experience an influx of candidates?

Cook

The range of professions covered by the term cook is extremely wide, from the kitchen assistant to the great starred chef.

Robotisation has already been widely used in kitchens since the 1960s, making it easier to cut food in various ways, to knead dough or to beat egg whites. Artificial Intelligence is now entering ovens, to determine the right baking conditions. The trend will continue towards refrigerators and other household appliances. All will be connected and operate in a synchronised way, which will reduce the tasks of the kitchen staff accordingly.

Fully automated kitchens already exist in the prototype state[266]: the robot, having been notified of the order, gets hold of the ingredients, mixes them, cooks them, and places them on a plate ready to serve. In some hotels, more as an attraction than anything else, omelettes are made by a robot (which even dares to flip them, most of the time successfully). Many trials are underway to further automate fast food: the type of food served seems to be ideal for this exercise. A hamburger-flipping robot has been around for several years. Automated fast food

---

[266] For example Spyce, the result of the efforts of 4 MIT students
https://www.youtube.com/watch?v=byDmDWq7wc8

kiosks are already available in Shanghai or California[267]. Many Japanese restaurants have very high levels of automation, from taking orders to delivering the dish on a conveyor belt (or, better still, a miniature train), to making sushi in the kitchen[268].

If we leave aside the elite of the great chefs and the task of creating new dishes, which will undoubtedly remain for some time the prerogative of humans, the other tasks all have the potential to be automated in the medium term. Here again, only economic considerations might preserve employment for a time in cases where wage savings cannot justify investment in automation equipment. It can therefore be assumed that the extreme automation of kitchen professions will occur first in countries with high labour costs or labour shortages.

Hairdresser

Hairdressers hold a job that is strategic in the current context. Their clientele is demanding and very sensitive because hairstyle is closely linked to appearance and identity. Customers make individualised requests, sometimes based on examples that almost always end up being customised and modified. And even if the haircut is standard, even if it consists in shaving the person's head, its physical implementation is difficult to achieve. Finally, a certain category of customers go to the hairdresser not only for the maintenance of their hair but also for a good chat. Hairdressing therefore seems to combine all the obstacles to automation.

To the great relief of the many hairdressers and barbers around the world, hairdressing should remain a sector shielded from automation for a long time to come. The buoyancy of demand closely matches the demographic trends. That said, the occupation is in the category of occupations that are easy for humans and difficult for machines. The low level of technical skills required and the high level of competition do not

---

[267] https://www.foodbeast.com/news/artificial-intelligence-could-change-the-fast-food-industry-in-a-major-way/
[268] See, for example, the Genki Sushi chain, which exports its format to all the countries where it operates.

make it possible to ensure a high income – with the exception of the few stars of the hairdressing industry.

Cashier

The cashier's tasks essentially consist in recording purchases made and collecting payment. Payment, particularly electronic payment, no longer requires human intervention; recording purchases requires less and less.

The progressive decline in employment started with productivity gains at cash registers, thanks in particular to the rapid reading of barcodes by scanners. The number of employees fell further when operations at the cash register were partially outsourced to customers themselves, on a self-service basis, under the remote supervision of a reduced number of employees. Customers benefit by significantly reducing their waiting time.

The final blow to the use of cashiers will come when purchases are automatically recorded in real time, thanks to different sensors, as soon as the goods are removed from the shelves. There will no longer be any cash register since the payment itself can be made from a mobile phone, or even automatically by detecting the identity of the buyer. Such systems already exist in supermarkets without employees that appear in embryonic form in the United States or China[269].

This automation takes place in a context where demand is itself is decreasing. Retail itself has never fared better, but most of it is being converted to online sales.

Cashiers and self-service employees, who still represent more than 3 million employees in the US, will disappear completely in the short to medium term[270]. The expected disappearance of the cashier's job will certainly penalise employees whose livelihood depends on it. But the job is very unsatisfying, often physically exhausting, with inconvenient

---

[269] AmazonGo in the USA and Hema (Alibaba Group) in China, among others.
[270] The Sapiens Institute gives the date from 2050 to 2066, which seems extremely late to us. We would be surprised if there are still cashiers in supermarkets in 10 or 15 years' time.

work schedules, and very poorly paid. Many will see the substitution of the human by the machine as a step forward for humanity.

Data entry operator

Data entry operators use their computer keyboard to manually enter data that usually ends up in the company's management systems.

It is one of the first occupations to have been outsourced to countries with low labour costs. It will also be, with a high degree of certainty, one of the first to disappear in the short term. Indeed, the most routine applications are already supported by RPA (Robotic Process Automation). This technology accurately replicates the tasks performed by an operator, without even having to do any programming – so it is very simple to implement.

For slightly more complex data entry, the requirements coincide with the most advanced faculties of Artificial Intelligence – optical character recognition and Natural Language Processing. For example, when entering invoices, the machine can read amounts (even handwritten ones) and identify the supplier's name or the subject of the purchase from the various text fields.

Data entry operators also work in an unrewarding and low-paid profession. While the profession does perform a basic economic function for the individuals who hold it, it does not correspond to a fulfilling activity that makes best use of the qualities of human beings.

Call centre worker

A call centre worker can perform various functions. In any case, their job is psychologically difficult and sometimes not very rewarding. In addition, when clients are individual consumers and not companies, their needs often arise outside normal office hours.

Telemarketers initiate the act of remotely selling a generally unsophisticated good or service. Their approach is extremely repetitive. Their ability to understand or persuade the client is sometimes limited. Telemarketers are doomed to disappear relatively quickly, replaced by a voice chatbot or other electronic communication channels. These substitutes, supported by the company's information systems, will be able to rely on all the information available and could to turn out to be more convincing.

Customer service agents respond to requests or complaints from customers who are generally dissatisfied. Queries have varying levels of difficulty. In simple cases and relatively closed scenarios, chatbots can also conduct most of the conversation thanks to the immense progress in Natural Language Processing. Cognitive virtual agents already know how to explore the company's databases to find, for example, a price, a forecast delivery date or the exact status of an order. Artificial Intelligence can even be followed by a personalised complementary service offered to the customer. And your initially dissatisfied customer ends up happy and converted into a new company champion, committed to the company's cause.

The benefits of replacing humans with machines are both an economic gain and an increase in service quality, as the machines are always available.

Customer service employees will disappear by phase and level of intervention. Only employees assigned to solving complex problems, technically or emotionally, will survive in the short and medium term.

Secretary or administrative assistant

The administrative profession entered its long phase of decline with the advent of information technology. The number of employees in the sector in the US today is about four million.

In the past, secretaries took instructions given verbally or scribbled on paper, typed them up and executed them. Artificial Intelligence is doing it on its own today. It can then identify and get in touch with people to be contacted, filter access requests, answer standard emails, make or confirm appointments, complete forms and inquiries, retrieve data and perform various analyses, produce expense reports, and book flights or hotel accommodation.

The fall in the sector will not only continue but accelerate, potentially sparing only the upper fringe of the highest value-added management secretaries. The speed of the decline might be offset in some economies by an increased need for administrative support. But secretarial and administrative assistants are generally doomed to disappear.

Accountant

There are about 1.4 million accountants and auditors in the US alone.

The most basic tasks of an accountant are reconciling invoices with orders, entering information, reconciling bank statements with the general transaction log, and filing and storing all documents. More experienced accountants prepare the company's financial records and management accounts, ensure that they balance properly and analyse them. They also ensure that new or amended accounting standards are correctly interpreted and implemented.

All these tasks fall within the privileged target of Artificial Intelligence, since accounting is a pure mathematical creation based on the collection and analysis of data. These tasks will therefore be carried out in the short or medium term by Artificial Intelligence. Even the introduction and application of new rules will require a limited number of experts whose conclusions can be learned by the machine and disseminated. Except for the roles of supervision and legal responsibility for the company's accounts, the number of employees in the accounting sector is expected to decline in the medium term.

Financial analyst

Financial analysts provide guidance to businesses and individuals making investment decisions[271].

However, data acquisition and processing are exactly the areas where Artificial Intelligence excels, far exceeding human capabilities in terms

---

[271] This definition, like a few others in this chapter, is drawn from the US Bureau of Labor Statistics.

of detecting correlations and making predictions. Nouriel Roubini, the economist who against all odds predicted the 2008 financial crash, says: "There were tens of different signals that would eventually lead to a tipping point."[272] But Artificial Intelligence does not miss these different signals. Once the infrastructure is in place, it does better than economic and financial analysts and can easily do without them. It should be noted, however, that the Oxford study [273] attributes greater difficulty to automating them, perhaps because of the human validation required depending on the importance of the decisions to be made, or because of the difficulty of initial implementation.

Financial advisors, who assist individuals and companies in the management of their financial assets, are in an even more vulnerable situation. Multiple consulting bots – the roboadvisors – are already emerging in the start-up landscape, with a value proposition of replacing emotions with data, but ensuring the customer is in the driving seat[274]. The financial advisor is no match.

Financial advisors should disappear completely in the short term. Financial analysts may survive for some time depending on the expected impact of the analyses to be conducted. In the meantime, they will be very strongly augmented, which should reduce their workforce unless there is a significant increase in activity.

Claims adjuster, appraiser or examiner

The insurance business is structured differently depending on the country. In general, claims adjusters, appraisers and examiners evaluate insurance claims and decide how much, if anything, the insurance company must pay in response to the claim. They take note of and analyse the circumstances of a claim, record the damage, quantify the

---

[272] https://www.theguardian.com/business/2009/jan/24/nouriel-roubini-credit-crunch.
[273] Frey and Osborne study of 2013 [14].
[274] Connect is one example among many others:
https://www.crossbridgeconnect.com/

damage, investigate the causes and establish responsibilities, while trying to be as objective as possible throughout the process.

Most of these tasks involve the expert's perception for estimating the level of damage and databases to quantify the repair or replacement. The capabilities at work here coincide with those of Artificial Intelligence. The search for causes and the establishment of responsibilities may take longer to automate, similarly to the work of a judge.

Claims adjusters and examiners will be greatly augmented by Artificial Intelligence in the short term, creating a financial gain for all parties and a speed of processing much appreciated by victims of damage[275]. This significant augmentation of experts by machines should reduce the number of people in the profession, unless the volume of insured persons increases very significantly in territories where the current coverage is low. The final disappearance of claims adjusters and appraisers, claimed to be inevitable in the short term by the Oxford study, can only be fully achieved when different stakeholders' responsibilities can be assessed – a difficult task.

Manager

Manager is a term that encompasses a wide variety of jobs. Generally speaking, the manager directs and supports their team and is accountable for the results.

As far as Artificial Intelligence is concerned, it can make predictions, inform decisions, check outcomes and highlight possible explanatory factors. However, AI does not know how to lead a team of men and women: inspire them, encourage them, understand their deep motivations, or manage conflicts. It would not be seen as a legitimate manager today anyway – this is the human premium at work. AI knows how to establish winning strategies in well-defined environments, but does not understand the environment in which a company or other institution operates. With current technologies, it cannot decide on a

---

[275] Lemonade insurance works on this model of doing everything "instantly": https://www.lemonade.com/

team's priorities and even less craft a strategy that it would itself decide to adopt. Moreover, AI is not morally or legally responsible – only a human being can take this responsibility as of today.

Managers will certainly be augmented by Artificial Intelligence, but not replaced in the near future. It is likely that the manager's value – and therefore their income – will increase.

Legal assistant

The legal assistant, or paralegal, is an assistant specialising in law who can write procedures and reports, but also, depending on the country and practice, carry out research on case law or doctrine.

All these operations are time-consuming for humans, but relatively easy to perform for Artificial Intelligence: almost instant reading of thousands of pages, infallible memory, identification of relevant passages thanks to semantic understanding, and generation of summary notes.

At the end of this very unequal battle, legal assistants are condemned to see their numbers fall in the short or medium term.

Lawyer

It will be long before an AI delivers a passionate argument in the courtroom – the robot in a toga is still generations away. But arguing a case is only a small part of the lawyer's activity.

All the work of reviewing the file and researching case law, as we have seen with the legal assistant, will inevitably fall within the remit of Artificial Intelligence. This can provide simulated judgments and encourage settlement rather than going to court. It will enable quicker and better-accepted compromises, for example for divorce settlements, saving considerable time and money.

Some lawyers specialise in business law. In 2017, an Artificial Intelligence[276] was put into competition with 20 business lawyers to review a set of non-disclosure agreements. The AI was able to identify more legal problems in these contracts than the average lawyer. In addition, while humans had to spend an average of 92 minutes, the AI only took... 26 seconds! Officially, the lawyers who took part in the test were delighted at the prospect of being augmented and being able to focus on more interesting aspects of the profession.

The risk for these lawyers, even if they seem in denial for the time being, is that this augmentation will become more and more important until they are partially replaced. Lawyers' fees are a great incentive to find technological routes to at least a partial substitution.

Lawyers, therefore, will be significantly augmented, although some of their functions are currently not automatable, such as negotiation and persuasion. Unless there is a significant increase in activity due to the decrease in cost, the profession's workforce should decline. It is more difficult to predict the evolution of their income.

Doctor

Today, doctors must study for many years to understand and learn something as important as the functioning of the human body, its diseases and the corresponding treatments. It is only after this that they eventually undertake a specialisation. The effort required of them is immense. Doctors must then apply their knowledge while managing the human relationship with their patients.

Tomorrow – in other words, in perhaps 20 years' time – Artificial Intelligence will be able to diagnose diseases with much greater precision than humans[277]. AI will also recommend a therapeutic plan, incorporating the latest advances in science; the plan can be fully customised as part of precision medicine.

---

[276] The AI was the one of the start-up LawGeex.
[277] See Part 1 Chapter 4.

Doctors will be augmented by AI for diagnostic and therapeutic tasks. Some predict that doctors will turn into luxury nurses, more available and cheaper than current doctors[278]. This would indeed happen if the initial training, after becoming shorter and less demanding, makes the profession less selective and open to more candidates. The role of the physician would evolve and they could spend much more time catering to the patients' emotional needs. The profession would be organised in such a way that physicians could refer patients to a specialist in case of medical doubt. With a larger number of doctors and lower fees, access to medicine could be facilitated in territories with less coverage today. There would no longer be any medical desert, either in advanced or developing countries.

Facilitating access to medicine and augmenting doctors with AI already exists in Ping An's "One-minute Clinics" in China[279]. These unmanned kiosks, which look like photo booths, welcome patients for a consultation. The patient is first managed by an AI which collects symptoms and medical history before making a preliminary diagnosis. A real doctor, online, then joins the consultation and confirms or modifies the diagnosis and prescriptions. A small adjoining cabin serves as a pharmacy, also without staff. According to Ping An, their medical AI, driven by data from 300 million consultations, can recognise about 2,000 pathologies; the adjoining pharmacy can store about 100 of the most requested drugs. Ping An aims to deploy about 1,000 of these kiosks by the end of 2018. This is thought-provoking, even in the West.

AI will not completely replace doctors, but it will probably significantly change the profession. The impact on the total workforce is uncertain, but income should decrease with de-skilling.

---

[278] This is Kai-Fu Lee's prediction in particular and it is not devoid of common sense.
[279] https://www.mobihealthnews.com/content/ping-good-doctor-launches-commercial-operation-one-minute-clinics-china

Caregiver

Caregivers ensure the physical and moral comfort of patients under their care, supporting them in the activities of daily living and contributing to their well-being. Their intervention is both very physical, helping patients to overcome a sometimes-diminished autonomy, and deeply relational.

Some of the physical tasks, particularly those requiring real strength to help patients move, can be at least partially robotised. But many interventions, particularly body care, are far too complex to be automated and robotised in the short to medium term. As to the relational part, it remains largely in the human domain even if robotics and Artificial Intelligence are venturing into this field – as we saw with your aunt Stephanie[280]. There is still a high human premium.

As the population is aging, it is no coincidence that the number of caregivers is increasing in most developed countries. The trend towards more care and caregivers is likely to continue. Anticipated demographic changes will of course be a driver. An even more important driver will be the social changes that many are calling for in the era of Artificial Intelligence: to let machines do the machine work so that humans can focus on being human.

The trend will be the same at the other end of the age spectrum, with childcare.

All healthcare professions should see an increase in their workforce. There is no objective reason why the level of income, which is rather low today, should increase, unless there is a shortage of caregivers or a significant societal change.

Teacher

The teaching profession in most countries of the world is very similar to what it was in the 19th century: the teacher, in a one-way process,

---

[280] See Part 1 Chapter 4.

imparts their knowledge to the 20, 30 or 50 students who are in the classroom listening to them. Teachers are also overwhelmed by a series of administrative or para-pedagogical constraints that consume a lot of time.

However, it is now understood that the transfer of knowledge is only a tiny part of the teacher's role. In addition, the personalisation of teaching is one of the keys to success. Artificial Intelligence will help considerably in this respect. With a very detailed understanding of what knowledge the student has or has not acquired, AI will guide the student towards the desired learning outcomes by taking the path most appropriate to his or her strengths, preferences and tastes, pace and abilities. It will recommend appropriate exercises and projects, and organise the necessary revisions.

AI will also take over all the tasks usually assigned to teaching assistants, such as answering administrative questions or basic questions about the course content. In fact, in 2017, an educational assistant named Jill Watson was put to work online at the University of Iowa with great success for an entire term...until it was revealed that it was an Artificial Intelligence[281].

In this transformation, the teacher will not disappear – or at least not for a while. Although AI technically helps with subject-by-subject teaching, and while it can provide basic tutoring, it actually has no understanding of what it teaches and will not always be able to rise to the level of the questions that students might ask.

Above all, AI lacks the ability to truly understand, inspire, motivate, congratulate or comfort students – in other words, to meet their socio-emotional needs while orchestrating their learning. Today it can only simulate, which is a second best but still has its limits.

As teachers are relieved from a large number of time-consuming tasks, and as they benefit from insights provided by AI, they will be able to

---

[281] https://www.businessinsider.com/a-professor-built-an-ai-teaching-assistant-for-his-courses-and-it-could-shape-the-future-of-education-2017-3/?IR=T

spend more time with each learner and significantly increase the impact of their work.

The teaching profession will evolve in a very significant way but will not disappear. Only teachers who have not been able to adopt technology will quickly disappear. The time freed up by machines will help them strengthen the supervision of their students. The change in the total number of employees and in their compensation remains uncertain, as there is a buoyant demand in most countries.

Computer scientist

The computer scientist's extensive ecosystem covers many professions, from data scientists to Machine Learning engineers or researchers, through database, server or network administrators; developers of all types; programmer analysts or software architects. They almost all share the characteristic of being in high-growth sectors with labour shortages, ensuring sustainable employment prospects. In the short term, the need is even greater due to the countless projects for digitising data and implementing Artificial Intelligence.

Only basic developers could see their jobs threatened in the short or medium term by Artificial Intelligence, for the simple reason that it is also learning to code! Coding is one of the simple activities that AI can learn and implement. Multiple solutions already exist to generate the basic code automatically from functional instructions. As far as developers are concerned, they must spend considerable time keeping abreast of the evolution or the replacement of computer languages, mastering the latest programmatic advances and adopting the multiple libraries available.

At the very top of the scale, only ten or twenty thousand researchers[282] worldwide are at the level necessary to advance the science of Artificial Intelligence. This is a golden opportunity that does not seem to be about

---

[282] http://www.jfgagne.ai/talent/

to dry up. The best researchers are headhunted by the ten or so leading companies in the market. They have superstar status.

The various IT professions, with the possible exception of certain tasks prone to automation such as basic coding, constitute a sustainable and attractive employment sector.

Artificial Intelligence ethicist

This activity is completely new. It perfectly illustrates the new type of jobs that will come along with, and supervise to a certain extent, the deployment of Artificial Intelligence.

In a context where the possible abuses are numerous and potentially catastrophic, the ethicist will help define and implement Artificial Intelligence as humans wish it to be. It will guide the design, construction and use of AI.

By definition, this activity will remain human. The headcount will be limited but the role will be important.

News presenter

The news presenter, on the TV, is usually in charge of reading the news convincingly between two television reports. The presenter also conducts interviews with their guests.

A Chinese channel has already digitised two of its star presenters and let the avatars present a news bulletin[283]. The faces and expressions, voice and intonation of the avatars were modelled on the originals. They are still relatively easily discernible from their human models, but it is only a matter of time – and probably very little time.

The human added value is negligible for the task of presenting news – except perhaps a little credibility, for those who still believe that human presenters will be more likely to tell the truth than a machine and less

---

[283] https://www.cnet.com/au/news/watch-this-creepy-ai-anchor-talk-like-a-real-person/

likely to be themselves manipulated. The huge advantage of avatars is the ability to update the news bulletins in real time and not to carry outdated information in pre-recorded shows.

The avatar itself is not at all able to conduct interviews today, and this is unlikely to be resolved quickly. The interviewer asks relevant questions, carefully listens and interprets the answers, highlights contradictions or a lack of clarity and builds on the interviewee's replies – all of this is beyond the machine's competence today (except perhaps the instant comparison with past statements). However, while the ability of Artificial Intelligence to generate syntheses of information is still imperfect, it is increasing at high speed: the role of AI could therefore increase.

Unless there is a very high human premium that is difficult to anticipate today, the general-purpose news presenter will disappear in the short or medium term. The interviewer function, which can be completely dissociated, will remain.

Actor

Star actors can fetch compensation of tens of millions of dollars for their appearances. This is a strong incentive to digitise them, which has other advantages. The physical presence of the actor is no longer necessary, and with it a large number of obstacles disappear: coordination constraints, reluctance to perform stunts, mood swings, illness or even death.

Star Wars fans must have noticed the appearance of Peter Cushing, a hero from the original 1977 film, in the recent episode Rogue One. However, Rogue One was released in 2016, and Peter Cushing died in 1994. Technology was very effective in superimposing Cushing's appearance onto his acting double ... of course with the consent of his estate. Similarly, one can easily imagine another 50 years of new episodes of Mission Impossible, with a Tom Cruise still as heroic and admired – but at a much lower cost.

The phenomenon is still very marginal, and there is undoubtedly still a human premium. But there has been considerable technical progress in image technologies. In addition, the public is increasingly accustomed to special effects and computer graphics, they appreciate animated films, and their loyalty seems to go more to franchises than to the actors of the moment. Actors should keep this in mind.

Footballer

As we have seen, robot footballers have encountered varying levels of success[284]. Humanoid robots are struggling. Robots on wheels can impress with their technical and tactical mastery - but it's a different sport, since these robots are not humanoid.

Professional human players can therefore be reassured. The most talented amongst them will continue to attract crowds and earn fortunes for a long time to come – but the others, outside the elite, will probably still have just as much trouble making a living. Eventually, robots will improve in agility, run faster than humans and shoot right under the cross bar from a distance of 80 metres, but spectators will probably still be willing to pay to see their fellow humans on a football field.

The human premium comes into play amidst human effort and victory, as well as in suffering and defeat. Haven't we loved circus games since the dawn of time? Are there not spectators left to encourage women and men lifting weights that must feel heavy to them but are laughable in terms of the machines' capabilities? Don't we still enjoy seeing 8 athletes running 100 metres at the modest speed of 40 kilometres per hour? How we look at human performance in sport is disconnected from the incomparably superior performance of machines.

The examples above are naturally very limited given the existence of hundreds of different types of jobs. They give an emotionless account of what large predictable changes jobs are likely to go through. Some

---

[284] See Part 1 Chapter 3.

cases will see people thrive; others will give rise to real human hardship and suffering. These examples are intended only to stimulate critical reflection for major career choices. This is the subject we will now discuss.

Chapter 10.   A framework for career choice

I n the previous chapters, we explored in detail the key questions to be asked. We then looked at some consolidated global employment forecasts. Next we reviewed 23 examples of jobs with very different destinies, some destined to disappear, others promised to grow.

It is time to summarise and formalise a career guidance framework. This framework is aimed both at young people preparing to enter the labour market and at professionals who already have a career of however many years behind them and who wish – or are forced – to evolve. The purpose of this framework is to facilitate and guide reflection before decision-making. By and large, it is a synthesis of the methodology already examined in detail. Despite the prevailing uncertainty and the rapidly changing situation, it enables us to identify some major trends that need to be taken into account.

The main criterion used is the sustainability of employment. In parallel, the level of income is discussed as far as possible. To avoid adding to the uncertainty, this framework covers a horizon of only 10 to 20 years and is based exclusively on technologies available today – or at least accessible with incremental improvements.

From this framework, additional conclusions will also be drawn about the influence of time, the relevance (or not) of maintaining a "median" attitude, the usefulness (or not) of resisting the adoption of augmentation, and finally the existence of a final criterion for job selection.

The five questions

The series of questions to be asked drives our framework.

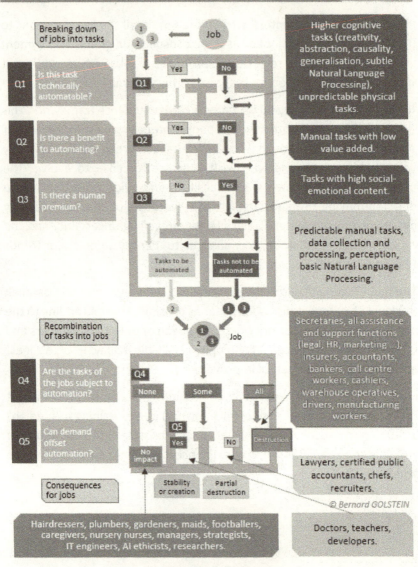

Figure 4: Does this job have a future?

The job is first **broken down into** elementary tasks, which are filtered through the three automation questions.

Is the task technically automatable? To answer this question, we must rely on our comparison of human and AI capabilities in terms of mental processes[285].

The answer will be negative – the task is not technically automatable – when the higher functions of the following different mental processes is activated: reasoning (abstraction, causality, generalisation), creativity (especially radical creativity), natural language processing (fine and non-routine communication), emotions (behaviour with a high socio-emotional content). A negative answer will also be given for a number of physical tasks that are not predictable or require high levels of dexterity or balance. Thus, jobs that are not currently automatable include hairdressers, electricians and plumbers; managers, strategists and researchers; and in part lawyers and computer scientists.

On the other hand, the answer to the question of whether a task can be automated will be yes, as soon as the mental processes implemented are mainly memory and attention, perception, the search for patterns or correlations in the data, prediction, speech recognition and synthesis, summary and semantic extraction, creativity by imitation or by exploring a field of possibilities, and finally the ordinary cases of motor skills. And if the answer is yes, we must move on to the next question.

Is there a benefit to automating? The answer is negative as soon as the cost of implementation exceeds the savings achieved and there is no other performance impact. A large number of low-paid manual tasks fall into this category, such as basic warehousing or basic production activities in small organisations, or cooking in small establishments. In these cases it is not cost-effective to automate.

In all other cases, there is an interest in automating, whether for an economic gain (e.g. replacement of a bank employee), a performance gain (e.g. replacement of a border control officer), or both (e.g.

---

[285] Refer to the whole of Part 1 Chapter 3.

replacement of a taxi driver). And when the answer is yes, we must continue with the third question.

Is there a human premium? The answer is yes if the law requires it (for example by restricting the circulation of autonomous vehicles for a time), but especially if socio-emotional factors favour humans. Some parts of the jobs of doctors, teachers, psychologists or life coaches fall into this category.

In all other cases, there is no human premium. At this stage of the decision tree, the task is bound to be automated sooner or later.

The initial job must now be reconstituted by grouping together the initial tasks. The job may even be subject to a deeper recombination, for example by adding entirely new tasks, getting hold of others from jobs that have themselves been abandoned, or even dropping tasks that would no longer be considered essential. **Are the tasks constituting the job going to be automated?**

If the automation is total, i.e. if it concerns all the tasks constituting the job, which is rare, the job disappears. If there is no automation at all, which is just as rare, employment is maintained. If automation is partial, there is one last question to ask to get a sense of what will happen to the job.

Is the intrinsic demand for this job promising? If the answer is no, then the headcount in that job is doomed to fall. There will inevitably be job destruction. It is a bad choice of career or a field where it will be difficult to maintain oneself. If, on the other hand, demand is strong, for example in the case of partially automated IT professions such as programming, then despite this partial automation, it may remain a good field for a while.

Change as the only constant

The variables that make up our framework are constantly evolving. As a result, none of the answers to the five questions are fixed and the conclusions for individual jobs are continually evolving too. But while the framework is dynamic, the general trend does not change: the propensity for automation increases inexorably over time. Let us see how the answers to the first three questions evolve over time.

The technical possibility of automation increases over time with incremental innovations. The quality of machine translation or semantic understanding, for example, increases steadily with continuous innovation. And the situation can change very quickly! Just 15 years ago, two researchers from MIT and Harvard stated that it was extremely unlikely that an autonomous car would be able to "execute a left turn against oncoming traffic", as the manoeuvre was so complex that it would be difficult to discover all its rules. Their book was about the new division of labour between computers and humans [286]. They were therefore at the forefront of thinking about automation, yet they were caught off guard by technological advances. Their misadventure is recalled by the authors of the Oxford study of 2013, which has already been cited several times[287]. These very authors, in their study, mention social intelligence, creativity and perception as obstacles to automation. However we have already had the opportunity to note that, over the past few years, the situation has changed in each of these three areas. The technical possibility of automation can also take a leap forward with a radical innovation. For example, if Artificial Intelligence acquires common sense or understanding of context, its ability to process natural language will increase considerably.

The gain from automation is also a variable which changes over time. When we talk specifically about economic gain, it results from the difference between a benefit and a cost, each of which is variable. As a country moves up the development ladder, wages increase; the downside of enrichment is that jobs are more exposed to automation because the potential saving on wages becomes more attractive. If wages increase for other reasons, for example because there is a shortage of labour for a particular job that is too uninteresting or too painful, then conditions also become more favourable to automation. At the same time, the cost of automation decreases as experience is

---

[286] Levy and Murnane, *The New Division of Labor* (2004).
[287] We take this opportunity to reiterate that it is worth reading, particularly for its brief history of the impact of technology on work [14].

gained in the automation process, or even as the automation process itself is automated. Indeed, today automation is an operation that requires a high level of human intervention, but machines will gradually take on more of it. Finally, of course, the non-economic gain from automation tends to increase with the efficiency of the technology. For example, the more effective the medical diagnosis by AI, the stronger the incentive to automate.

The human premium is also changing with the law and mindsets. Today, aeroplane pilots, surgeons and social companions retain a human premium. But the day will come when flying a human-piloted aircraft will be considered particularly reckless, as if you were being asked today to land without radar and air traffic control on a day of thick fog. Radar sees what escapes the naked eye; Artificial Intelligence will see what escapes biological intelligence. The day will also come when being operated on by a human being will be considered very reckless and crazy. The day will finally come when social robots will be widespread in our homes. Some Asian countries are pioneers in this field, while other societies find it grotesque at the moment. Perhaps pet robots will supplant pets – they will not only be able to offer company but also provide many other services. This does not mean, far from it, that the human relationship will be devalued; it will simply have found an acceptable alternative in the event of unavailability. If there are not enough teachers, doctors or coaches, Artificial Intelligence can partly make up for their absence.

Few people are willing to recognise and accept the prospect of change. The most frequent reaction is the outright denial of the drastic changes to come in one's own profession. Whether translators or lawyers, anaesthetists or accountants, everyone finds something in their profession that they think will protect them from substitution. There are still financial advisors who believe that the human component of their profession is too strong for them not to be significantly affected, for the simple reason that they are still the ones that the population turns to when the stock market is yo-yoing. This may be the case today, but in our opinion not for very long.

The permanent change of the framework will be accompanied by the permanent change of professions. It will not simply be a matter of changing employers while keeping the same type of job, but of changing jobs. This is illustrated by the McKinsey Global Institute's study, highlighting the risk that nearly 375 million people will have to retrain by 2030[288]. The problem will be only beginning, with a rate of change potentially becoming so rapid that human beings could no longer adapt to it.

The inversion of the Goldilocks principle

In the famous children's tale, little Goldilocks arrives in a cottage whose occupants seem to be away. On the table she sees three bowls of porridge and finally picks the one that is neither too hot nor too cold. She then goes for a nap and picks the medium bed which is neither too hard nor too soft. From her preferences for what is *just the right amount,* the *Goldilocks principle*[289] was born. It is the heir to Aristotle's "golden mean" and to the Latin "in medio stat virtus[290]".

This easy-to-understand principle applies empirically to a wide range of disciplines, from developmental psychology (the infant focuses on events that are just complex enough) to medicine, marketing, mathematics and economics (ideal economic growth is just strong enough, but not too strong). In astrobiology, exoplanets in the Goldilocks zone are those that are neither too close nor too far from their stars, so that temperature conditions are favourable for life to flourish.

With Artificial Intelligence, the Goldilocks principle applied to employment is turned on its head. If the job is too median, either in its intrinsic positioning or in the level of expertise which its holder needs to apply, there is a good chance that it will be in danger.

---

[288] See the explanation in Chapter 3 and the MGI study itself [11].
[289] https://en.wikipedia.org/wiki/Goldilocks_principle
[290] "Virtue is in the middle".

Jobs that are sufficiently close to Artificial Intelligence benefit from the extraordinary aspiration it provides. Closest to its core, AI researchers are both the inventors and explorers of modern times. They are also the new stars that television shows and companies compete fiercely for. Also very close are computer engineers and data scientists. They implement Artificial Intelligence, in industry after industry and company after company. They are overwhelmed with work, and there is no reason why it should stop any time soon because technologies are constantly evolving and skills are still not sufficiently widespread. In their wake, data analysts also participate in the great transformation, as well as programmers. The ecosystem is complemented by all the peripheral professions already mentioned, such as AI ethicists. It also includes the countless business experts who facilitate the entry of AI into their field. They are not computer scientists, at least not by trade, but they know how to analyse and break down their business so as to make it accessible to Artificial Intelligence, which they help to train. They are financiers, logisticians, biologists, warehouse operatives or Go players. They provide initial training to the Artificial Intelligence models, and offer their expertise in the service of new or difficult cases: they are the ultimate business reference for AI implementation.

On the other hand, far, very far from Artificial Intelligence, some jobs thrive precisely on this distance: artists and other radical creators, for example, derive their legitimacy from their humanity, their imagination, their sensitivity, their vulnerability. Athletes, when they are not illegally augmented, play the same game.

Between these two extremes, life is more complicated. The polarisation of trades and wages did not have to wait for Artificial Intelligence to emerge, but AI did exacerbate the trend. Artificial Intelligence gradually nibbles at jobs in the field, especially the most predictable cognitive or manual jobs. Over time, this large furrow in the middle widens, Artificial Intelligence can begin to replace certain jobs that it was only augmenting, and then to augment those that we thought were totally beyond its reach. The Goldilocks zone of employment is a perilous place to be.

The same phenomenon takes place with levels of expertise. Let's go back to our translators' textbook case and start with average translators. The quality of their translations is increasingly surpassed by that of Artificial Intelligence. The trend is obviously not in their favour. Only expert translators will survive – the ones who can convey the subtleties of the original language in the target language – or at the other end of the spectrum, the ones who charge so little that they will still attract some clients, despite the questionable quality of the translation. Take average cooks. They are not starred chefs or even renowned chefs, a status that would confer a certain immunity. Neither are they cheap enough to be shielded from automation. Finally, take average teachers. If their contribution is limited to knowledge transfer, then they are the main target of Artificial Intelligence. Talented educators, on the other hand, are out of the reach of Artificial Intelligence because of the remarkable socio-emotional support they provide. At the other end of the spectrum, older students who support children with homework through cheap tutoring are not in immediate danger either.

For partially automated jobs, therefore, expertise sometimes gives a respite and sometimes even solid and lasting protection. It is precisely this level of expertise and high performance that everyone must aspire to when starting a career, for more peace of mind. At the other end of the spectrum, taking a low-cost position can certainly confer an economic advantage, at least temporarily. But the median position, which could be described as the Goldilocks position, is very vulnerable.

The inversion of the Goldilocks principle also seems to apply to salaries. With the polarisation of employment, with this large furrow that is widening in the middle, average wages will tend to disappear. Traditionally high-paying jobs that escape automation (e.g. IT specialists or managers) will keep their high salaries. The relative de-skilling of professions that will have been largely augmented (such as doctors in the medium and long term) will make those professions accessible to a greater number of people and subject to greater competition, which will cause a reduction in their income. Trades with historically low wages, now subject to an even more competitive environment, are unlikely to see their income increase. Even the more relational professions of care, healthcare and education, with a rapidly growing demand, will probably remain low-paid unless there is a significant societal change.

The adoption of augmentation

For a given task, as we have seen, the initial augmentation is often the prelude to a subsequent substitution. However, this risk does not mean that we should refuse augmentation by Artificial Intelligence; quite the contrary. To refuse it would be to sideline oneself early.

Tomorrow, what will a doctor be worth if they turn down assistance by Artificial Intelligence in diagnosis? They will be dumped by their patients. What will a teacher be worth if they continue to offer the same unique programme to their class, foregoing adaptive learning? They will inevitably be discarded. What will a recruiter be worth if they choose not to do a preliminary screening of candidates applying for a job offer? They will be overwhelmed and eventually let go. It is therefore essential, in order to remain competitive, to adopt Artificial Intelligence technology. AI will not immediately replace these professionals, but doctors, teachers and recruiters who do not adopt AI will certainly be quickly replaced by those who have adopted it.

In scientific research professions, whether in life sciences, physical and chemical sciences, earth sciences or climate sciences, augmentation by Artificial Intelligence has already taken on such importance that laboratories can no longer do without these skills to provide quality research.

Aware of this situation, some professions are getting organised. The American College of Radiology, to mention only one, has created its own Institute of Data Science. Radiologists are at the forefront of the upcoming upheavals.

Augmentation may well seem double-edged, with an initial advantage and a subsequent risk. Refusing it would only speed up the professional's de facto exclusion from the mainstream workforce.

In praise of passion

The career choice framework is a useful selection tool based mainly on the presumed sustainability of employment. But its permanent and rapid evolution adds to the already significant uncertainty. While the propensity for automation increases inexorably, uncertainty may arise from a pace of automation that could be faster or slower than predicted. Income will also evolve, probably in a rather negative direction for many.

This is not very good news, but it strongly encourages us not to keep sustainability of employment and projected income levels as exclusive criteria for career selection.

It will also be of great importance, as it is today, to allow yourself to be at least partially guided by your passion. Passion is most conducive to the emergence of excellence or expertise that, in addition to high job satisfaction, will also provide better employment conditions. Passion will allow us to endure the ups and downs that the future certainly holds. It might very well place us in ideal conditions if new professions appear in a field related to the job already chosen by passion, opening up new perspectives.

Identifying this passion to begin with, and following it afterwards, will be prerequisites to fulfilling the mission that everyone will set for themselves. This mission or *raison d'être* will be part of the new compass that parents must contribute to equip their children for success in the 21st century. This is what we will see in the third and last Part.

Work: takeaways

Four visions of the future

When we consider the future of work in the medium and long term, four competing visions stand out. The most **optimistic** vision refers to Augmented Intelligence rather than Artificial Intelligence. It points to the extraordinary opportunities AI offers to free humans from routine, mundane, painful or degrading activities. The **historical** vision simply sees Artificial Intelligence as the driving force behind the latest industrial revolution. Staunchly following the Schumpeterian school of thought, it firmly supports the idea of creative destruction. Activity and growth will return with renewed stamina, as they always have in the past. The **pessimistic** vision believes that this time, it is different. Humans, destined to become inferior in every respect to AI, will gradually lose their added value. Jobs will become scarce, inequalities will skyrocket. A tiny dominant minority will coexist with a majority of "useless" people. The **radical** vision acknowledges that the end of jobs is inevitable, but it trusts that human genius will invent a new social contract with a novel way of redistributing wealth, perhaps based on Universal Basic Income. With their material needs provided for, humans will engage in other activities that will allow them to thrive or contribute to societal well-being.

In reality, the future is impossible to predict, and may contain elements of all four visions.

A task-based model

In the shorter term, for some activities covered by current jobs, AI will partially or totally replace humans. To assess the impact of AI on jobs, we must first look at the lowest level: the level of tasks that jobs are broken down into. If a task is **technically automatable**, if there is a **benefit** in automation and if there is no **human premium** in performing it, then it is destined to be automated.

Is the task technically automatable? The answer is found in the comparison between the capabilities required by this task and the existing capabilities of Artificial Intelligence. More than half of the tasks performed in a professional context can already be performed by Artificial Intelligence, with today's technologies.

Is there an expected gain in automating the task? This will often be an economic gain, but there may also be a significant increase in the effectiveness of the task. The benefit from automation quite clearly differentiates between cognitive tasks, whose marginal cost of implementation is almost zero, and manual tasks, whose cost of implementation can be increased by the deployment of robots or other physical equipment. The lack of economic gain will almost never be an argument for cognitive tasks.

Is there a human premium? Mindsets, but also sometimes laws, may not always be ready for certain tasks to be performed by machines and not by humans. This is still the case for many socio-emotional tasks.

Even if a task has been through all the filters and is guaranteed to be automated, there might still be a long road to implementation, several years or up to a decade, as is customary in such transformations.

Jobs with a future

Once the tasks are recombined into occupations, it becomes possible to assess the impact of automation on employment in the short and medium term.

To assess the impact of automation on work in the short and medium term, it is prudent to run the above filters on each job, and particularly on its component tasks. But if we are to put forward some general rules, then it can be cautiously argued that jobs most likely to be automated include manual, routine and predictable jobs, such as truck driver, production worker or warehouse worker; secretarial, assistance and support jobs of all kinds, such as legal assistant or call centre agent; and data collection and analysis jobs, such as accountant or financial advisor, even if they are highly valued today.

Occupations least likely to be automated include manual and physical jobs that are unpredictable or have very low added value; jobs involving deep social interaction, such as coaching, caring or managing; highly creative jobs; and jobs containing higher, non-routine cognitive tasks, such as strategist, researcher, engineer or computer scientist.

A proper assessment of employment sustainability also requires knowledge of changes in underlying demand. Demand can be strong enough that it offsets the impact of partial automation on jobs. The health, education and care sectors will benefit from such an upward trend, as will the IT sector.

If job sustainability is the main assessment criterion, then at a relatively comparable level of qualification, one is better off as a hairdresser than a cashier, as a chambermaid than a waiter, as a plumber than a mailroom operative, as a nursing assistant than a legal secretary, as a childcare worker than a call centre agent, as an IT specialist than an accountant, and as a lawyer than a financial advisor. But Artificial Intelligence, in its impact, blurs the traditional boundaries between manual and cognitive occupations, or between low-skilled and highly skilled occupations. Keeping the same job sustainability criterion, one is better off as a tree pruner than an insurance expert, as a crane operator than a bank employee, as an electrician than an administrative manager, and as a fitness coach than a market research analyst. Finally, without being destined for complete automation, some professions such as lawyers, teachers or doctors will evolve in a very significant way.

Artificial Intelligence is the death knell for all that is median in the world of work. To survive, a job will have to be either close to Artificial Intelligence or as far away as possible. The expertise required should be either very high or so low that automation will not be justified. Income will also be bimodal: high wages will remain high for jobs that survive, while average wages will probably decrease, leaving a gaping space in the middle.

The permanence of change

All the parameters of our models vary over time. What cannot be automated today may become automatable in the short or medium term. What is socially or psychologically unacceptable today may be fully adopted in one or two decades – particularly with regard to the status of robots and Artificial Intelligence in social interactions. Jobs, therefore, will be increasingly likely to be automated. And individuals will probably have to change professions and completely reinvent themselves several times in their lifetimes. This has major implications for the education system, which we will explore in Part 3.

Part III

Education

Chapter 11.   Paradigm shift

A s the era of Artificial Intelligence dawns, people are looking for an education system that will be able to adequately prepare future generations. What, in particular, can formal education offer?

Formal education is not new. When writing was invented 5,000 years ago, its complexity required the training of a literate elite. However, this highly specialised learning could no longer take place outside of a dedicated setting: this is how school was born. This respectable institution has lasted for generations and took its present form in the 19th century. Now, under the influence of Artificial Intelligence, it is facing a new inflexion point.

The end of a paradigm

The end of 19th-century education
It was in the 19th century that modern school emerged in the Western world. It broke with the previous model that primarily served the Church and the State, catering mainly to boys from the upper strata of society and characterised by the paucity of its educational methods.

National school systems were set up, underpinned by social and economic objectives and not without nationalist ulterior motives. School became more democratic: Jules Ferry made it secular, free and compulsory in France in the 1880s, and around the same time primary school became compulsory in Great Britain and the United States[291], almost a century after Prussia. Even if school lasted only until the age of 10 or 11 for the majority of children, young boys and now young girls were flocking to school to be educated. A victim of its own success,

---

[291] In the United States, laws making primary school compulsory were passed state by state between 1852 and 1917.

school now had to be industrialised to meet the demand of both students and a society in search of new productive resources.

Very quickly, the few progressive theories that had emerged in previous decades and centuries, or that still popped up here and there, were discarded. The aspiration to personalise education did not stand up to the constraint of industrialisation. The progressive and natural child development advocated by Rousseau, against the beliefs of his time, was put on hold. The educational principles of Pestalozzi, treating children as such and not as miniature adults, were abandoned. The visionary practices of Maria Montessori, calling for completely individualised and free child development, using the physical manipulation of objects[292], were marginalised.

Indeed, school at the end of the 19th century had to operate like a big factory. Education, to begin with, was purely instruction: it was about imparting knowledge from the outside by forcing it into the brains of children in one way or another. The main pedagogical objective was to inculcate successive layers of knowledge in the most effective and scalable way possible.

Therefore, the appropriate method of instruction was systematic and uniform, teacher-centred, using standardised teaching materials, but never focused on the learner. The student had now become one anonymous individual amongst 30, 40 or 60 other learners in the classroom. Teaching evolved from individual to collective. Students used to sit next to each other in rows from the teacher's desk to the back of the classroom. All learners faced the teacher, who was sitting at their desk or standing next to the blackboard. The teacher would impart quasi-sacred knowledge. They would address students unidirectionally, and students were meant to religiously absorb the teachings. The students' main objective was to memorise the knowledge, to recite it, to use it in exercises, never to dare question it, and finally to regurgitate it during exams. The tyranny of grades replaced – at least partly –

---

[292] These principles of free and spontaneous development were themselves wrong, as multiple modern studies have shown, but they had the advantage of promoting personalisation and pleasure.

physical bullying. Pupils would go to school from morning to late afternoon, as their parents would go to work; the former learned facts by heart while the latter fulfilled their professional duties.

And then, when compulsory schooling was over, some, usually the least fortunate, would go on to apprenticeship or directly into working life; others would go through the intermediate stage of secondary school, or even university. All were equipped to work until retirement – or more likely until death. Everything was fine in this industrial age[293].

Fortunately for us, the education system has since drastically evolved. Theories of pedagogy, supported by the cognitive sciences, have made considerable progress. But there are still remnants of the 19th-century education system in many countries. It should be remembered that many children still do not have access to school. Even for those who do, classes of 50 or 60 students are not unheard of. It is not uncommon to hear a whole class repeat their teacher's words in a perfectly synchronised monotone. Other problems persist. Teacher training in the subjects taught, but not in the art of teaching, is unfortunately a frequent reality. The nearly exclusive emphasis on the transmission of knowledge is almost a general rule. The extreme focus on memorisation and discipline, reinforced by the tyranny of exams, is still widespread.

This sometimes leads to amusing situations. In many countries, foreign language teaching, for example, is still based on grammar and translation rather than on modern communicative methods. Some learners have studied the target language's grammar rules and vocabulary so much that they have a better grasp of them than native speakers – but they are unable to utter a single sentence that they have not previously memorised. Although they know the entire dictionary, they can't say a word in the target language! In the most populous country in the world, some 5-year-olds are reportedly taking advanced literature courses; they memorise hundreds of verses and recite them

---

[293] For more information on this very brief history of education, see http://history-world.org/history_of_education.htm or https://en.wikipedia.org/wiki/History_of_education or even better, the specialised books.

without even understanding their meaning, and this has been going on for thousands of years.

But this system inherited from the 19th century is doomed to collapse in the era of Artificial Intelligence. The socio-economic objective and nationalist ulterior motives remain. However, the fundamental assumption on which the current system is based, namely the relative stability of knowledge and trades over time, is being shattered. We must now educate for jobs that do not yet exist, and be prepared to abandon several times during our lifetimes jobs that have become obsolete[294]. How can we do this? And how can we ensure, more generally, that learners learn the right things?

Three pillars of the new educational paradigm are gradually emerging. Is the knowledge taught obsoleted too quickly, is it available outside of school, and does it no longer guarantee that we will achieve our life objectives? Then we must stop focusing exclusively on knowledge, especially if it is not transferable, and refocus instead on more sustainable assets: **timeless skills**. Is initial education (school and university) no longer capable of equipping an individual for an entire lifetime? Then education must become **lifelong**. Are traditional teaching methods not as effective as we would like them to be? Then we must be willing to be guided by **the modern educational arsenal** that science and technology make available to us.

From knowledge to skills

Knowledge falls into (relative) disgrace
For centuries, as we have seen, education has been synonymous with the memorisation of knowledge. This has been even more true since the coming of age of modern school in the 19th century. The knowledge being imparted is often specific to a particular field. It is all the less transferable as it is most often taught superficially, for example by rote

---

[294] 65% of the jobs that will be performed in the future by children entering primary school today do not yet exist. This number is cited in many reports including the World Economic Forum report [28] but we were unable to identify the root source.

learning, rather than in a deeper way. In contrast, for knowledge to be transferable, its general principles must be well understood and assimilated, and its applicability and use cases well mastered. Then the learner can be set free from particular examples and become able to generalise[295].

However, knowledge is most commonly introduced during classes, learned by heart, served up again during various exercises and finally regurgitated during exams. Therefore, knowledge is taught to exams – and often wrongly so, since the exam does not necessarily measure real or useful learning. The widespread practice of cramming adds to the problems: many of the skills or knowledge memorised at the last minute without necessarily being understood do not survive for long after the exam.

The brightest minds have never liked this focus on specific knowledge. During his first triumphant visit to the United States, Albert Einstein failed Edison's test asking for the value of c, the speed of light[296]. "I do not carry such information in my mind since it is readily available in books," he replied to the journalist who was interviewing him[297]. The year was 1921 – when he received the Nobel Prize.

What would Albert Einstein say a century later? Many young and old minds are still cluttered with information that can be found very easily with an internet search. Google, today, knows everything or close to it: the date of Elizabeth II's coronation; the proper spelling of *dilemma*, *fluorescent* and *idiosyncrasy*; the engineering principles of an electric car; the theories of learning; and of course the speed of light. Knowledge has become a commodity.

---

[295] See a more detailed description of transferable knowledge in "Education for Life and Work: developing transferable knowledge and skills for the 21st century" [55].

[296] https://www.nytimes.com/1921/05/18/archives/einstein-sees-boston-fails-on-edison-test-asked-to-tell-speed-of.html

[297] From the NY Times, May 18, 1921
https://en.wikiquote.org/wiki/Albert_Einstein

Moreover, as we progress through time, knowledge challenges us on two fronts. At the vanguard, the volume of knowledge available is soaring. New inventions, new discoveries, and new practices are added to the mass of knowledge. We are in the middle of a real explosion of information.

At the rear, the speed at which knowledge expires is also steadily increasing. Old knowledge is becoming obsolete: some is found to be inaccurate ("no, the infant's brain is not a blank page at birth"); some ceases to be used because the corresponding practice itself ceases ("one no longer plans a waterfall project but adopts agile management"); some is integrated into a larger chunk and no longer needs to be mastered on a stand-alone basis ("these modules are managed by a library of pre-existing functions, so it is no longer necessary to worry about them"). Knowledge, like a radioactive substance, decays and has a half-life – the period that marks the moment when half of its initial quantity has disappeared[298]. We cannot rigorously establish the half-life of all knowledge. But according to some estimates, the half-life of an engineering degree, for example, was 35 years a century ago, 10 years in the 1960s, and today could reach barely 5 years at most[299]. Some claim that half of the specific knowledge provided in the first year of a four-year technical course is outdated even before the student receives his or her diploma[300].

The resurgence of timeless skills

Under these conditions, it is useless to acquire specific knowledge at the wrong time and in the wrong way, since it is largely destined to become obsolete before being put to use. It is also imprudent to focus on mastering a particular field: in an era of permanent change, this strategy is no longer a guarantee of a stable career, financial independence or even life satisfaction. What is invaluable in a changing context, however,

---

[298] The interested reader will be able to look at Samuel Arbesman's book: *The Half-Life of Facts: Why Everything We Know Has an Expiration Date.*
[299] See Shane Parish's blog post at Farnam Street
https://fs.blog/2018/03/half-life/
[300] The information is contained in the British report "Solving Future Skills Challenge" [26].

is the actual skill of learning: knowing how to learn. Being able to use the information learned and apply it appropriately, sometimes in adjacent areas, is an essential complement to the ability to acquire knowledge.

In the new educational paradigm, therefore, learning to learn becomes the highest priority. It must be supplemented with the cognitive capacities that allow us to make sense of the volume of information we are faced with, and to understand and analyse the world. These cognitive skills include reasoning, critical thinking, and problem-solving skills. In the 1921 interview in which he willingly admitted his ignorance of the value of the speed of light, Albert Einstein rightly stated: "The value of a college education is not the learning of many facts but the training of the mind to think."[301] Let us add the cognitive capacity of creative thinking, closely linked to curiosity and imagination. The same Albert Einstein, who never ran out of critical and relevant comments on the knowledge-based educational model, illustrated his point in another interview in 1929: "Imagination is more important than knowledge. Knowledge is limited. Imagination encircles the world."[302]

As we move into a new era, other skills, formerly much less valued, take a prominent place among the timeless skills: these are non-cognitive skills. These can be divided into intrapersonal and interpersonal capabilities. Intrapersonal capabilities relate to oneself: am I able to manage and control myself properly; am I in the right mindset to learn and progress? Interpersonal skills are about our interactions with others: are we properly equipped to communicate and collaborate effectively, to thrive in relationships with others and to enable them to thrive as well?

These cognitive and non-cognitive skills, taken as a whole, have gained the ill-defined title of 21st century skills[303]. They are timeless, while

---

[301] See note 296.
[302] "What Life Means to Einstein: An Interview by George Sylvester Viereck" The Saturday Evening Post (26 October 1929)
[303] https://www.linkedin.com/pulse/21st-century-competencies-education-towards-ai-proof-life-golstein/

specific knowledge or skills must be either renewed or completely lost. We will see with our 21st Century Compass why some of them are even more relevant in the era of Artificial Intelligence, and how to develop them.

From initial education to lifelong learning

The permanent need for training

The challenge is not only to provide children and young adults with appropriate initial education, including timeless skills. In addition, with the increasingly rapid upheavals in technology, jobs and society in general, this initial education is no longer sufficient to equip an individual for a lifetime. Yet this is how the system has worked so far: the first part of life was devoted to learning, and the rest of life to work and the implementation of initial learning.

As we saw earlier, even the most optimistic institutes studying the future of work are qualifying their forecasts of full employment by 2030 by specifying that nearly 400 million people should change jobs[304]. However, to change jobs (and not just employers or industries), learning new skills and knowledge is a prerequisite. This is particularly true if the job you are looking for is different enough from your previous one to shield you from the new wave of automation that is already on the horizon.

Employers also testify to the need for new competencies in the broadest sense, i.e. including knowledge and skills. When surveyed by the WEF[305], they said they expect that only 58% of the main skills used in 2018 will still be in use in 2022 – which means that 42% of the existing skills of the labour force will have to evolve in this very short period of time[306].

To change jobs, and because the jobs themselves change, it is therefore necessary to continue training as adults. Lifelong learning refers to the

---

[304] See in particular the results of the McKinsey Global Institute study [53].
[305] World Economic Forum.
[306] The WEF survey covered a panel of companies employing about 15 million people [28].

addition of this continuing training to initial education. Its importance is such that the International Labour Organization advocates the recognition of a *universal right to lifelong learning,* "formal and informal, from early childhood and basic education to adult education and training"[307].

The stakeholders involved in lifelong learning

Multiple stakeholders are involved in lifelong learning. First, states are obliged to carry out their responsibility – including financial responsibility – to prepare their people for the future. Companies look to secure future human resources while taking adequate care of their current employees. Service providers create new educational opportunities. Finally, of course, individuals are invited to take charge of their own destiny and training. Success is only possible if the various stakeholders converge to meet a twofold challenge: to support the transition of the working population as a *whole* to the jobs most in demand, while ensuring that *each individual* is on a trajectory that is both realistic and adequate for their needs.

States are involved in lifelong learning at very different levels. Singapore, for example, is conforming to its tradition of proactiveness and active socio-economic planning. Its SkillsFuture programme aims to enable Singaporeans, regardless of their age or professional situation, to "achieve their full potential" while contributing to the transition of skills and professions. Training, along with advice and funding, is an essential part of this. For 23 targeted industrial sectors, transformation maps indicate the economic prospects, describe the hundreds of jobs available and the skills needed, show the pathways from one occupation to another, suggest training paths and provide reminders about the corresponding funding. In addition, in order to promote initiative and individual responsibility in training, each citizen over 25 years of age had their personal training account credited with an initial amount of S$500 (about €365) in 2015. The account can be used at the sole discretion of the account holder – whether for courses in computing, cooking or

---

[307] See the ILO report "Working to build a better world" [32].

Korean[308]. Overall, a quarter of the Singaporean working population benefited from SkillsFuture in 2018[309].

Other states are careful not to be too prescriptive about the most appropriate type of training for each individual. They also believe that they are not in the best position to choose the best training and jobs, and leave this up to the market. Therefore, they essentially finance the training via previously certified organisations. As an example, France, through the Compte Personnel de Formation (CPF), grants an annual credit of 12 to 24 hours of training to anyone over 16 years of age and in the workforce. This credit of hours will be replaced from 2020 by a monetised contribution to an individual's training account of between 500 and 800 euros per year depending on the circumstances.

Sometimes, it is the industry trade associations that actively organise their own evolution. Given our analysis of the evolution of work[310], it should not be surprising to find an initiative led by the federation of the financial sector in Belgium. The employees of the banking sector, which is expected to be over-staffed, are encouraged to retrain as nurses[311]. Bankers who leave are offered paid training to become nurses or caregivers.

Companies naturally play a major role in continuing education. They aspire first and foremost to satisfy their own needs for human resources, given the ongoing profound redefinition of jobs under the influence of technology [312] and market forces. According to the WEF report mentioned above[313], at least 54% of employees will require significant or very significant training by 2022. However, the employers surveyed stated their intention to focus more on their best employees, especially those who are already in leadership positions and whose work will be increased by new technologies, rather than on employees at risk of

---

[308] The renewal of the initial $500 appropriation is under discussion.

[309] http://www.skillsfuture.sg/NewsAndUpdates/DetailPage/a35eccac-55a5-4f37-bd2f-0e082c6caf70

[310] See all of Part 2 on Work.

[311] https://www.lemonde.fr/economie/article/2018/12/29/en-belgique-des-banquiers-incites-a-devenir-infirmiers_540342525_3234.html

[312] See all of Part 2 and in particular Chapter 10: A framework for career choice.

[313] See note 306.

losing their jobs. This strategy, which raises the question of the moral responsibility of companies towards their employees, may also be short-sighted. Existing employees often possess an informal knowledge of the company – which does not appear in any manual or procedure – and a demonstrate an invaluable loyalty.

There are of course exceptions, and not always where you expect them. Amazon funds up to $12,000 per year in training for each of its hourly-paid employees with more than one year of seniority[314]. It therefore targets employees at the bottom of the scale, typically handlers and other logistics workers. The sectors covered by the subsidised training do not necessarily have a link with the company itself, but rather with the sectors of the economy with the best opportunities: health, IT, transport and skilled technicians. Amazon is thus taking care of its image – which has been quite damaged in the past – while ensuring the support of current employees and the ability to attract future employees into these difficult roles.

The renewal of the professional educational offer
To facilitate lifelong learning, the professional training ecosystem is undergoing a profound transformation, both within companies and amongst service and technology providers.

Within companies themselves, the function of the "Learning & Development" department is gradually changing in nature. L&D teams were once producers of educational content, often pushed somewhat perfunctorily to employees. It is now more and more common for content production to be decentralised or outsourced. L&D teams are refocusing on engineering and implementing learning environments and systems. Learning must be social and take place in a psychologically safe and engaging environment. For each employee, learning needs to be an effective and enjoyable experience, as if they were an external customer. Moreover, learning must be psychologically safe, along with any experiments conducted in order to identify better decisions and outcomes; the notion of failure does not belong here. In the most sophisticated companies like Google, L&D teams conduct experiments on training itself. For example, a small team can spend a few months studying the drivers of human motivation that lead an individual to

---

[314] https://www.inc.com/scott-mautz/amazon-is-paying-its-employees-12000-to-train-for-a-job-at-another-company-its-brilliant.html

create educational content and disseminate it throughout the company; various modalities are tested until the most effective one is identified and adopted for the entire organisation.

Technology providers are aligning themselves with the evolving needs of the market. Thus, many new types of training platforms, such as ClanED or Gnowbe, are making their way into companies to revitalise their internal training. The new platforms, in line with current trends, enable social learning (learning together with other employees), often in bite-sized chunks (segments of a few minutes each), searchable anywhere and at any time, and leaving the employee a lot of freedom over which content to target.

Training institutes, from technical institutions to universities, provide an increasing share of their courses to audiences with prior professional experience. They no longer restrict their recruitment to fresh graduates from secondary education. Some universities even make lifelong learning one of their main missions, and no longer an ancillary service[315]. Experienced professionals follow university courses, full-time or part-time, such as MBAs, to advance their careers. Others return to their passion after following a professional training program, even if occasionally it may seem a step back from their initial training. Thus a marketing manager may turn into a baker, or a former trader convert to a farmer.

New players are emerging with innovative educational offers. Coursera, EdEx and Udemy, for example, invented and launched MOOCs – low-priced Massive Open Online Courses – less than 10 years ago. Unfortunately, their success so far has been mixed[316]. Some of these MOOCs have since pivoted to in-company certification training. Other new entrants have positioned themselves as providers of short training courses designed to fill the gap in the skills most in demand. This is the case with General Assembly[317], which offers mainly digital skills training.

---

[315] This is the intention of Northeastern University, for example. See note 303.
[316] Massive Open Online Courses, or online courses open to all, with high attendance and low prices. Unfortunately, the surveys showed the high drop-out rate of these courses and especially the fact that they attracted mainly existing graduates who wanted more qualifications, rather than new students in higher education.
[317] https://generalassemb.ly/about

Companies, especially the smallest and most in need of ready-to-work personnel, have reconsidered their opinion on short qualifying training courses: they are now highly valued. Micro-degrees or even nano-degrees or bootcamps lasting a few hours to a few days are making their way to the top alongside Bachelors' or Masters' degrees lasting 3 or 5 years.

Leave no one behind

The reluctance of most employers to fund the training of the most vulnerable employees highlights a moral problem but also raises a legitimate question: which individual training paths are likely to succeed? In other words, given a starting point, what are the destinations that can be targeted with a reasonable chance of success? Organisations as diverse as O*net[318] in the United States or the Lee Kuan Yew Center for Innovative Cities in Singapore seek to identify the preferred pathways between jobs, mainly on the basis of the similarity of the tasks performed or the skills required. The question arises in similar terms about the redeployment of low-skilled employees to IT and data science occupations. In response, some vow to "leave no one behind". Here are a few examples.

Bit Source, a Kentucky-based website development company, has managed to convert "coal miners into data miners"[319]. It has succeeded in making the transition from miners to high-tech employees in a region where industrial activity had declined.

Yoann Fol's Dathappy[320], based in France and Singapore, provides outstanding training in data analysis for low-skilled employees. A short theoretical training course is followed by real and concrete customer projects, invoiced below market rates but rigorously supervised and giving full satisfaction to customers. After their training, new recruits become mentors themselves for subsequent students.

Also in France, Simplon[321] markets itself as a network of solidarity and inclusive labs that offer free digital training. Their preferred target is to

---

[318] Under the protection of the U.S. State Department of Employment.
[319] Read Bit Source's presentation on their website
https://www.bitsourceky.com/about-us
[320] See http://www.dathappy.com/
[321] https://simplon.co/

unlock talent "far from employment, or originating from underprivileged territories, with a gender parity objective". Thus, Simplon caters to women; refugees and fresh migrants; young people Not in Employment, Education or Training (NEET); the disabled; and project owners in social enterprises.

General Assembly is not the least committed among these pioneers. Its CEO reports with passion and commitment[322] how former truck drivers have been trained in basic data analysis. Reportedly, the most difficult aspect was convincing the truck drivers themselves that it was within reach. To achieve this, General Assembly resolved to conduct dedicated training sessions for them, not only to properly calibrate learning, but above all to increase learners' confidence. The absence of more qualified classmates kept discouraging comparisons and negative psychological influences at bay.

Even AI Singapore, a Singaporean state entity responsible for driving Artificial Intelligence policy in Singapore, hires Artificial Intelligence apprentices. Initially equipped with simple Excel skills, apprentices are transformed into data analysts and entry-level programmers.

Not all training can succeed, of course. Without a solid foundation in mathematics and computer science, it is not possible to become a researcher in Artificial Intelligence. But in this field as in others, there are, at least in the short term, jobs that are accessible to many through successful training. Learning paths that are likely to succeed are sometimes assessed in terms of a minimum share of common skills – for example, if an individual has mastered half of the skills required for a new job, the transition has a reasonable chance of being successful. This is obviously a somewhat simplistic line of reasoning and more research on this subject would be required. It should be noted, however, that often psychological barriers are the highest – and they can be overcome.

Lifelong learning is in full swing, involving a multitude of old and new players. It will undoubtedly continue to grow. Skilling, reskilling, and upskilling are about to become the new norm.

---

[322] General Assembly Conference in Singapore in 2018.

From lectures to the modern educational arsenal

Experiential education replaces the lecture course

The lecture course symbolises the old educational paradigm. Pupils packed into a classroom or students in a lecture theatre are the passive recipients of often abstract knowledge that they must ingest. Regardless of the teacher's goodwill, this traditional method is ineffective for at least two reasons. Firstly, the content of the teaching is undifferentiated, while each learner has different needs. Secondly, the passivity of learners considerably limits their ability to fully absorb and internalise what they are taught.

The lecture course is now subject to an additional constraint. In the new paradigm, formerly almighty knowledge increasingly gives way to timeless skills – those that do not go out of date, as their name suggests. Can these new subjects be taught in a traditional way? Not really. Some of the target skills are difficult to teach and difficult to learn, and totally incompatible with traditional educational methods. Grit, creativity, empathy or collaboration are not imparted through a lecture to passive students in a classroom or theatre. You have to experience them to understand them, to evaluate yourself, to practise and improve.

The most sophisticated teachers and professors embed these skills into their courses, moving very quickly from initial presentation to practice. Group work allows for collaboration and empathy. The design of a new service or the invention of a new fictional world allows you to exercise your creativity. Life or school experiences are used to reflect on resilience. We will see how much this matters to educators whose explicit goal is to develop clearly identified timeless skills and to nurture a well-defined learner profile.

Younger students will take part in practical work and group projects. Slightly older students will sign up for numerous internships: taking their first steps in business, administration or research during a "discovery" internship in their teen years; immersing themselves in their host organisation during long-term internships lasting six months to one year, during college years. This is what Joseph Aoun, President of

Northeastern University, calls experiential education[323] : integration between classroom experience and real-world experience. The subject being taught must be experienced in real conditions to be genuinely understood and worked on.

Using science to inform education

The change in educational paradigm includes a new role for science in informing teaching. There was a time when we were less well equipped to evaluate the results of educational policies or practices. Decisions – when made consciously – were then essentially intuitive, "philosophical" or dogmatic. Today, science can validate or invalidate our practices and inform educational choices.

Language teaching is a good example. The ability to learn a foreign language decreases with age, with a very significant drop from puberty onwards. The reasons for this superiority on the part of children are essentially physiological: language-learning capabilities diminish as sensitive periods for phonological and grammatical learning come to an end. Moreover, there is high individual variance among adults learning foreign languages; from puberty, a differentiation in language learning ability sets aside a small minority of more gifted learners from a struggling majority. In contrast, children, even infants, are all linguistic geniuses – there are no exceptions, except in the event of health problems. It is therefore surprising that so many resources – time, energy, and financial resources – are being devoted to trying to teach languages to adults aged 18 to 88, when these resources would be more wisely and effectively allocated to children. Science also teaches us that children are born with the ability to recognise and differentiate all the sounds produced in all human languages, but that this ability disappears if particular sounds are not used in the child's environment during the sensitive period, that is, until the age of 12 to 18 months. Thus, the Japanese have great difficulty distinguishing between the sounds [r] and [l], because they have neither in their own language, but rather a single intermediate phoneme. If a family considers this ability important, then it is essential to nurture it in the early years! Finally, science teaches us,

---

[323] See note 303 and in particular the video of Joseph Aoun.

again for language learning, that the amount of language heard and produced, as well as the amount of feedback received, are essential factors in learning. Therefore, it is impossible to really learn without "producing" (i.e. without generating sentences) or receiving feedback (i.e. without mistakes being corrected). Other factors common to all learning, such as attention, commitment, motivation and consolidation, also come into play. All these learning factors are well known and scientifically documented. Consequently, embarking on a teaching or learning effort without taking them into account is not only ineffective but also highly objectionable in our enlightened contemporary context.

Last, science can inform educational policies[324]. We discussed previously how the training pathways from one job to another and their effectiveness are still insufficiently supported by scientific evidence. More research is needed to evaluate the performance of each of the pathways, determine the field of possibilities and, to the extent possible, improve people's perspectives. Perhaps Artificial Intelligence will be able to answer these questions, given its unique ability to identify correlations, before the detailed reasons for them are understood.

Technology greatly enhances teaching effectiveness

The modern educational arsenal includes at least two massively effective new technological tools: Artificial Intelligence and virtual reality.

We have already seen Artificial Intelligence at work with your children in Part 1[325]. Our two AI-powered tutors, Tom and Kate, were in charge of guiding your children's teaching, in parallel with school. Artificial Intelligence was also used to support teachers in the school system. The most fundamental contribution of AI to education is the personalisation of teaching, as opposed to an identical lecture for the entire class. Humans give the learning objectives to the AI, which in turn determines how best to achieve them for a given learner. It thus takes into account the learner's exact level of understanding and knowledge and their pace

---

[324] See requalification paths earlier in this chapter.
[325] Read or re-read the section on the impact of AI on education, Part I Chapter 4.

of learning; in other words, the learner's real needs. It also integrates the learner's preferences: learning paths[326], or areas of interest that can serve as a useful pretext for learning. The AI follows the learner's progress towards their learning objective, continuously and positively assessing how well the various elements have been learned, adjusting the path as progress is made, and reviewing past topics just at the right time to best consolidate knowledge.

Another tool is making its way into the teacher's toolbox: virtual reality, with all its variants. Let's explain the various nuances in one sentence. Virtual reality immerses the subject in a completely synthetic digital environment; augmented reality inserts digital objects or captions onto a real background, often with the objective of providing information about the surrounding environment; and mixed reality anchors objects that are virtual, but that fit naturally and could be real, in a real environment. These technological achievements have multiple pedagogical virtues. When a young child draws a lion in her notebook and witnesses how it comes to life and runs across the savannah, a shiver of excitement seizes her, her attention is completely mobilised, her engagement is total and her imagination is strongly evoked[327]. When students see the functioning of a complex system in a real situation, whether it is the engine of a motorcycle to be repaired or the heart of a patient to be operated on[328], the teaching is contextualised, concrete and effective. In the few cases mentioned above, technology contributes to providing a real immersive experience while remaining in the traditional learning environment of a classroom or a school. These pedagogical virtues are also tapped into when raising awareness amongst the general population: for instance, the staging by a well-

---

[326] While science informs us that there is no learning style corresponding to different neurological functioning, there are many preferences expressed by learners about the type of pedagogical support (written, video, oral) that they particularly like.
[327] See the coloring and animation of the lion
https://www.youtube.com/watch?v=QCceCt7bvFw
[328] The heart in augmented reality
https://www.youtube.com/watch?v=x9D9eIWZZNgM

known weather channel of a hurricane and a flood in mixed reality is the most effective early-warning and sensitisation message[329].

Other more diffuse and perhaps more unexpected technological tools also belong to the modern educational arsenal: learning videos and video games. Video games are often criticised as they are likely to become addictive and increase social isolation. However, when responsibly used, they remain excellent at developing the ability to focus. Moreover, their designers often build in the notion of progressivity in learning. As a matter of fact, they do it better than many professional educational software programs: players get to move from one level to the next after training and mastering a skill, i.e. an additional competence. Not all games are violent. Some, like *Minecraft*, boasting 90 million monthly players[330], are the heirs to traditional construction games. As for the learning videos, available on the main distribution platforms, they are in line with the times: short, interesting, entertaining, and concrete. They manage to bring subjects considered unglamorous to a young audience of enthusiasts. They also boast subscribers by the millions.

As just discussed, three main trends mark the end of the educational paradigm born in the 19th century. This paradigm was characterised by a period of initial training covering the first 15 to 25 years of life. Learning was centred on knowledge, which in turn was mainly imparted through rote learning and memorisation. In the new paradigm, knowledge takes a step back and leaves a major role for skills. Learning is initiated in early childhood and continues into adulthood, destined to last for a lifetime. Finally, teaching methods are informed by cognitive sciences and make use of state-of-the-art technology.

The stage is set. Skills and knowledge will be taught with a modern pedagogical arsenal on a lifelong timeline. The question now becomes:

---

[329] The Weather Channel excels in this exercise. See the hurricane (https://www.youtube.com/watch?v=bRkXPuGAHkE), the tornado, or the fire, hailstorm etc....
[330] September 2018 value.

what are the fundamentals that will guide education, especially initial education, to enable humans to thrive in the age of Artificial Intelligence? The answer lies in the 21st Century Compass.

Chapter 12.   The 21st Century Compass

As you make your way through this series, you are probably starting to appreciate the great upheaval that is beginning to take place... the scale of which will be unprecedented. We saw in Part 1 that Artificial Intelligence, little by little, is surpassing human beings – its creators – at an increasing number of human mental processes. We then found out and took stock of the consequences for the world of work in Part 2: humans will certainly be augmented in some jobs, at least initially, but it seems almost inevitable that machines will gradually replace us within a few generations.

This is where it is worthwhile, once again, to remember why Artificial Intelligence was introduced, why we have jobs, and why we have an education system. In principle, all three have a common objective: to provide us with a better life. Granted, the definition of a satisfying life, let alone a better life, varies greatly among individuals – and Maslow shed light on how needs can be prioritised, with his well-known pyramid. Some will undoubtedly point out how we insatiable humans seem destined to always want more. Details may vary, but the fundamental principle of aspiring to a better life seems universal. Artificial Intelligence is not an end in itself. Work is not an end in itself. School is not an end in itself. All of them converge towards this aspiration for better health, more comfortable material conditions, more happiness and greater fulfilment.

This is also the purpose of the 21st Century Compass that we are about to introduce here. Its objective is to facilitate navigation in our new, ever more uncertain and changing environment, in which a new force has emerged: Artificial Intelligence. It is not only intended to guide school behaviour, but rather to make its usefulness felt throughout life. Even better, its implementation will help create the conditions necessary to shape the world of tomorrow. The Compass is intended to be the educational reference system that will ideally equip each child from their early formative years; its understanding will be further developed and its effects will be felt throughout life. Its design is a direct result of the evolution of the world catalysed by Artificial Intelligence and reflected in the world of work.

Presentation of the Compass

The 21st Century Compass brings together the skills and knowledge essential for a better life in today's and tomorrow's world. It also includes an indication of the direction to be chosen and the steps needed to get there.

The compass is focused on the **ability to learn**. We now know that meta-learning, or learning to learn, is much more a science than an art. Simple rules informed by cognitive science make it possible to drastically improve its effectiveness.

The compass is based on **foundational knowledge**. Taken separately, foundational knowledge is insufficient; but if not acquired or improperly mastered, it might jeopardise professional and personal life. Foundational knowledge includes *literacy*, or the ability to use and communicate written information in everyday life; *numeracy*, or the ability to create and use mathematical information and ideas; and *digital literacy*, or the ability to use digital tools effectively and appropriately.

The compass is flanked by two sets of skills. On the right, three essential **cognitive skills**: *critical thinking* allows us to make rational decisions; *creative thinking* invites us to imagine what does not exist yet; and *interdisciplinary thinking* gives us new perspectives by linking *a priori* separate domains. On the left, three fundamental **socio-emotional skills**: *resilience*, essential to manage life's hazards and know how to recover; *empathy*, necessary for a deep and sincere human connection; and finally *collaboration,* since almost all human achievements result from the involvement of several people.

Last but not least, the compass needle points to the **moral North**. Our actions will be guided firstly by *personal ethics*, delimiting the roads we are willing to take, and secondly by a *purpose,* defining our mission in the world.

The moral North may evolve. But the other components of the Compass are very stable. Most of them consist of skills sometimes referred to as timeless. They can accompany an individual throughout their life, even in the midst of a whirlwind of change.

Other pieces could have been added to the compass. All the pieces could have had additional components. But with a necessarily limited quantity, the ones we have chosen are the most relevant.

The Compass is not an end in itself, but rather a beginning. It is a robust launch platform. As a general-purpose tool, its broad coverage provides the necessary qualities to adapt in most circumstances. However, it does not prohibit diving deeply, on demand, into a specific domain or expertise – quite the contrary.

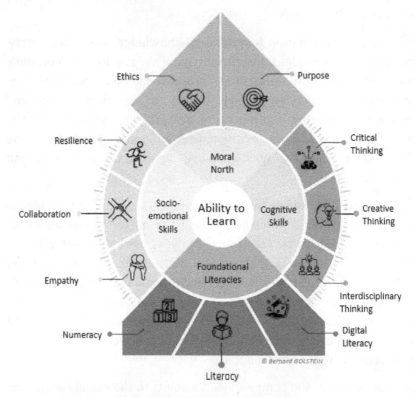

Figure 5: The 21st Century Compass

The Compass and Artificial Intelligence

Looking at the Compass, you might be thinking that almost nothing it offers is specific to the era of Artificial Intelligence. Wouldn't the characteristics highlighted have been just as legitimate 10, 20 or 100 years ago?

It can be assumed that none of the components of the Compass would have been harmful in other times. But let us look at how they are particularly appropriate in the coming years.

First of all, the magnitude and pace of the changes on the horizon cannot be overemphasised. The *ability to learn* will therefore be essential in a constantly changing environment.

The key components of the Compass will help us define how we want to live in the coming period. The *purpose* will be an opportunity for everyone and for society as a whole to formulate the *raison d'être* and meaning we wish to set for our lives; it will be particularly important to address it, as the end of work as we know it will leave a huge emptiness to be filled. *Ethics* will guide all our decisions, which will be all the more essential as malicious behaviours threaten to be amplified by Artificial Intelligence. *Critical thinking* and *creative thinking* will allow us to reflect deeply, meaningfully and creatively on this world we want to shape.

Multiple components of the Compass will help us make the most of machines. Let us always keep in mind that their positive effects on our lives promise to be immense. To this end, *foundational knowledge – literacy, numeracy* and *digital literacy* – will be an essential starting point. They will be complemented by the *Moral North* and the *cognitive skills* already used to choose and design our future.

Some of the Compass' skills will provide us with protection in a world that will be increasingly dominated by Artificial Intelligence. This is the defensive side of the general approach. *Critical thinking* and *digital literacy* will help us to unravel the true from the false in our complicated world. *Resilience* will be a valuable shield to overcome the inevitable hazards to which life will increasingly expose us.

Other skills will also give us the opportunity to differentiate ourselves from Artificial Intelligence by exploiting those capabilities where we maintain an undeniable superiority over the machine. This can be described as the offensive side of the approach. As you may remember from Part 1, AI's *creativity* is limited to imitating or exploring possibilities, while ours is much more prone to divergent thinking. Similarly, AI remains a great specialist, unable to generalise outside its narrow field of intervention or to build bridges between different fields – which justifies our interest in exploiting *interdisciplinary thinking*. As for *collaboration* and *empathy*, they will allow us to benefit from the enduring human premium[331] and will constitute an affirmation of our humanity. Let us not forget this: even when Artificial Intelligence perceives a human emotion or simulates one in return, it does so with great algorithmic talent but without experiencing or truly understanding anything. Only humans can go deeper into the emotional analysis of others by supplementing superficial perception with appropriate questions; only humans are genuinely capable, for now and for the foreseeable future, of determining the appropriate response to a human emotion.

Thanks to the Compass, therefore, we will be able to determine our path while keeping in mind the big picture, we will be able to make the best use of the possibilities offered by AI, we will equip ourselves with safeguards, and we will even strive to develop the strengths that differentiate us from machines.

The Compass and life

Intuitively, we would expect a good command of the various elements of the Compass to predict success in achieving life's objectives, particularly in the areas of life satisfaction, work, material well-being, health and emotional relationships.

---

[331] The human premium has been defined at length in Part 2. It consists in assigning tasks to humans for reasons other than technological, since machines would be capable of performing them.

The effects of cognitive skills have been the most studied to date. They are positively correlated, in a systematic but somewhat modest way, with the achievement of desirable life outcomes. The correlation is clear for academic success and in general for professional success. That said, there are multiple instances of personal failures of individuals endowed with high IQs – which significantly contributed to the recognition of socio-emotional skills two or three decades ago.

With cognitive intelligence held constant, emotional and social intelligence always provides an advantage. Self-control, empathy, optimism and other characteristics, detected early on in life, were found to be significant predictors of positive outcomes[332]. The group of skills collectively known as conscientiousness (working hard, being responsible and well organised), which appears indirectly in the Compass as resilience, seems to be the one socio-emotional skill most correlated with success in life. The impact of conscientiousness is such that it surpasses IQ as a predictor of success.

According to a group of experts convened by the US National Research Council in 2012, the rigorous assessment of the impact of 21st century intrapersonal and interpersonal skills remains insufficient[333]. Overall, and regardless of specific skills, the best predictor so far of work and life success is the number of years of study. But be careful: this is a result based on statistics from the distant past. The methods that were previously effective are not indicative of future success in the upcoming period.

Finally, it should be noted, at the risk of causing confusion, that the external aspects of success in life are not strictly correlated with ethical posture. Even if we like to think that sooner or later, perpetrators of unethical actions are caught by society (and there are indeed many who languish in prison), this is not systematically the case. You can "succeed in life", with complete impunity, despite ethically reprehensible behaviour in business, politics and society. Conversely, you can also be

---

[332] See Daniel Goleman's multiple references for "Emotional Intelligence" [19].
[333] See the National Academies' report entitled "Education for life and work" [55].

perfectly ethical and live in painful poverty. Admittedly, multiple studies at country level show that a higher level of integrity is correlated with a higher level of development[334]. However, at an individual level, the enlightened self-interest approach, claiming that we must be ethical at least out of self-interest because it improves our own lot, will often be proven wrong.

The Compass and the world of work

For several years now, the world of work has been expressing needs that resonate strongly with the Compass.

Thus, in its aforementioned 2018 report on the Future of Employment[335], the World Economic Forum interviewed companies representing a total workforce of more than 15 million employees in a diverse set of sectors and countries.

The demand for skills by 2022 singles out the following top five in decreasing order: critical analysis and innovation; learning strategies and active learning; creativity, originality and initiative; technological design and programming; and critical thinking and analysis. Despite a difference in terminology, four of these five competencies are included in the Compass in the form of learning ability, critical thinking, and creative thinking. The only one not in the Compass (although it is partly covered by digital literacy) is the specialised skill of technological design and programming.

The next five skills in the World Economic Forum survey are: complex problem solving; leadership and social influence; emotional intelligence; reasoning, problem solving and idea generation; and systems analysis and evaluation. Again, the spirit of these competencies is reflected in the Compass: our empathy and collaboration cover emotional

---

[334] Many studies point out that the level of corruption has a strong negative impact on GDP per capita, such as
https://www.researchgate.net/publication/287348821_The_Impact_of_Corruption_on_GDP_Per_Capita
[335] The Future of Jobs report 2018 [30].

intelligence and to some extent leadership and social influence; our interdisciplinary thinking includes systems analysis; and the other points are slightly redundant compared to the cognitive abilities already mentioned in the first five places in the ranking.

At the end of the day, the only major difference between the first ten skills identified by the World Economic Forum and those of the Compass is the presence in the latter of an intra-personal skill: resilience. In addition, the Compass includes an ethical and philosophical direction and recalls the need for foundational knowledge. Let us also take due note that the business world may be less advanced than it thinks. As much as business leaders seek 21st century competencies, it is very common for recruiters and mid-level managers to hire for the exact knowledge and skills required to hold the job on offer, with immediate applicability.

Besides these minor differences, there is therefore a remarkable convergence between the Compass, a key success factor and guide for the individual in the 21st century, and the needs expressed by the world of work.

The Compass and school systems

The overlap between the Compass and most existing school systems is less compelling. Traditionally, school does not educate in the components of the Compass, nor does the Compass guarantee success at schools as they currently operate.

Indeed, most school systems still give a prominent place to knowledge. Students continue to be tested on a vast amount of knowledge that they must take in and be able to repeat back on exam day, sometimes at the cost of significant and inappropriate cramming. At best, some cognitive skills are also developed.

But things are gradually evolving. Thus, the international PISA standard[336], which assesses and analyses the educational performance of students in the OECD and beyond, introduced in 2015 an additional dimension that reflects current developments. PISA used to focus on the core subjects of reading, mathematics and science. It now also includes collaborative problem solving, and it will include a measure of creative thinking from 2021 onwards.

The results for the 2015 collaborative problem-solving test are enlightening, especially in relative terms: in other words, how a country scores relative to what was expected given its students' individual performances in science, reading and mathematics. The countries with the best relative performance are Australia, Japan, Korea, New Zealand and the United States: two Asian countries and three English-speaking countries. The students from Japan and Korea were already very strong individually and are even better at working together. The students in the United States were below average individually, but their excellent collaborative skills enabled them to enter the top group for absolute collaborative performance! On the other hand, some countries had a good individual performance but fell down collaboratively: this is the case for the four Chinese provinces that participated in the event. Finally, some countries were below average individually and did even worse collaboratively: this was the case for France.

School systems are also changing, some leading the way, others clearly lagging.

Singapore
Singapore often leads the pack. In the latest edition of PISA[337], Singapore not only finished first in the world in each of the three categories for 15-year-olds – science, mathematics and reading – it also worked its way to the top of the table for collaborative problem solving. Success factors include a well-trained, well-paid and highly respected teaching staff; a

---

[336] Programme for International Student Assessment
http://www.oecd.org/pisa/
[337] The latest results published are those of the 2015 edition. The 2018 results will be released in 2019.

continuous search for good practices and pedagogical objectives in line with the times; and the way education is so highly valued by the local population.

A clear educational strategy accompanied the country on its development journey, characterised by relevance and successful implementation. The first phase (1959–1978), motivated by the country's survival, laid the foundations for a coherent and homogeneous system. The second phase (1979–1996), aimed at efficiency, considerably increased the quality of basic education and reduced failure. The third phase (1997–2011) coincided with Singapore's transition from industry to a high value-added service economy. The "Thinking Schools, Learning Nation" program was implemented, and cognitive skills such as critical thinking began to complement knowledge.

Singapore, in the educational field as everywhere else, never feels it has made it and can rest on its laurels. The questioning and the quest for improvement are permanent. Beyond PISA, the country acknowledges the efforts needed in soft skills and creative thinking. Challenge accepted! From 2012 a new educational framework, "Student Skills and Learning for the 21st Century"[338], has guided the entire programme. In 2019, Singapore announced a further adjustment of its school system with a reduction in the importance of examinations, a reduction in the very high pressure at school, and better personalisation of the curriculum for students. In parallel, efforts to develop digital skills and creative thinking are ongoing[339].

Finland

Finland is also used to being top of the rankings. The overarching educational principles are very different from those of Singapore, with a low number of hours, very low anxiety related to school, and very

---

[338] "21st century competencies and student outcomes", https://www.moe.gov.sg/education/education-system/21st-century-competencies

[339] See in particular the description of Singapore's Digital Makers' Program and the emphasis on creativity.

strong pedagogical freedom granted to teachers – who are themselves also highly respected. Finland's greatest pride is the homogeneity of its results, regardless of the social background or geographical location of its students.

The most recent change undertaken by Finland grants increasing importance to multidisciplinary projects, which make it possible to address all subjects on a given issue, rather than the traditional approach of studying individual subjects.

France

France has traditionally had a very strong knowledge bias in its school system. However, much to everyone's dismay, students' results when it comes to evaluating that knowledge are in freefall, regardless of the benchmark. France has fallen into the wrong half of the PISA rankings, and is sometimes even at the bottom of the pile. In other national assessments – in mathematics, for example – today's best students are barely at the level of the worst students thirty years ago[340]. Schools are also unable to offset social inequalities. These results are deeply worrying for the country that boasts the fourth largest contingent of Nobel Prize winners, the second largest contingent of Fields medallists in mathematics... and one of the proud recipients of the 2019 Turing Prize with Yann LeCun.

France has often tried to reform its system, increasing the mistrust and reluctance of the teaching staff. The latest reforms are a step in the right direction, with increased investment in small classes and pupils in difficulty, the change in the format of the baccalaureate, greater emphasis on the contribution of science in teaching, and a greater proportion of collaborative work.

United States

The American K-12 is not known for its excellence. The results of the PISA assessment confirm this: in 2015, young students from the United States ranked below the OECD average in all categories. Actually, all

---

[340] The remark is from S. Dehaene, quoted by Le Monde
https://www.lemonde.fr/societe/article/2019/04/05/mathematiques-le-niveau-des-ecoliers-plonge_5446009_3224.html

categories except one: collaborative problem solving. They actually rank third in relative performance at collaborative problem solving. This is no coincidence.

In the early 2000s, an American non-governmental organisation, the Partnership for 21st Century Learning, invented the concept of 4Cs. It describes the 4 essential skills believed to be essential for modern education, each starting with the letter C: *Creativity, Critical thinking, Communication* and *Collaboration*[341]. In 2010, 21st century skills were included in the standard curriculum for public schools, the Common Core [342] . From early childhood onwards, communication and collaboration activities are practised in the classroom and formally evaluated – a guarantee of their actual importance in the system.

This is not in vain: in any subsequent international gathering, Americans often stand out for their ability to communicate and collaborate.

The IB system

Of all sizable school systems, it is undoubtedly the International Baccalaureate[343] (IB) system that is most in tune with the Compass. Just as the French system is knowledge-based, so is the IB system student-centred. Unlike others, the IB system is not a national system, but a transnational one. Created about 50 years ago, it has been adopted by about 5,000 schools worldwide and covers school ages from 3 to 19 years old – that is, from kindergarten to the end of secondary school.

The objective of the IB programme immediately sets the tone: "How can we be sure that we are leading [students] into work life with the skills they really need in order to thrive, succeed and be happy?". The program aims for the development and success of students beyond the strictly academic framework.

The entire curriculum is guided by the objective to nurture each student according to the "IB learner profile"[344]. Students are trained to become *inquirers, knowledgeable, thinkers, communicators, principled, open-*

---

[341] http://www.battelleforkids.org/networks/p21
[342] https://en.wikipedia.org/wiki/21st_century_skills
[343] https://www.ibo.org/about-the-ib/
[344] https://www.ibo.org/benefits/learner-profile/

minded, altruistic, risk-takers, balanced, reflective. This is not merely a list of words. Teachers have all their educational practices firmly anchored in the objective of the "IB learner profile" [345]. It is also immediately apparent that mastery of knowledge is only one of the ten components of the profile.

As just demonstrated, aside from the IB system, the content of the Compass is significantly different from that of most school systems. This is precisely why the Compass should not be interpreted as being opposed to the different school systems. Instead, it should be welcomed as complementary. It is a reference point towards which school systems have begun to slowly steer. If the Compass comprises the qualities and characteristics necessary for success in life and work, why not teach them at school?

When to teach the Compass?

Learning during sensitive periods of childhood
The Compass requirements are best implemented from an early age and refined throughout life. The earlier the practice is carried out, the easier it will be; the longer it is instilled, the more automated the associated processes will be in the brain until they become perfectly natural and almost unconscious. They will already be firmly established when the relentless decline in brain plasticity begins.

In addition, a small number of Compass pieces are associated with sensitive periods of childhood: they must be learned during these periods, failing which they might never be acquired with the same effectiveness.

The foundational knowledge of literacy and numeracy are among these pieces to be learned during childhood. Language acquisition, if not achieved in the early years of life, will never take place, as demonstrated by the extreme difficulties of feral children or children brought up in

---

[345] In one of the IB schools we visited, a teacher devotes each week to one of the attributes or subattributes, using a variety of age-appropriate activities.

complete isolation. Similarly but less radically, learning the alphabet is much easier at an early age – and it is obviously the first stage of literacy.

Sensitive periods for cognitive abilities

Executive control, and more specifically working memory, is essential to the learning ability featured at the heart of the Compass. Executive control must be developed young and has an impact on the rest of life. This was the conclusion of a longitudinal study that monitored 1,000 children from birth to age 32. It found out that the level of self-control in childhood was a linear predictor of success in adulthood in terms of physical health, personal finances, lack of addictions and crime[346].

Other studies[347] suggest that cognitive abilities in mid- and end-of-life are strongly correlated with cognitive ability at age 20, but not with education or education-related activities that may take place after that age. The effect of education on cognitive abilities thus plateaus at the end of adolescence, reinforcing the need to improve the quality of initial education.

Sensitive periods for socio-emotional capacities

Similarly, as Daniel Goleman, author of the first masterpiece on emotional intelligence[348], points out, "the emotional lessons we teach children at home and at school shape our emotional circuits, making us more capable or more unsuitable for the basic practice of emotional intelligence. This means that childhood and adolescence are critical to establishing the essential emotional habits that will govern our lives."

Indeed, like cognitive intelligence, emotional intelligence is a biological and more particularly a neurological phenomenon. Some traits have an innate component – for example, at least partially, character traits such

---

[346] Self-control in childhood predicts health, prosperity and public order [18].
[347] See Influence of young adult cognitive ability and additional education on later-life cognition [52].
[348] There are many editions of Goleman's book. The later ones have been enriched with data from neuroscience that explain the mechanisms at work. A significant part of the elements reported here come from Goleman's work [19].

as confidence or shyness, cheerfulness or melancholy[349]. Other traits are particularly acquired during periods of maximum brain plasticity (until adolescence) or even before if this corresponds to a specific sensitive period. The ability to calm down, or even empathy, is acquired and cultivated from the first months of life. The prefrontal cortex, which plays an essential role in executive control mechanisms such as inhibition (i.e. self-control), matures in late adolescence, between the ages of 16 and 18. These sensitive periods make it possible to work on the associated socio-emotional skills.

Beyond childhood and adolescence

However, it should be kept in mind that a significant part of the Compass can be acquired, developed and cultivated throughout life.

The *growth mindset* holds that at any time, effort and persistence allow learners to develop and progress. No basic abilities, talents or traits are fixed, let alone at their innate level. Believing in this premise is often a self-fulfilling prophecy: one learns better when one thinks that learning is possible. According to this principle, it is never impossible or too late, as long as we are aware of the need and really want to learn and change, within the limits allowed by biology. This learning is achieved through personal experiences and targeted therapeutic or educational actions[350].

Finally, a small number of cognitive and socio-emotional abilities increase with age[351]. In the cognitive domain, verbal comprehension or listening skills increase between adolescence and middle adulthood. The same applies to certain socio-emotional capabilities, such as conscientiousness or the ability to please.

We have thus outlined the main characteristics of the Compass and explained why it is so relevant to the age of Artificial Intelligence. We

---

[349] Having an innate component does not mean being immutable: these traits can change.

[350] The most impressive cases of "emotional rehabilitation" are observed in post-traumatic stress situations and demonstrate that relearning is possible.

[351] The examples hereafter are drawn from scientific studies cited in the National Research Council report: Education for Life and Work [55].

have confirmed its relevance to the strong demand from the world of work, and highlighted the lasting discrepancy between the Compass and the existing school systems, although the gap has largely begun to reduce. The time has now come to get at the pith and marrow of the Compass, so as to better impart it to the learners of the 21st century.

Chapter 13. The fundamentals

The 21st Century Compass, which we introduced in the previous chapter, is built around a solid central structure. First of all, it includes a base made up of **foundational knowledge**. Literacy, numeracy and digital literacy are the indispensable foundations on which the rest of knowledge is based. The heart of the Compass is formed by the **ability to learn**, which has been considerably illuminated in recent decades by cognitive sciences and neuroscience. Finally, the top part points to the **moral North**, including ethics and purpose. The moral North is intended to guide us in our actions and decisions, just as the North Star guides us geographically.

These three parts, with their different natures, make up a foundation, a means of change and an overarching direction. Let us now look at the details.

Figure 6: The fundamentals

Ability to learn

At the heart of the Compass is the ability to learn.

Awareness of the importance of this ability is not new. As early as the 1970s, the futurist Alvin Toffler stated his prophetic aphorism: "The illiterate of the 21st century will not be those who cannot read and write, but those who cannot learn, unlearn, and relearn."

What is newer, however, is the scientific knowledge of the mechanisms of learning. One of the most advanced scientists studying these mechanisms is the French cognitive and neuroscientific psychologist Stanislas Dehaene. He identified four pillars of learning: attention, active engagement, feedback, and consolidation. They will only be outlined here, without going into the detailed scientific approach that proves their validity, but we cannot recommend strongly enough a more in-depth reading of the field[352].

Attention

Paying attention amounts to pointing a powerful spotlight at the object of attention. When one's attention focuses, a cascade of reactions is triggered in the brain that increases the ability to process the signal, from simple perception to learning.

Conversely, lack of attention will often lead us to miss phenomena, events or information that are nevertheless evident as soon as our focus is on them again. Distraction or excessive stimulation of the senses have the same effect as lack of attention.

Especially among the very young, even if they are not yet equipped with speech, attention makes social learning possible. When an adult indicates, often with a simple glance, that a particular object or phenomenon deserves attention, the child automatically switches to learning mode. Here again, in a beautiful demonstration of their trust in the adult, the child activates the mechanisms in the brain that amplify the perception and processing of the information to which their attention has been drawn.

Active engagement

A passive brain does not learn, or only learns very little. This observation alone explains in large part the failure of lecture courses – which have, nonetheless, been the symbol of the school system for centuries – as opposed to active pedagogies.

The active learner mobilises different brain areas, in the frontal cortex, and thus unlocks learning. The young or not-so-young learner is engaged in their cognitive processes; their curiosity has been stimulated. They think, make hypotheses, compare the results with their predictions, look for solutions. It is a process of effort and risk taking. For maximum commitment, the difficulty of the task must be high enough to generate interest, and low enough not to risk discouragement.

---

[352] To that end, read *Apprendre!*, by Stanislas Dehaene [17].

Feedback

Learners' mistakes are often stigmatised and their role in learning deeply misunderstood.

However, error is one of the main learning mechanisms! If the brain is a Bayesian inference engine, meaning something that updates the probability of a hypothesis as evidence or information becomes available, it can only adjust its model by comparing expected results with reality. And when it realises its mistake, the surprise generates a series of reactions in the brain that amplify learning. Thus, an infant stares longer at a totally unexpected scene than the one to which they have become accustomed or one that they anticipated; electroencephalograms confirm a characteristic peak of activity that indicates surprise.

But make no mistake: error is only beneficial as long as the feedback is given in the right way. Of course, the error should not be viewed negatively, as evidence of a weakness or failure, but as a learning opportunity. The quality and accuracy of feedback determines the quality of learning.

Consolidation

While it is awake, the brain accumulates a considerable amount of data. What does it do with the data, and where does the data go? Every time you sleep, the brain carries out a great consolidation project. It sorts the data that needs to be stored and transfers it physically, after an accelerated re-viewing, to a deeper area of the brain. In doing so, it frees up brain resources for the coming day, and reinforces the memories it has stored in an appropriate area.

Consolidation during sleep is beneficial not only for the formation of new memories, but also for bringing clarity to ideas. It is not only a popular belief; it is also a phenomenon measured experimentally, by comparing the ability to generalise abstract concepts with and without sleep.

Another method of consolidation is spaced repetition. After each learning process, people's performance at memory retention tasks decreases over time. But if we repeat a cycle of consolidating this knowledge, reactivating it and then sleeping, then the knowledge becomes a little more anchored in memory. Thus the concept of spaced repetition was born about a century ago: reviewing knowledge at strategic intervals to memorise it better, with an emphasis on the most fragile knowledge.

How to learn to learn?

In order to learn to learn, it is necessary to develop each of the learning catalysts described above. It is therefore required for the learner or the teacher, to begin with, to be aware of the four pillars and have a sufficiently detailed understanding of them. One cannot guess the considerable importance of this unless one studies it, and it is all too easy to completely misinterpret it!

After understanding the pillars, it is necessary to practise each of them.

Both **attention** and executive control[353] develop spontaneously with maturation, but their development can be accelerated through training and education. Paying attention is in itself a form of training for young children. A multitude of activities improve children's executive functions: computer games, other games, physical activities such as gymnastics and martial arts, yoga and meditation activities, and finally school education itself! The practice of music, which involves sophisticated motor coordination, is also recognised as very beneficial. As for the teacher, they should strive to capture and maintain the child's attention and avoid exposing the child to an environment loaded with excessive visual or auditory distractions.

To encourage **active engagement**, many common-sense solutions are appropriate: practical work, discussions, small group projects – all approaches that require people to be actively involved. Beware of misinterpretations! Dehaene describes the case of a school principal who, believing that he was encouraging his students to become actively involved, had pedals installed under their desks. Active engagement is

---

[353] Executive control is a set of functions that are necessary to focus and think, when an impulsive response would be inappropriate. Basic executive functions include cognitive flexibility, inhibition and working memory. Accepted practices improve their development for children [18].

intellectual, and can be done without any physical movement[354]. On the other hand, it must encourage cognitive effort, with well-calibrated activities (sufficiently difficult but not impossible). Educational activities must be structured in such a way that they meet the pedagogical objective while leaving room for commitment from the learner.

To enable the learner to benefit from **feedback**, it can be useful to help them understand the positive side of errors beforehand and thus to completely take the drama out of errors – it is thanks to them that learning can take place. Knowledge tests then appear in an entirely new light: they become an opportunity to test your knowledge and continue learning. Unfortunately, this is not the current connotation of tests and examinations, which are usually reduced to a mark or grade, and not always followed by the necessary corrective action. As we have understood, each error, if it is to be useful, must be the subject of benevolent but precise and high-quality feedback.

The brain itself is in charge of the **consolidation** process. But we must not disrupt it. Sleep is essential. The main recommendation is to respect the learner's biological rhythm. When infants take naps several times a day, they consolidate their knowledge – it is a period of intense activity and not a momentary cessation of activity. Preventing the naps would be seriously detrimental to the baby. When a teenager has difficulty getting up early, there is no point in forcing them to do so – it is much better to try to adapt school schedules. Finally, when an adult stays awake late and fights against sleep to keep their commitments, they are not doing themselves any favours – it would be better, if possible, to have a short night's sleep and wake up early, armed with greater clarity of mind. The second recommendation related to consolidation is to distribute learning: it is better to revise frequently and in small doses than to devote a longer but one-off period to it.

Metacognition
To the four pillars put forward by Stanislas Dehaene, we will add the importance of reflecting on one's own learning as soon as a sufficient level of maturity is reached. In a report covering decades of research in

---

[354] The anecdote is also reported in *Apprendre!* [17].

learning sciences, the American Academy of Sciences concludes that a metacognitive approach to education is effective[355]. This metacognition, or reflection on knowledge, is "above" the subjects to be learned. It involves not only applying learning strategies but doing so in a conscious way and looking at one's own capacities to learn in different contexts[356].

Kimberley Tanner offers recipes to promote metacognition[357]. These are questions to ask before, during and after learning activities. For example, before class, we can think about what we already think we know, the questions we have at this stage and what we are trying to learn from the class. During the class we may wonder what thoughts come to mind, whether some elements seem confusing, or whether we are able to distinguish between the big picture and the details. The post-course reflection may give rise to other questions: what the essence of the course was, what was really interesting, how what we understand now is different from what we thought we knew, whether we still have questions, what to focus on, etc. There are other sets of questions to ask during the actual learning or homework, during the knowledge tests, and at the end of the course.

Tanner opens her article with a nice quote that will allow us to conclude: "Learning how to learn cannot be left to students. It must be taught."[358]

Ethics

The advent of Artificial Intelligence requires a new world to be built. This needs everyone to have a strong moral reference. Ethical questions arise at all levels.

---

[355] For more information, refer to the National Research Council's "How People Learn" (2000) https://www.nap.edu/catalog/9853/how-people-learn-brain-mind-experience-and-school-expanded-edition

[356] See the introduction to metacognition proposed by Nancy Chick of the Center for Teaching at Vanderbilt University, from which some of the elements presented here are derived: https://cft.vanderbilt.edu/guides-sub-pages/metacognition/

[357] See https://www.lifescied.org/doi/10.1187/cbe.12-03-0033

[358] The quote is from M. D. Gall and colleagues.

First of all, what ethics should we give, in very concrete terms, to the systems we design today to make our lives easier? Machines must apply some kind of rule, whether explicitly programmed or learned from examples – which forces us to answer all the questions we have carefully avoided until now.

The emblematic case is the so-called trolley problem. Imagine, for a moment, that the brakes of an autonomous car suddenly give way, when it is driving at full speed. Pedestrians are crossing the road at that very moment. Who should the car save amongst passengers and pedestrians? The car cannot save everyone and therefore it has to make a choice. How will this autonomous system decide who should live and who should die? Addressing this problem of the "Moral Machine", French researcher Jean-François Bonnefon has collected 40 million simulated decisions from millions of people around the world[359]. The survey demonstrates that some preferences are universal: sparing humans rather than animals, saving as many people as possible, and favouring children. But there are also individual preferences and even quite strong cultural preferences. The group defined by researchers as the Southern group is committed to saving women, people of high social status and healthy people. The Eastern group, mainly from Asia, places more emphasis on the elderly and law-abiding individuals. The Western group exhibits a preference for inaction: that is to say, to let the car just follow its initial path.

Car manufacturers are already faced with these complicated choices in the design of their vehicles. A luxury brand thought it was a good idea to announce that it would first save the passengers in its cars. By doing so, they caused such an outcry that they had to state a new official position and claimed that they had initially been misunderstood[360]. Another manufacturer suggested that vehicle owners should be allowed to configure their own vehicles themselves. As soon as the context

---

[359] See its dedicated website http://moralmachine.mit.edu/ or the article in *Nature* https://www.nature.com/articles/s41586-018-0637-6 [50].
[360] https://jalopnik.com/now-mercedes-says-its-driverless-cars-wont-run-over-ped-1787890432

becomes personal, altruistic preferences instantly fall through the cracks: the most common decision is to save the passengers, if you or your loved ones are in the car!

Ethical issues will pile up as autonomous systems become more and more numerous. When law-enforcement or security robots become a reality, what rules will they be endowed with? Will they be armed? How should they step in, concretely, if an individual threatens someone else's life? An obvious advantage of robots is that they can be programmed to take the first bullet: they will have the luxury of fighting back rather than attacking first.

Setting up the legal arsenal

States are beginning to reflect on the legal arsenals to be put in place regarding the design and use of Artificial Intelligence. The principles are far from universally shared: first because ethics is not universal, and second because some states themselves use AI for highly controversial social regulation purposes.

Can we tolerate a state use of Artificial Intelligence which, with disregard for fundamental human rights, aims to subjugate individuals? Should an algorithm be allowed to make or strongly suggest a decision – for example, the refusal of a bank loan – without being able to explain it? What should we do with this other algorithm, which is fed during its supervised learning with countless human biases that are prevalent in society, such as disadvantages for women in job offers and members of certain ethnic communities in court decisions? Is it even reasonable to entrust court decisions to machines? All these questions must be addressed from an ethical perspective.

As we have described in detail in Part 1, Europe is undoubtedly leading the pack in protecting the rights of its citizens[361]. In April 2019, it adopted its "Ethics Guidelines for Trustworthy AI", which is only indicative at this stage but is probably intended to play a more binding role in the future. According to its recommendations, AI must not only be lawful, by complying with existing laws and regulations, but also be

---

[361] For more details, see Chapter 5 of Part 1, and more specifically the section entitled "Ethical safeguards".

ethical, by adhering to fundamental rights, and basic principles and values. The ethical objective puts humans at the centre, which translates into principles of benevolence, non-malevolence, human agency, fairness and transparency.

Beyond the law

The legal arsenal is making good progress. This is positive, because the law usually signals an absolute minimum with which it is essential to comply. But ethics goes far beyond compliance with the law.

What is legal is not always legitimate. Outside the AI world, tax avoidance is legal for individuals and companies, but is not ethical for either of them. Selling cigarettes to adults or sugary drinks to children is still allowed, but it is not ethical. Sending non-recyclable waste to countries that do not have the means to process it is also unethical, if we stretch the concept a little.

Similarly, many choices related to AI would benefit from being analysed through an ethical lens. In China, the world's second-largest AI superpower, the most represented industry among the top 100 AI companies is security[362], particularly facial recognition. Given the way facial recognition is used in China – social regulation and monitoring of ethnic groups – is it ethical to invest in it? Some Western fund managers have begun to ask themselves the question[363]. Taking part in any digital activity in China implies storing your data there; however, under cybersecurity laws, the Chinese state could get hold of them on request. Does a business opportunity justify accepting this constraint? Google employees certainly opposed their management's plan to comply with government constraints in order to re-enter the Chinese market – and it was the management that eventually gave in. In the United States too, many Google, Microsoft and Amazon employees oppose the use of their technology for American military projects – and sometimes push back against their leaders.

---

[362] https://www.technologyreview.com/f/613296/what-you-may-not-understand-about-chinas-ai-scene/
[363] https://www.economist.com/business/2019/04/06/google-and-the-ethics-of-business-in-china

Artificial Intelligence is progressing rapidly, and many cases will arise where only personal ethics will help make the right decision. The stakes are immense. It is the hallmark of AI to make do with paltry means – a computer and an Internet connection – to launch virtual atomic bombs[364]. Most of the time, the circumstances will be new, so there will be no laws dealing with the subject at hand. In other cases, there could be existing laws but they might be circumvented. As with the shattering news of the first genetically modified baby in early 2019 in China, the authorities will sometimes claim not to be aware and will quickly get rid of the apparent culprit – but Pandora's box will be open.

Ultimately, only a very strong ethical sensitivity permeating society, characterised by familiarity with ethical reasoning, will perhaps prevent catastrophic decisions.

Building the world of tomorrow

Even more important directions will have to be determined: those that will shape the world of tomorrow. According to Gabor's principle[365], "everything possible will necessarily be implemented" – in the sense that technological progress is an unstoppable force. Is it not dangerous that more and more ideas like human agency and individual free will are being transferred "from the philosophy department to the engineering department"[366]? How can we preserve our human agency and keep in mind the other principle, the one that Gargantua passed on to his son Pantagruel in Rabelais' masterpiece[367] almost 500 years ago: "Science without conscience is but the ruin of the soul"?

What respective roles will we want to give to human beings and machines? Will we be able to realise the dream of a world where humans are more human precisely because machines do their job as

---

[364] See Part 1, Chapter 5, in particular the section on "Openly malicious use of AI".

[365] Hungarian physicist and 1978 Nobel Prize winner:
https://en.wikipedia.org/wiki/Dennis_Gabor

[366] Remarks by Yuval Noah Harari in a debate in Stanford:
https://www.wired.com/story/will-artificial-intelligence-enhance-hack-humanity/

[367] The Life of Gargantua and of Pantagruel, pentalogy by Francois Rabelais.

machines? What values will we want to promote? Many decisions will have to be made that will not only be the responsibility of AI ethicists, but of society as a whole.

Will an attempt be made to grant humans their own private preserve, even if progress as such is very difficult to control? In everyday life, will it be tolerable for individuals' decisions to be *de facto* controlled by algorithms whose recommendations are less and less verified or questioned, or which strengthen filter bubbles and open the way to all kinds of manipulation? In the world of work, with humans destined to be gradually replaced by machines, will decision-makers follow any logic other than the merely economic to decide on the pace of change and the support to give to the employees affected? Will society agree to implement the vision of the Radical, expressed in Part 2 of this book, or conversely will it evolve towards that of the Pessimist? According to these two visions, the end of the work as we know it is inevitable. The Pessimist sees an explosion of inequalities and an untenable situation for a large part of humanity. But according to the Radical, human genius will be able to give birth to a new social contract and a new model for the redistribution of wealth[368].

In parallel, the day will certainly come when robots will also have rights. Perhaps they will ask for them, or more likely humans will decide to grant them some. Some futurists have already started addressing these questions. Tomorrow, the contribution of the whole of society will be required.

The challenge remains to determine and apply ethical principles that will enable humanity to flourish in the age of Artificial Intelligence. To this end, education in ethics for all strata of society seems essential.

How to teach ethics?

Ever since Plato, people have been trying to figure out this central question of ethics education. A common approach in systems advocating freedom of thought is to teach not predefined values or norms, but rather the process of ethical reflection. The development of

---

[368] See the discussion between the four friends in Part 2, Chapter 6.

ethical competence is reflected in the ability to think critically, to form a judgment that can be defended by ethical argument, and ultimately to ensure consistency between that ethical judgment and one's actions. Plato's school of thought hypothesises that it is the quality of reasoning, and not inculcation, that must lead to the sovereign good.

This reflection can take place at school. The first step is to become aware of and ignore the illusions or deterministic processes that influence thought. As a second step, reflection leads to a logical conclusion which is extended to make informed and consistent choices. Then, through education in culture and the humanities – literature, history, sociology – one's thinking gains finesse and perspective, extracting itself from its temporal and spatial context. Confrontation between ideas, and openness to contradiction in debates between students, directly feed the thought process. The entire process is benevolently guided by teachers' methodological interventions or incentives to challenge other opinions.

This approach is adopted, for example, in the International Baccalaureate's course in "Theory of Knowledge", or epistemology. It is essentially a course in critical thinking with ethical ramifications. This subject is not just a façade: it involves 300 hours of classes during the last two years of secondary school and success in the exam is a prerequisite for receiving the IB qualification. Reflection begins with deconstructing how we know what we think we know and how we think we know what we know, and analysing and trying to remove the biases that affect our knowledge. This leads to a critical examination of multiple subjects, from *in vitro* fertilisation to autonomous vehicles. It can be followed by role-playing, for example in debates where each party is tasked with defending a given position in the context of an ethical dilemma. It is a natural forum to address emerging issues related to Artificial Intelligence.

Moreover, this educational approach to the process of ethical thinking cannot, by its very nature, accommodate any restriction on freedom of thought. Committing to this process already amounts to choosing the ethical framework in which we position ourselves. Once this choice is made, good-quality ethical reasoning must logically lead to human-centred values. But not everyone accepts this system of thought. Some authoritarian regimes, including some of the greatest powers in Artificial Intelligence, impose from the outset a different ethical paradigm in which national interests rather than individual freedoms prevail. Ethics is not universal, it is cultural. The deep implications of different existing ethical foundations are such that a clash of civilisations based on Artificial Intelligence is far from improbable. As AI does not stop at physical boundaries, the confrontation is likely to be even more violent.

Raison d'être

Keynes, in his 1930 paper, did not stop at announcing technological unemployment [369]. He added: "This is only a temporary phase of maladjustment. All this means in the long run that mankind is solving its economic problem. (...) This means that the economic problem is not – if we look into the future – the permanent problem of the human race. Why, you may ask, is this so startling? It is startling because if, instead of looking into the future, we look into the past, we find that the economic problem, the struggle for subsistence, always has been hitherto the primary, most pressing problem of the human race (...). If the economic problem is solved, mankind will be deprived of its traditional purpose."

The opportunity to find one's purpose
There you go: for centuries, the struggle for economic survival has been one of humankind's main concerns. Work was propelled into the role of a default *raison d'être*. In doing so, it obscured the search for any higher purpose for our time on Earth. With the drastic transformation and perhaps the disappearance of work in the traditional sense of the word, it is high time we had another look at our real purpose.

Keynes went on: "Will this be a benefit? If one believes at all in the real values of life, the prospect at least opens up the possibility of benefit."

---

[369] The Moderate referred to it in Part 2, Chapter 6, to illustrate how old predictions about the end of work are and how potentially erroneous they can be.

Purpose, once identified and put to use, is expressed through the continuous effort to make a significant impact on the world, on society or on someone's life. It is both a quest and an achievement that provides deep satisfaction. It is also known to improve the physical and mental health of those who have had the opportunity to discover and devote themselves to it[370].

The end of jobs and employment does not mean the end of work. There are still countless things to do, which may not earn remuneration in the traditional sense of the word. Advancing knowledge for those who wish it, or building, painting, fulfilling one's dreams. Thriving without concern for material needs. Strengthening one's humanity by applying its fundamental principles. Caring for others, for loved ones, for the community, for the common good. Educating, transferring to the next generation, empathising, supporting.

Daring to embrace one's purpose

However, Keynes could not help but express his doubts: "Yet I think with dread of the readjustment of the habits and instincts of the ordinary man, bred into him for countless generations, which he may be asked to discard within a few decades." He did not believe in the ability of humans to free themselves from work as a pure source of income.

Generation X, born between the mid-1960s and mid-1980s, seems to have proved him right. When they decide to act in accordance with their thoughts and values, Gen X members often wait until the middle of a traditional career – or even beyond – to abandon the traditional path in favour of a more meaningful alternative. This generation retains an astonishing ability not to deviate from a course that nevertheless feels inadequate. They are drained rather than uplifted by their professional or social environment and are acutely aware that it is a poor use of their time and energy. Are they trapped by economic constraints? Social pressures? The daily routine?

Keynes would undoubtedly be happy to see that Millennials, and even more so Gen Z, born between 1995 and 2010, seem to have much less

---

370

https://greatergood.berkeley.edu/article/item/can_purpose_keep_you_alive

apprehension than their elders about favouring meaning over other possible attributes of work – and increasingly early in their professional careers[371]. Here a young business school graduate embarks on a career not in finance but in sustainable development. A young engineer gives up their traditional career in a large corporation. The "cognitive dissonance between corporate realities and the climate imperative" is often a trigger for reflection, for increased attention to initial or later career path decisions, or even for voluntary withdrawal from the world of work. In addition to the fight against climate change, other issues mobilise young people from the very beginning: the inclusion of different social and ethnic groups, and increased access to energy, vital care, essential banking services and the digital world.

Even years before they enter professional life, Gen Z do not hesitate to assert their aspirations, and in the process they shake the old world. For example, the young Swedish girl Greta Thunberg was barely 15 years old when her Friday school strike won considerable media coverage. At lightning speed, she succeeded in rallying young people from all over the world to the fight against climate change. All the while she kept criticising the entire political class very harshly for their inaction in all the prestigious forums she had been invited into, from national parliaments to the COP and the World Economic Forum.

Fostering the emergence of purpose
What can parents do to foster the development of purpose?

First and foremost, they must monitor their own advice. Their recommendations most probably represent what they have suffered from or missed out on, and what they benevolently want their offspring to benefit from. However, the *raison d'être* is eminently personal. No one can take responsibility to design it for someone else. Nor might they even comprehend someone else's purpose. Just accepting it unconditionally is a very supportive thing to do. One should also bear in

---

[371] https://www.lemonde.fr/campus/article/2019/04/16/une-perte-de-sens-totale-le-blues-des-jeunes-ingenieurs-face-au-climat_5450927_4401467.html?xtmc=sense_quete&xtcr=12

mind that there is no particular age when purpose emerges, and that it may change significantly as people mature.

Perhaps the most important role of parents is to create choices, to broaden the range of possibilities. They should not hesitate to encourage their children's curiosity and commitment, stimulating and satisfying their thirst for discovery. The more diverse and varied the fields explored are, through reading, media, speaking to people or direct experience, the more likely it is that the elusive *raison d'être* will be discovered. What is it that motivates you to the point of repeatedly justifying significant sacrifices? What makes you react the most; what is it that seems so shocking that you are compelled to act? What is the uplifting topic that you could talk passionately about for hours – even if everyone else is bored?

Finally, parents will want to provide courage. You only live once and it is dangerously easy to be dragged into just living everyday life until the end, without daring to attempt your true objective, because of material constraints or the ease of remaining in your comfort zone, because of pressure from parents or society, or for any other reason. Regrets may be as bitter as they are useless and unproductive. Too late is too late. If, in contrast, we can develop a society that is more open to exploration and setbacks, if we can identify sufficient safety nets, then we must not hesitate to think outside of the box, favour boldness over insipid ease, and favour strong aspiration over other people's desires for us.

Be careful not to wield excessive influence on your children, introduce as wide a range of interests as possible, and instil courage: these are three useful things that parents can do to help their children, young and old, gradually discover their purpose.

Foundational knowledge

Necessary knowledge

The transmission of knowledge is the area on which school has traditionally focused. Although the importance attached to it has long been disproportionate, it is nevertheless undeniable that any activity requires a certain amount of knowledge, including specialised knowledge or know-how, that must be either already mastered (which will become increasingly rare) or subject to being acquired (which will become more and more frequent). Moreover, knowledge, when it is deep enough to be transferable, becomes even more valuable by strengthening our learning machine.

Knowledge underlies the other elements of the Compass. Expertise is necessary for creative thinking, as we will find out. In addition, knowledge is a foundation of critical thinking as well as of ethics: the mastery of a reasoning process is useless in the absence of the subject matter to exercise it on or the material to feed it.

Let us make no mistake: knowledge is necessary. The only word of caution is the risk that it might displace the other elements of the Compass or would be learned for the wrong reasons (examinations!) and in the wrong way (superficial cramming!).

Last but not least, some knowledge serves as a basis for all the rest; we will call it *foundational knowledge*. Its most recent addition is *digital literacy*. We will explore it in depth after briefly mentioning the more traditional *literacy* and *numeracy*.

Literacy and numeracy

Let us recall that *literacy* refers to the ability to use and communicate written information in everyday life. *Numeracy* refers to the ability to create and use mathematical information and ideas.

These definitions therefore go far beyond the ability to count or read and write. The skills at work are typically those measured internationally by assessments such as PISA[372], or the TIMMS and PIRLS tests for numeracy and literacy respectively. There is an equivalent for adults, the PIAAC assessment, also organised by the OECD[373] on a ten-yearly basis. For adults and children alike, there are wide disparities even within the advanced OECD countries.

---

[372] See the discussion in the previous chapter in the section: "The Compass and school systems". Continental and regional assessments also exist.
[373] Organization for Economic Cooperation Development, gathering 34 democracies with market economies as well as 70 non-member economies.

This foundational knowledge, taken in isolation, is very inadequate for anything beyond day-to-day living. But it is absolutely essential because it is a prerequisite for accessing all other knowledge. Literature is an essential gateway to culture and the humanities, themselves key areas for shaping the world of tomorrow. Its role is equally important in almost all of the Compass's areas of expertise. Numeracy is one of the main gateways to science and technology. It is also required for anyone who wants to be actively involved in the development of Artificial Intelligence.

To improve the quality of literacy and numeracy training, the key success factors are known to be: a well-trained and socially valued teaching staff, the use of the 21st century arsenal of technological means and scientific methodology, and interventions adapted to children's specific needs.

Digital literacy

Every year, in the final year of primary school in her International Baccalaureate (IB) school, Laura, the teacher, asks her young students to give a presentation on the tree octopus. Known by its Latin name of *octopus paxarbolis*, the species, native to the West Coast of the North American continent, is in danger of extinction. Fortunately, it is very well documented on a dedicated website that students can immediately navigate to online. The home page includes a general description with a photo of the animal in its natural habitat. The News section reports amongst other things a relevant scientific discovery just a few weeks old, as the date shows, as well as a series of recent information published on a weekly basis. The subject seems to be topical. However, the best students spend very little time on their presentations. Because *octopus paxarbolis* is a hoax made up from scratch[374] – and becoming aware of this is the only purpose of the exercise.

Thirty years after the invention of the Internet, the ability to use digital technologies is often a matter of survival in daily life, in school and at work. Amongst older generations, some are inevitably victims of the digital divide – they will have great difficulty, at best, in penetrating the

---

[374] https://en.wikipedia.org/wiki/Pacific_Northwest_tree_octopus

digital world. But most other people are gaining a sense of control. In fact, hardware has become more user-friendly and often works perfectly from the moment it is turned on; websites and applications provide such an optimised user experience that the user is guided effortlessly through their intuitive journey. In addition, there is a meta-competence in the use of digital technology: one video messaging system is very similar to another, all e-commerce sites work in pretty much the same way, registration or payment procedures for any website have become standardised – so ease of use necessarily increases with digital consumption. Minor difficulties in adapting from one application or version to another are increasingly easy to overcome. Even website development has become easier: almost anyone can now create a website and put it online without writing a single line of code.

Yet the impression of control is misleading. Digital literacy, taken here in its broadest sense of effective and appropriate use of digital technologies, is very unevenly distributed. Reading sports news or financial information on one's mobile application, engaging in social media or listening to music on a streaming site is not what is called being digitally literate. Ironically, the least aware of their weaknesses are... *digital natives*! The concept, invented in the early 2000s, assumed that anyone born in the 1980s and sufficiently exposed to digital technology would have spontaneous and automatic competence. Studies conducted a decade later would disprove it, dispelling the myth of digital natives: they are not intrinsically competent, they largely overestimate their level of competence, and they benefit greatly from training when it is provided to them[375].

Being digitally literate is not limited to using one's consumer equipment or popular applications. Word processing and presentation applications, spreadsheets and their latest developments, and collaborative tools for information sharing, planning, co-creation, ideation and analysis, have all become part of the indispensable repertoire in the academic and

---

[375] See for example Sam Nataraj's study [29] or the article from the EDCL Foundation (http://ecdl.org/policy-publications/digital-native-fallacy).

professional world. Soon, virtual reality, 3D printing and of course Artificial Intelligence technologies will be added.

Beyond the functional knowledge of applications, it is wisdom of use that really characterises digital literacy. The tree octopus hoax is far from recent – it even dates back to 1998! However, many still fall for it and many more are deceived by its more sophisticated heirs. As for *deepfakes*, these hyper-realistic fakes produced by Artificial Intelligence[376], one needs be particularly savvy and trained to be able to spot them. In the new arms race between fake-generation and fake-detection technologies, the former still has an edge.

How is digital literacy taught? By increasing exposure to digital tools and simultaneously supporting learners. In Laura's class, the last year of primary school, all the pupils have tablet computers. They know that all the knowledge of the world is within their reach via their Internet connection. What Laura and the other teachers teach them for the rest of their schooling is to make sense of this information. And, more importantly, to assess its truthfulness. They are asked to identify three presumably independent sources for any given piece of information before they can conclude that it is trustworthy. But you can never be sure.

Over the years, the pupils learn to understand, identify and manage the various dangers associated with the digital world. What are the privacy risks of leaving personal information on the Internet? Is confidentiality really respected in supposedly closed groups? Can an apparently harmless encounter turn into a serious security threat? Can we be manipulated by being drawn inside a filter bubble or by being the victim of a deliberate fake? Beyond the risks, what is the digital etiquette in an online discussion or working group?

What was true for digital technology in general is being reproduced and amplified with Artificial Intelligence. 20 years ago digital natives appeared; today *AI natives* are born. They are immersed in Artificial Intelligence, but they have no reason to understand it spontaneously –

---

[376] See Chapter 4 of Part 1 on the risks of Artificial Intelligence.

quite the contrary. Cynthia Breazeal, a professor at MIT and a leading specialist in personal robots, recounts the anecdote of a group of young children gathered around an Alexa device – Amazon's virtual assistant. Upon getting asked a question it doesn't comprehend, Alexa simply answers that it didn't understand. A very positive child answers back: "It's okay, we'll ask another Alexa."

Cynthia Breazeal and her team have developed a remarkable programme to democratise AI education for K-12 (kindergarten to twelfth grade) [377] . The programme covers both the general understanding of AI and the algorithmic and ethical concepts. The modules, carefully adapted to the age of the young learners, alternate between online and offline activities. For example, in a school in Philadelphia, more than 200 students address ethics through the design of an improved version of YouTube in a workshop. As they reflect on the topic, they end up identifying multiple stakeholders with different objectives, and realise that their design can favour or penalise one or the other. This helps them become aware of the ethical responsibility of AI designers. Elsewhere, young learners build robots in which each component is a technical learning exercise: sensors, memory, programming – having specified the design objectives themselves. Elsewhere still, students explore algorithmic logic on their computers through highly accessible and interactive games that link a familiar activity to a model of Artificial Intelligence. Using rock–paper–scissors, they understand reinforcement learning; using musical remixing, they study probabilities and random variables; using vegetable sorting, they see the different classification algorithms at work and understand their logic (without having to write a single line of code).

Ultimately, in the most advanced institutions in the world, in America, Asia or Europe, digital learning is multifaceted. Schools have *fab labs*[378], 3D printers and other learning and creative materials, as well as programming or advanced training modules that do not require writing

---

[377] https://www.media.mit.edu/projects/ai-ethics-for-middle-school/overview/
[378] *Fabrication laboratories* or manufacturing workshops where digital technologies (3D printers, etc) allow students to design and create.

any code. Soon, learners will be familiarised with Artificial Intelligence. Namely, they will learn to differentiate between major algorithmic models; they will know their respective use cases, strengths and weaknesses, to the point of assessing the relevance of an algorithmic class to a given problem. In the long run, they will be able to have a lively discussion with the machine and disagree with its conclusions if it has been set up wrongly! They are also taught to guard against its risks – even when the concern is more about the nature of the technology and the data used, as in the case of bias[379], than about deliberate malicious intent. Their learning will be complemented by data literacy, where they get to learn to manage, analyse and interpret data. At each stage, they take a step back, questioning what the machine offers, its limitations, the precautions to take when using it, and how to interpret the results.

Of course, schools like Laura's may seem privileged and tuition fees are high; some schools on the East Coast of the United States may also seem elitist. But other configurations of digital education exist. At Singapore's public schools, which are almost free of charge, all schools that so desire are equipped with a playful programming platform[380]. As the heir to traditional building games, it puts programming within the reach of the youngest. Teachers are carefully trained and use the platform to make their students think about innovative solutions to real problems. The achievements of primary school children are celebrated by the authorities and proudly displayed in special public events. Another public programme launched by Singapore is AI4K[381], an acronym for "AI for kids", reserved for children aged 10 to 12. The half-day in-class initiation is preceded by online activities and raises awareness about all the aspects of AI mentioned above.

In schools, fab labs or programming workshops around the world, the educational objectives extend far beyond learning a language like Scratch or Python, or mastering a particular technology – these will

---

[379] See Chapter 5 of Part 1 on the risks of Artificial Intelligence.
[380] micro:bit (https://microbit.org/)
[381] https://www.aisingapore.org/industryinnovation/ai4k/

probably be obsolete within a few years anyway. The real aim is to teach an understanding about digital creation, to teach transferable methodologies, to encourage children to collaborate on digital projects, to enable them to stand back from technology, and to build self-confidence in this first stage of digital literacy that will develop throughout life. In short, the objective is to build an identity as a user – and to some extent an identity as a designer – for digital technologies and Artificial Intelligence.

Chapter 14.   Socio-emotional skills

The sides of the 21st Century Compass are equipped with three cognitive skills and three socio-emotional skills. We will discuss cognitive skills in the next chapter, and socio-emotional skills right now. Let's see what they are, why we have selected them and especially how to teach them.

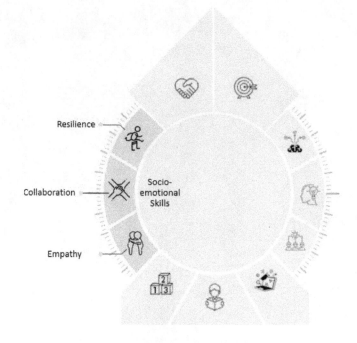

Figure 7: Socio-emotional skills

What exactly are we talking about?

Skills that are sometimes poorly defined

Cognitive skills determine our ability to process information; the most important are memory and all the aspects of reasoning.

Socio-emotional skills encompass everything else; that is why they are sometimes referred to simply as non-cognitive skills. In practice, they relate to emotions and social connections. They include two main subsets: intrapersonal capabilities, focused on self-control, and interpersonal capabilities that characterise our interactions with others.

As for 21st century skills, they sometimes refer only to socio-emotional skills, sometimes to all the cognitive and non-cognitive skills that seem appropriate to our century, and sometimes even include knowledge.

There is a multitude of cognitive and socio-emotional skills. While the multiplicity of skills is real, the impression of profusion is reinforced by the fact that the terms are imprecise. Many of them are almost synonymous and refer to the same concept (such as flexibility and adaptability, or collaboration and teamwork), or have a high degree of overlap.

Finally, some skills are different in nature from others. Some are called reflective: employed mainly in psychology, they are experimentally "discovered" using factor analysis, during the development of a model with independent dimensions. This is the case for the very common model of the Big Five personality traits[382]. Five dimensions (openness to experience, conscientiousness, extraversion, agreeableness, and neuroticism) were identified and then named in a model that best reflects psychological diversity. Each of these dimensions is itself made up of intercorrelated personality facets. Conscientiousness, for example, is usually characterised by resilience and perseverance, a strong work ethic, seriousness and reliability, self-discipline, methodicalness and organisation.

On the other hand, some other sets of skills are not reflective but formative: this means they are made up from scratch and include whatever their creator wants to include. The skills identified by the World Economic Forum or by the O*Net database fall into this category – and that is why they may appear less rigorous.

---

[382] https://en.wikipedia.org/wiki/Big_Five_personality_traits

Since the Compass is limited to six skills (three cognitive and three non-cognitive), drastic choices had to be made about the most meaningful and relevant of them for our use. They are not necessarily homogeneous and may come from several different frameworks.

Independent skills

Cognitive skills are completely independent of socio-emotional skills. Have you ever met an extremely intelligent person, in the sense that she has a high IQ, but who completely lacks socio-emotional qualities? Brilliant in her concepts and thinking, this person suddenly finds herself clumsy in social settings, obviously uncomfortable or even completely out of place, sometimes having difficulty in her friendships or intimate relationships, unable to understand the emotional environment in which she is immersed and often unable to clearly identify, express and control her own emotions?

At the other end of the scale, don't you remember a very ordinary individual in terms of cognitive abilities, who on the other hand seems like a real emotional magician? He has no equal in understanding and reading characters or situations, building strong and lasting relationships, integrating into groups, preventing or managing human crises without apparent effort, and persuading people with finesse. He seems at peace with himself and satisfied with his life, forgives quickly, and does not ruminate about small incidents which after all are not worth it and are easy to overcome.

Entangled skills

Yet, although cognitive and non-cognitive skills are completely independent, the mutual effects of one on the other are multiple.

When a strong negative emotion takes hold of us, be it anger, fear, anguish, anxiety or pessimism, it is because an external signal has reached the emotional part of our brain and has been interpreted by our amygdala. The amygdala in turn discharges into the prefrontal cortex, the location of executive control. Its intensity can be such that it deeply disrupts executive control, paralysing working memory, inhibiting attention; in short, preventing us from thinking properly. So the negative emotion causes us to lose all our intellectual capacity. On the other hand, strong motivation or mild stress, both positive emotions, can improve the functioning of cognitive or motor skills, sometimes leading their lucky recipient to the highest level of performance in a state of absolute bliss called "flow".

Reciprocally, cognitive abilities can also help us with our emotions. When we are seized by a negative emotion, such as violent rage, there are two main strategies for trying to overcome it. The first is to literally turn away from the rage, by having fun or thinking of something completely different. The second, on the contrary, aims to confront rage by attacking its cause. This is where cognitive abilities come to the rescue. Does the cause really justify such an angry response? Is there a different interpretation, a different point of view that would mean the emotion deserves to be reconsidered? In these cases, reason can tame emotion.

Resilience

In the summer of 2016, Alex Honnold was training to make the first *free solo* ascent of the mythical El Capitan, that is to say without any kind of assistance: by himself, without any belaying system or protective equipment. For the first time in his life, Honnold, who is almost infallible (otherwise he would already be dead), fell and got away with a slight compression of his vertebrae. He didn't give up. A few weeks later, he fell again and twisted his ankle. His recuperation period was short-lived: he continued training on a climbing wall wearing an orthopaedic boot. On April 30, 2017, his friend Ueli Steck, a mountaineering legend, died in the Himalayas. But nothing could stop Honnold. On June 3, 2017, he became the first and so far only person to conquer El Capitan in a free solo climb[383].

Honnold is an extraordinary character. Others like him are known for their resilience: Tiger Woods, who won a major golf tournament after an eleven-year gap interspersed with a series of personal indiscretions and multiple back operations; Elon Musk, whose first three rockets blew

---

[383] His story is told in a documentary film, "Free Solo", which won an Oscar in 2018.

up and whose fourth, when all funds had run out, became the precursor to SpaceX's tremendous success; the Apollo 13 astronauts, whose return to Earth was objectively miraculous; and the Salvadoran fisherman who survived 438 days lost at sea.

But neither life's trials nor resilience are exclusive to exceptional people. The loss of a loved one, academic failure, a project that does not want to materialise, or a sudden layoff are challenges that ordinary people face – and they often demonstrate amazing resilience.

Definition
Resilience is the ability to recover from a setback, frustration, failure, loss or personal tragedy, and to get on with life.

This ability to bounce back quickly from an often-unexpected event with initially very negative effects is one of the strongest predictors of success in life. It is considered one of the components of conscientiousness, which a recent study identified as most predictive of long-term success among socio-emotional skills[384].

Related skills are found in the immediate neighbourhood of resilience, such as mental strength, determination or grit. Their sometimes-subtle nuances do not prevent these related skills from being largely correlated with resilience. Mental strength refers to the ability to manage stress, pressure and change. Determination means resolve, firmness, and intensity of the will to achieve an objective. Grit[385] is defined as passion and perseverance towards long-term goals. Unlike resilience, these related skills do not assume the existence of a failure to overcome, but they signal a strong desire to achieve a goal, no matter how difficult it may be.

Resilience and related skills are based on other qualities such as self-control, deferred gratification and optimism. Self-control helps to avoid

---

[384] See the study already cited on Education for Life and Work [55].
[385] *Grit* has been widely studied by Angela Duckworth, who identifies it as one of the most important conditions for success in school and beyond. See her excellent Ted Talk:
https://www.ted.com/talks/angela_lee_duckworth_grit_the_power_of_passion_and_perseverance?language=en

being overwhelmed by negative and incapacitating emotions in the event of failure. Deferred gratification consists in accepting and even preferring a less satisfactory present situation in view of a much more favourable future state [386]. Optimism and a generally positive perspective on a given state of things prompts us to take advantage of the difficult situation to learn from it and overcome it. These qualities enable us not only to bounce back after a failure but also, to a certain extent, to alter the course of events and put ourselves in a position to prevent failure from occurring.

Why resilience is important

The road ahead is laden with pitfalls. Avoiding failure may not be possible for everyone in the years and decades to come.

Change, as we have seen in detail in Part 2, will take place at an ever-increasing pace and intensity. Technology will solve humanity's most important challenges and greatly simplify daily life. For those who are properly equipped, these changes will be a boon. But for everyone else, and this might be the majority, there certainly is an uncertain future ahead. Technology is likely to have a devastating effect on employment as we know it today. The workforce will decline in many trades. There will be no guarantee that new opportunities, yet to be discovered or invented, will arise in sufficient numbers to feed the displaced workforce.

In addition, some events will take an unexpected turn, at least for those on the receiving end. For example, individuals may be led to believe they took all the necessary measures to ensure a comfortable future, only to find themselves caught in a whirlwind of unanticipated disruptive phenomena. Imagine the banker, engineer, developer, or doctor who successfully completed their difficult and prestigious studies, only to realise after ten years of practice that their job is out of their control. They could see their profession disappear or, in a more likely scenario,

---

[386] The most famous example is an experiment conducted on 4-year-old children, letting them choose between a marshmallow now or two marshmallows in fifteen minutes. The children who chose to wait turned out to have better life outcomes than the others.

undergo a profound metamorphosis. Who knows if these conscientious professionals will see their competitive advantage in the labour market reduced or wiped out to the point of being expelled from the workforce?

Being excluded from the world of work, sometimes completely unexpectedly and before society has redefined the role of work, can be highly destabilising. Resilience will then be vital in order to move on and retain some peace of mind.

How to teach resilience

Like other socio-emotional skills, resilience may appear to some as an innate trait, if not immutable, at least difficult to change. Fortunately, this is not the case. There may be a genetic component that determines a baseline level, but it is always possible to cultivate resilience.

The starting point is undoubtedly to accept the event that triggered the failure or drama. Often, this is an externality: a third-party event over which one has no control. This is not a call to give up action and passively accept being tossed around as events unfold. But some facts are very clearly beyond our control. For most of us, this will be the case with the rise of Artificial Intelligence[387]. There is no point in seeking after the cause and ruminating at length about what life would be like without this blow. It is preferable to build the new reality into one's reasoning and to focus on how best to react to it – this is the only element that is within our abilities and to which we must devote our time and energy.

Adopting an optimistic vision of the future and striving to maintain hope clearly makes it easier to bounce back. Acknowledging that the negative event does not reflect an irremediable personal flaw is the first step towards turning the situation into a learning opportunity. In addition, tough as it may sound, adversity is often necessary for the development of resilience. More generally, how can this temporary hard blow be transformed into long-term success? What to learn from the event? How to adapt? Which strategy to adopt or which skills to develop? Belief in one's chances drastically increases the probability of successfully

---

[387] This obviously does not mean that we cannot try to forge a better world, but we must recognise that many will not necessarily have their destiny in their own hands.

coming out the other side. Confidence in one's abilities has a profound positive effect on the abilities themselves. Being endowed with a solid *growth mindset,* as amply studied by Carol Dweck, makes ambitious personal development possible. Simply believing in the possibility of this development increases the chances of success. Faith in oneself is strengthened by celebrating one's achievements and even efforts, if they are not successful yet. In a school experiment, simply explaining to students how neurological mechanisms underpin learning, with practice strengthening neural pathways and thus performance, contributed significantly to the increase in students' scores[388].

Clarity about one's purpose also increases resilience. Any adult, if they can discern their long-term mission and contribution to society, would be more likely to return to action and future plans in the face of chaotic, adverse events. Any child, if they are helping their peers, putting their qualities and strengths to a positive use, would feel an increased sense of usefulness and accomplishment. Both adults and children can more easily overcome the difficulties they face.

Finally, the support of the social environment forms the ultimate bulwark in the ability to bounce back. A damaged person's social network sees them in a good light, reminds them of their talents and successes, and enables them to find themselves again and develop future projects. It serves as the last pillar when all others collapse. And when the reasons for hope seem to have disappeared, the members of the network are still there to provide precious comfort in the form of friendship or unconditional love – the very essence of humanity.

Four of the main elements in building resilience are therefore: acceptance of the negative event and focus on the solution; positive vision and confidence in one's ability to develop or find a solution; confidence in one's purpose; and support from a strong social network. These principles are best cultivated from childhood, when neural plasticity allows for better anchoring, but can also be developed during adulthood.

---

[388] Carol Dweck summarises many of her studies at a Stanford conference: https://www.youtube.com/watch?v=hiiEeMN7vbQ

Empathy

"My mother was the single most important influence in my life. I saw her struggles as a single mom. She taught me the values of hard work and responsibility, but also of compassion and empathy – being able to look at the world through somebody else's eye and stand in their shoes." This message for Mother's Day 2013 was delivered by a gentleman called Barack Obama. Obama demonstrated empathy throughout his political life and attributed much of his success to it[389].

A multitude of concepts behind a catch-all term

At first look, empathy is defined as the ability to understand others' feelings and / or to experience feelings oneself. But behind this synthetised definition there exists a total lack of consensus. Passionate debates among experts have abounded for the past two decades. Even Barack Obama, quoted above, uses the same word to refer to different concepts and sometimes makes questionable distinctions between empathy, sympathy and compassion. One researcher has been able to distinguish eight closely related but conceptually distinct phenomena that can claim to be a form of empathy, depending on circumstances and studies [390]. Sometimes these eight different phenomena are experienced in turn during the same social interaction.

To simplify matters to the extreme, there are two main families.

Cognitive empathy refers to the understanding of others' internal states, thoughts and feelings. This is often achieved by imagining this state through **perspective taking**, by putting oneself in others' shoes, either by projecting oneself into the other person's situation or by trying to

---

[389] See the countless references to empathy in Obama's speeches:
http://cultureofempathy.com/Obama/Quotes.htm
[390] This is Daniel Batson, author of the article that is reprinted in the first chapter of *The Social Neuroscience of Empathy* [20] (2009, MIT Press).
https://www.researchgate.net/profile/Nancy_Eisenberg/publication/2487026
18_Empathic_Responding_Sympathy_and_Personal_Distress/links/02e7e539
bd3a87471b00000000/Empathic-Responding-Sympathy-and-Personal-
Distress.pdf

guess the other's point of view in the other person's situation. It is not a feeling or emotion but indeed a fully cognitive state.

Emotional empathy, on the other hand, consists in producing an appropriate emotional response to the other person's emotion. This response may be the same emotion as, or a different emotion than, that experienced by the person who is the object of empathy. Emotional empathy begins with detecting and identifying the other person's emotions (also called **empathic accuracy**) and continues with acknowledging the other person's feelings (which is no other than **sympathy**). It might possibly continue by adopting the posture of others under the effect of mirror neurons (**mimetic empathy**). It may evolve into compassion for others (**empathic concern**), or a personal feeling of discomfort and stress (**empathic or personal distress**), which is self-centred.

Why empathy is important
The emergence of the era of Artificial Intelligence brings for many humanists the unexpected opportunity to put humans back at the centre of our lives. In their vision, machines do machine work and humans take care of fellow humans. This scenario, rich in increasingly intense interpersonal relationships, requires more mutual understanding, solidarity, collaboration, justice and morality; in short, more of the skill that underlies all the above characteristics: empathy.

Empathy has multiple intrapersonal and interpersonal benefits in all circumstances[391]. On a relational level, empathetic people have a social life that they find more satisfying. They also make it more pleasant for other people to interact with them. When receiving empathy, they can distinctly feel how others' feelings adapt to their own. They are comforted by the fact that their emotions elicit an appropriate emotional reaction, and find this more rewarding than having their

---

[391] Mentioned by William Chopik in his article "Differences in Empathic Concern and Perspective Taking Across 63 Countries":
https://www.ipearlab.org/media/publications/ChopikOBrienKonrathInPress.pdf

position or condition actually understood from an intellectual point of view.

Empathetic individuals are also more likely to engage in socially beneficial actions: they are driven by a need for justice, they engage more often in volunteering, give more to charities and help people in need. When they act under the influence of empathy, their action is altruistic. On the other hand, if their action is motivated by empathic distress, their help is primarily aimed at satisfying themselves, by giving themselves a clear conscience. But in both cases, regardless of their motivation, they contribute[392]!

Empathetic people also control their aggressiveness or anti-social behaviour, reducing its potentially negative impact on society. In contrast, the absence of empathy (and in particular of emotional empathy) is the characteristic of psychopaths.

Empathy is a success factor for many professions today where rapport with others is necessary, such as sales, coaching, and management. Empathy plays a key role in all collaborative endeavours. In collaborative situations, particularly when accompanied by negotiation, studies show that cognitive empathy is generally preferable to emotional empathy. By analysing the situation rationally and from several points of view, the overall results of collaboration can be better than those obtained by emotional response, which tend to irrationally favour one group over another.

Finally, on a personal level, empathetic individuals tend to be more satisfied with their lives, have higher self-esteem and be more emotionally intelligent.

Ultimately, members of a more empathetic society experience a more satisfying interpersonal and intrapersonal life while contributing to the improvement of society – an ideal dynamic when Artificial Intelligence emerges. As we have seen in Part 1 of this book, AI is probably more effective than humans in terms of empathic accuracy. It is also able to

---

[392] On the contrary, too much personal stress can cause the person to turn away without helping.

simulate empathic concern by producing emotional responses. But this simulation is obviously only superficial, and machines do not understand what it is about. Until Artificial General Intelligence is achieved, only humans can produce a deep and subtle empathic response.

How to teach empathy

Some features of empathy can be detected as early as the second year of life, suggesting a genetic predisposition that manifests itself as the brain matures. Infants experience the feelings of others by mimicry, at an age when they cannot yet clearly distinguish self from other. They soon adopt more sophisticated empathic behaviours, seeking to console a little brother or an older sister.

In addition to the innate disposition, it is now accepted that empathy training is possible for a long period of time: typically from the beginning of school until the university years, and even beyond that into adulthood[393]. Several pilot programmes have proved successful in schools, particularly in the United States, including in neighbourhoods considered very difficult. The programmes exist in different formats. Some are the subject of a specific course, entirely dedicated to interpersonal skills, personal and relational skills[394]. In other cases, these concepts are included in the regular school subjects.

The starting point, regardless of the learner's age, is to raise awareness of the concept of empathy – this awareness has an immediate positive effect on the level of empathy itself. The other fundamental step is to train the person to detect their own emotions, to identify them and to name them. This understanding is a prerequisite for empathic accuracy regarding others. It is often empathetic inaccuracy, i.e. a misinterpretation of the internal state and intentions of the other person, that is at the root of conflicts at school, on the street or at work.

Role-playing, where someone borrows the identity of a real or fictional character, is a proven way to increase both emotional and cognitive

---

[393] See Chapter 7 by N.D. Feshbach and S. Feshbach in the above-mentioned *The Social Neuroscience of Empathy* [20].
[394] See in particular the encouraging and somewhat exhilarating description at the very end of Goleman's book [19].

empathy. Another very effective approach is perspective-taking, which prompts people to become aware of someone else's position or internal state. This is one of the most classic exercises in working groups or in conflict resolution, where each side is asked to clearly formulate the other's position. Sometimes, social conflicts are filmed, and each participant is asked after the fact to describe their feelings and opinions at each stage; this description is then shared with the opponent, so that each person can compare their interpretation of the other's position with the version given by the other person themselves.

Other factors have been identified as empathy augmenters. They are as diverse as watching the misfortune of others or other distressing content, practising modelling the behaviour of others, music education or collaborative learning.

Thus, there are many opportunities to foster the development of empathy during childhood and adulthood.

Collaboration

When you are done reading this paragraph, put your book or tablet down for a few minutes, look up, look around you and ask yourself what in your surroundings is not the result of collaboration. In a book on cognition, Edwin Hutchins proposed this exercise and the only relevant thing he found in his own environment was a small stone placed on his desk[395]. What can you find?

You can now resume reading. Note that even this book, however solitary the practice of writing may seem, is the result of intense collaborative activity. The author's ideas were refined under the impetus of a group of experts that was gradually formed. From discussion to discussion, one-to-one or in small groups, the content of the book took shape. This was only the beginning. Thanks to specialised Internet platforms, the author was able to find one graphic designer in Pakistan to produce the book's diagrams and a second one in Serbia to create the cover. The

---

[395] The injunction appears in Hutchins' (1905) "Cognition in the Wild". The anecdote is reported by Patrick Griffin and his colleagues [42].

author hired an editor in England for the English version of this book. The talent of the latter proved to be such that under her influence, the author ended up reworking parts of the original manuscript. He also crossed paths with influencers; one wanted to bring quality content to his readers, and another wanted to reposition himself in the field covered by the book, so both of them actively participated in promoting the book. At each stage, these interactions comprised many of the elements of fruitful collaboration. They involved multiple conversations, implicit or explicit negotiation, minor adjustments or major changes of course. Some of the collaborations were paid for and others were not, some formal and some not, but all of them certainly proved mutually beneficial.

Collaboration beyond cooperation

Collaboration, as defined by Wikipedia, is "the process of two or more people or organizations working together to complete a task or achieve a goal". Wikipedia is itself an excellent example of such collaboration: participants who are only slightly coordinated but operating in a structured framework work together to produce a service that is economically valuable and accessible to everyone. Here, collaboration is not only about the complementarity of knowledge, but also, and above all, about the discussion that ultimately leads to the creation of a stable state: consensus on content. This approach has revolutionised the dissemination of knowledge. The result is the largest encyclopaedia and the fifth most visited website in the world.

Collaboration consists of several essential components. Communication allows the information to be shared in order to achieve the common objective. Cooperation ensures the distribution of tasks. But the final component that is needed is collective participation, which transforms simple cooperation into collaboration. The use of diverse perspectives and ideas leads to a result that goes beyond the simple juxtaposition of individual contributions. Parallel and separate work is replaced by overlapping and shared activities.

Why collaboration is important

Everything, or almost everything, is collaboration – apart from living as a hermit for individuals or in complete self-sufficiency for groups. Even seemingly solitary tasks, such as achieving individual sports performance, are rarely accomplished without the active involvement of a team – even if it rarely shares the limelight.

In the animal kingdom, wolves hunt in packs and ants build through a huge collective effort. At school, children do their first group work on the classroom benches and experience their first group dynamics in playgrounds or on sports fields. In an extremely popular video game, the builder players each bring their stone to the jointly built building; elsewhere multiplayer games involve concerted attacks to "capture the flag" or destroy an enemy ship. In an orchestra, musicians with egos sometimes as developed as their talent manage to come together to produce an exceptional performance. Aiming to fight global warming, renowned scientists, whose role is to guarantee the truthfulness of claims made, join forces with artists or popular influencers to spread the message to audiences that are otherwise difficult to reach.

As a result of globalisation and technology, collaborations are increasingly being organised between countries, or between nationals of several countries. This is particularly true in the field of science. Scientific papers now include lists of authors showing the diversity of the world, beyond the lab and the country of the main signatory. CERN, where the Higgs boson was observed almost half a century after its prediction, is one of the most successful European collaborations. The recent indirect observation of a black hole is itself the successful outcome of a global effort involving 200 scientists and six observatories, from Antarctica to Hawaii and from Spain to Chile[396]. Almost all modern space missions are international collaborations: from Apollo–Soyuz to symbolise the end of the Cold War, to the International Space Station today.

In the business world, collaboration is a key means of leveraging collective knowledge and skills. For example, multidisciplinary teams are set up to manage a range of products over their entire lifecycle. Beyond the company's borders, design is conducted in collaboration with customers or suppliers. The team must often manage conflicting issues:

---

[396] https://www.youtube.com/watch?v=1EZiOSZ4L2I

reducing an initial investment can increase a later operating cost or the eventual end-of-life cost; adopting an attractive but atypical design can generate production complications; lowering its quality criteria can backfire on the company by later damaging its brand image. Collaboration makes it possible to identify these problems early in the process, rather than suffer them when corrective action becomes much more expensive. Different perspectives are confronted, ideas flow and enrich each other, innovative solutions emerge, and the best compromises are found. The ability to contribute is considered so important that even a talented employee may be fired if they fail to engage in their organisation's collaborative efforts.

What will the advent of Artificial Intelligence change in this picture? On the one hand, individual users do have increased direct access to the growing capabilities of AI. On the other hand, the implementation of AI will require collaboration, particularly multidisciplinary collaboration, for the foreseeable future. Moreover, strengthening the human link necessarily implies an increase in collaborative practices. We can therefore take for granted that collaborations of all kinds, far from drying up in the era of AI, will actually multiply. They will be facilitated by a whole range of technological collaborative tools already in place, from working on shared documents to tools for ideation, co-creation, planning and communication.

How to teach collaboration

Given the importance of collaborative activity, it is surprising to note the reluctance to teach it explicitly. Why assume that this competence is acquired naturally, without any dedicated effort? And the positive and negative potential from collaboration is increased by diversity among the participants: while diversity can lead to the most fruitful collaborations, it can also lead to the worst outcomes when the ins and outs of collaboration are not fully mastered.

Good collaboration requires theory, practice, and of course feedback, as with all kinds of learning. INSEAD, a business school ranked among the best in the world, is famous for the study and project groups it forms from day one. These bring students together throughout their studies and are still fondly remembered at alumni meetings 20 years after graduation. The experience is indeed remarkable. Groups do not form randomly: INSEAD imposes their composition, selecting as diverse a membership as possible. For instance, a group may include an American lawyer, a French engineer, an Indian businessman, a Russian art critic and an English journalist. Large egos seem to be the only thing in common. The group is so heterogeneous in every respect that it seems to be designed to function badly – unless an incredible amount of hard work and goodwill is put into it, to deploy known collaborative techniques and to commit to frequent introspection and feedback sessions. When this finally works, the group becomes highly productive.

Working well together is first and foremost a matter of mindset. Appreciating the value of others and the value of teamwork predisposes people to collaborative success. Among the more technical skills required for collaboration, four stand out: good group management, communication skills, empathy and conscientiousness.

To function properly, a group must at least have a common objective, shared values, agreed operating rules, well-defined responsibilities and good interpersonal relations between its members. The simple awareness of this reality of group dynamics often allows introspection and corrective actions to be taken that improve team functioning. The life of the group traditionally goes through several phases. These have long been documented by research in Organisational Behaviour: Forming, Storming, Norming, and Performing[397]. These principles apply regardless of the age of group members. Even young children can benefit from these principles – although of course the theoretical presentation of the concept will need to be adapted.

Communication between the members of a group is a prerequisite for its proper functioning. A contribution is only valid to the extent that it can be communicated. It goes far beyond simply keeping informed. Each communication event has a purpose, a target individual or group, a most effective transmission channel, a most suitable format, and an appropriate tone. Communication skills can be developed from an early

---

[397] This theory of group development was developed by Bruce Tuckman in... 1965!

age and strengthened over the course of schooling and life. If English speakers are excellent communicators, it is because they practise appropriate activities: from the "show and tell" in primary school to the debates filmed in high school followed by feedback on their performance. They develop clear expression of ideas, control of body language, attentive listening and confidence[398].

We have already mentioned the essential role of empathy in social interactions. Within a group, perspective-taking ensures that other group members' positions are clearly understood. As well as helping to achieve the goals of the collaboration, empathy has a positive impact on the other person, who may be reassured or galvanized by having their contribution recognised. A good understanding of the team members' positions and motivations also helps subsequent negotiations to reach a conclusion.

Since the aim of collaboration is to achieve a clearly defined objective, each participant must be sufficiently conscientious to carry it out. We have already mentioned this conscientiousness: it is the socio-emotional skill most correlated with the achievement of positive results. It includes perseverance and resilience, the mechanisms and learning of which we have already described in greater detail.

Among all the socio-emotional skills, resilience, empathy and collaboration are the ones we have identified as the most relevant in the age of Artificial Intelligence. These can all be learned and developed explicitly. What about cognitive skills?

---

[398] https://www.nureva.com/blog/education/how-to-teach-communication-skills-that-go-beyond-words

Chapter 15.   Cognitive skills

The cognitive skills included in the 21st Century Compass are critical thinking, creative thinking and interdisciplinary thinking.

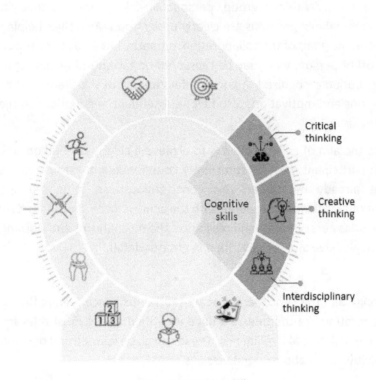

Figure 8: Cognitive skills

Critical thinking

What is critical thinking?

Critical thinking, defined simply, is the analysis of facts to form a judgment.

Robert Ennis, a professor at the University of Illinois, has devoted most of his research to this subject. According to him, critical thinking is reasoned and reflective thinking focused on deciding what to believe or do[399]. It therefore has four elements: it is reasoned (using rigorous reasoning skills); reflective (i.e. it is done in full consciousness); focused (goal-oriented); and targets doing and believing (i.e. any possible decision). Critical thinking includes both technical skills and mental attitudes or dispositions. In this sense it is broader than just a critical mindset, which is essentially the willingness of a person to evaluate a fact, without predicting their technical ability. Conversely, someone could have the technical capacity to think critically without the disposition to do so.

Ennis lists the dispositions or attitudes necessary for critical thinking. First, he highlights the genuine desire to form an accurate, justifiable opinion, without neglecting to explore all possibilities and examine all points of view. Next comes the care taken to understand and honestly present other people's positions. Finally, in an ancillary way, comes the concern for the other person, in particular in order not to intimidate them during the discussion.

Among the technical capabilities of critical thinking, Ennis first states the ability to clarify the problem: what is the question, what are the arguments set forth? Then he proceeds with the evaluation of the basis for judgment: what is the credibility of the source, and what is the credibility of the report or observation of it? He then moves on to reasoning itself: deduction, induction, and finally judgment. After the final clarifications and reasoning, the argument must be presented in a clear and sensitive way.

Why is critical thinking important?
For as long as humans have been communicating, there has been a need for intellectual self-defence tools. Critical thinking is undoubtedly one of them. Are the reported facts truthful, or at least likely to be? Is it even possible to know? If they are proven, do they really have the decisive importance we grant them? Are they generalisable? Is the reasoning

---

[399] https://education.illinois.edu/docs/default-source/faculty-documents/robert-ennis/thenatureofcriticalthinking_51711_000.pdf?sfvrsn=7bb51288_2

rigorous? Is the situation inherently difficult to interpret, or is there an intention to mislead? Over the years, it has been necessary to fight against lies and falsifications, against dogmas and conspiracy theories, against indoctrination and manipulation, against all fallacious reasoning, whether it be an unfortunate logical error or a deliberate intention to deceive.

Our era is particularly abundant in *fake news*: false information of all kinds. Technology in general and Artificial Intelligence in particular are no strangers to this, with the considerably increased ability to create increasingly realistic fake objects, images, sounds, videos, and texts.

Critical thinking, therefore, is more necessary than ever.

How to teach critical thinking
Critical thinking is one of the explicit target competencies of a growing number of school systems, from the American system (where the 4Cs, including critical thinking, are included in the Common Core) to the Singaporean curriculum.

The same choice arises as for many of the Compass's other skills: teaching in a dedicated course, separately from the rest of the curriculum, or doing so through traditional subjects, such as the humanities, social sciences or hard sciences.

The IB System's Theory of Knowledge course is an example of dedicated teaching[400]. Teachers explicitly teach critical thinking theory and go through numerous practical exercises. For example, they teach students to analyse information sources and discern the information presented. All kinds of propaganda materials are reviewed, with particular emphasis on fallacious reasoning, techniques of language manipulation, and recontextualisation of images, all within the framework of political objectives to be deciphered. Conspiracy theories can also be included in the programme, through case studies such as the September 11 attacks

---

[400] See Corinne Rousset's article, "Academic excellence, jousting and pedagogical pragmatism in Singapore" [27]. This article focuses on Singapore but is generalisable. We have drawn much of the material in this paragraph from it.

or Apollo missions. Sometimes students participate in small internal competitions of an unusual kind: each team is responsible for developing a conspiracy theory from scratch, the effectiveness of which will be judged by the other students. The exercise is pedagogically extremely effective.

Another particularly effective activity in critical thinking training is debating. Teams are formed and assigned to defend a pre-determined point of view, regardless of the actual opinion of the participants. Teams score one point for each correctly justified argument. Alternatively, teams are ranked according to the number of spectators whose minds they have changed between the beginning and end of the debate. This rhetorical exercise is primarily used for the applied understanding of critical thinking, to identify manipulative techniques and misleading arguments, or to fully realise the complexity of establishing the validity of any theory. It also enables students to discuss complex and sensitive subjects, for example the tension between utilitarianism and human rights or the highly variable nature of truth in writing history, depending on the perspective taken.

Critical thinking sometimes has an unexpected and undesirable consequence. Students eventually give in under the cumulative weight of masses of contradictory information flooding them. They tend to either doubt everything or put all information on an equal footing – both attitudes are to be deplored. Students are more easily convinced by conspiracy theories, which are themselves becoming more and more sophisticated and making tough demands of teachers. Some teachers shared with us that they could no longer use Holocaust denial as a study topic. From their classroom experience, the careful analysis of the documents and testimonies of this cataclysmic event, which is indisputable and barely three generations old, comes up against arguments that are increasingly difficult for ill-prepared teachers to refute. Negationist arguments are presented in a sufficiently credible, convincing, scientific and documented manner to resist the counterarguments of the insufficiently equipped teacher.

These anecdotes highlight that critical thinking, which is an ability to reason and a disposition of mind, cannot be deployed without solid knowledge. What makes it possible to refute Holocaust denial is not only an ability to reason, but also concrete historical or scientific arguments. Careful preparation is required to challenge, for example, the classic negationist argument that Zyklon B cannot be used in the confined volume of gas chambers. When the necessary knowledge is too advanced to be mastered by the critical thinker, it is essential that they call on an expert.

The other takeaway of the apparent limitations of critical thinking is the cruel reminder that in the arms race between the true and the fake, the latter still has a bright future ahead of it. Artificial Intelligence will be a dangerous ally, against its will, until its power can be used to detect forgeries.

Creative thinking

When a new working group is formed, a classic team building activity is the spaghetti and marshmallows challenge[401]. The objective for the participants is to build a tower as high as possible, topped by a marshmallow, in a strictly limited time. As for building materials, participants can make use of twenty pieces of spaghetti (uncooked and therefore rigid), one metre of string and a roll of adhesive paper. The results, says an expert on the subject, are remarkably consistent. The worst teams in this event are the young graduates of business schools. In contrast, the best teams consist of young graduates from... kindergarten. Why? Firstly, because little children collaborate better than their elders, without letting their egos interfere and without indulging as much in power struggles. Secondly, and more importantly, because little children apply one of the most effective creative processes: experimentation and iteration. Without *a priori* preconceptions or dogmatism, they explore structure after structure, drop those that are not suitable, invent new forms, bring about changes, and retain solutions that work. And they end up building very respectable towers.

---

[401] https://www.ted.com/talks/tom_wujec_build_a_tower?language=en

What is creative thinking?

Like many human mental processes, creativity is not short of definitions, covering similar but distinct aspects of the same concept. Most approaches agree on the notion of novelty combined with a certain usefulness. Ken Robinson, whom we will get back to later, soberly defines creativity as having original ideas that have value. Although the artistic field is the first to come to mind, creative thinking extends far beyond it. From everyday life to ingenious discoveries and inventions, from leisure to the world of work, any practice can emerge or evolve through creative thinking.

For a long time, conventional wisdom had it that creativity was a somewhat mystical process. This is obviously not the case: it is a cognitive process like any other, whose nature is just beginning to be deciphered by neuroscience. In the highly creative brain, three neural systems with complementary functions seem to be activated more intensely. The first system, called the *default* network, is involved when someone begins to imagine, daydream, let their mind wander – it generates ideas. We have already met the second network, known as the *executive control* network: it is activated when someone focuses their attention and rationally evaluates the ideas submitted to them. The third network, known as the *salience* network, acts as a switching mechanism between the default network and the executive control network; in other words, between the generation and evaluation of ideas. The most creative people seem to be those who can operate these networks together, whereas they usually operate separately[402].

Creativity differs significantly from intelligence. The latter, as measured by IQ tests, often uses convergent reasoning: it seeks to identify similarities. Creative thinking, on the other hand, uses disengagement (by distancing oneself from established ideas) and divergent thinking (a spontaneous, uncontrolled process of generating ideas). One of the currently most accepted theories on the relationship between intelligence and creativity is that of the threshold[403]: a minimum level of

---

[402] See "Robust prediction of individual creative ability from brain functional connectivity" [40].

[403] See "What do we know today about creativity?" [22].

intelligence is necessary to be creative, but beyond this threshold there is no longer a correlation between the two. Finally, to take two famous examples, Edison and Einstein, a brilliant inventor and researcher respectively, shared not only an extraordinary capacity for creative thinking but also delayed cognitive development in childhood.

Contrary to popular belief, and contrary to what even creativity experts considered obvious a few decades ago, most researchers today claim that creativity is not general but specific to a field[404]. Thus, creative individuals in absolute terms do not exist. Take your own case: perhaps you are very creative in designing scientific experiments, but much less so in designing a range of clothing, or vice versa; perhaps your creativity is highest when making wooden furniture but if you are forced to cook, you will follow the recipe step by step and make sure you do not deviate from it. Creative thinking requires a certain amount of expertise (even if, on the other hand, you can be an expert without exhibiting a shred of creativity). Using the example of cooking, prior knowledge of a wide range of ingredients, such as spices, allows them to be used in an innovative way.

Why creative thinking is important

Creative thinking is historically important because it is involved in all aspects of life and work. Researchers[405] have developed the 4C model of creativity. *Big-C* creativity, the eminent and radical creativity of Einsteins and Edisons, Picassos and Prousts, is the one that gets all the attention. Just after it, *pro-C* creativity refers to the creativity of a professional, such as a fashion designer, a process designer, a product manager or a customer segment manager. It should be noted that these creative positions determine to a large extent the performance of their company. The most successful companies are increasingly the most innovative; yet the most innovative are those that conduct the most

---

[404] This entire paragraph is based on Baer's very comprehensive article on the importance of creative expertise and all its consequences: "The importance of domain-specific expertise in creativity" [24].
[405] See the seminal paper by Dr. James C. Kaufman and Dr. Ronald Beghetto. https://www.researchgate.net/publication/228345133_Beyond_Big_and_Littl e_The_Four_C_Model_of_Creativity

experiments, and those that conduct the most experiments are often technology companies – such as Amazon, Google or Grab. Only technology enables the companies to conduct so many experiments and measure their results in near-real time. Next, *small-c* creativity describes daily creativity such as decorating a room, an innovative way to pack before a trip, or the outfit you assemble in the morning by combining different clothes. Finally, at the bottom of the scale, *mini-c* creativity is only really meaningful to the creator, like the first time a child assembles a construction set.

The acceleration of change in our society and our lives reinforces the need for creative thinking. We must constantly face new situations, solve new problems and overcome new challenges. Creative thinking allows us to maintain our ability to adapt and make the most of a complex and ever-changing environment. Let us remember that Artificial Intelligence will force us to rethink the world, the place of humans, their relationship with machines, and the social contract. Let us also keep in mind that AI is still in its infancy, and that to deliver on its promises, a series of radical innovations will be needed to advance the very technology making up Artificial Intelligence.

Finally, creativity is unique in that it allows humans to differentiate themselves from Artificial Intelligence. AI, as we saw in Part 1, excels in creativity through imitation – the kind that allowed it to finish the unfinished symphony. It is unbeatable in exploring the realm of the possible, which allowed AlphaGo to beat the world's best players and AlphaFold to identify protein configurations that minimise their energy. But when divergent thinking comes into play, Artificial Intelligence is powerless. Its algorithms do not allow it to achieve this today, which leaves humans with more exclusivity in the domain of radical innovation. Let's take advantage of this.

Although creative thinking is now recognised as essential among the skills of the 21st century, it is nevertheless seldom taught as such.

How to teach creative thinking
Before embarking on a journey to teach creative thinking, it is – alas – more relevant to ask why people end up lacking it. Indeed, at birth, almost everyone is endowed with creativity and happily expresses it

throughout early childhood. "We forget that back in kindergarten, we were all creative. We all played and experimented and tried out weird things without fear or shame. We didn't know enough not to. The fear of social rejection is something we learned as we got older. And that's why it's possible to regain our creative abilities so swiftly and powerfully, even decades later," as brothers Tom and David Kelley, innovation gurus, remind us[406]. But over the years, they add, fear takes over: fear of taking the first step, fear of being judged, fear of losing control, fear of the great unknown. Creativity disappears.

There are indeed many obstacles to creative thinking throughout life. The main one is encountered early on and is called education. "We don't grow into creativity; we grow out of it. Or rather, we get educated out of it," claims Ken Robinson in the most popular TED Talk of all time[407]. Parents discourage their "divergent" children from deviating from the norm at an early stage. The school system often stifles creativity by focusing on a certain type of skills, sometimes disregarding experimentation and almost systematically stigmatising mistakes. Most companies do not tolerate failure. Contrast this with Edison boasting, in his quest for the light bulb, that he had already found ten thousand ways that did not work. The social pressure to "succeed", finally, is immense, especially in Asian cultures, to a lesser extent in Europe, and even less so in America. This aversion to risk kills creativity in the making. From early childhood to adulthood, the whole universe seems to be conspiring to eliminate creativity.

The first thing to do in the search for creativity is therefore not to interfere with children's creative thinking: let them explore, dream, wander, test, undo and start again as they naturally do, while encouraging their creative journey. They take their first steps, without being aware of it, into the world of serendipity, a totally fortuitous encounter with elements not specifically sought. Serendipity, which paves the way to so many inventions and scientific discoveries, can only

---

[406] Tom and David Kelley are the inventors of Design Thinking and authors of *Creative Confidence* [35].

[407] https://www.ted.com/talks/ken_robinson_says_schools_kill_creativity#t-1138358

bless the curious, open and flexible mind, one that remains attentive to the unexpected.

There are also techniques to reclaim or stimulate lost creativity. The prerequisite – let us not forget – is to have a minimum of knowledge and expertise in the field at hand. A creative poet has no reason to be so creative in mathematics or car assembly if they are completely new to both areas. It is therefore necessary to ensure that this minimum expertise is real and relevant.

Other practices, which seem more generalist[408], are essentially aimed at taking different points of view or connecting ideas that are not usually related. For example, one study experimentally verified the effectiveness of even a short period of training in the following four techniques[409]: silence, with individual brainstorming; lines of evolution, with gradual associations from one concept to another; random connections, by linking two distant and randomly chosen concepts or objects; and SCAMPER, from the acronym for techniques that generate new ideas by Substitution, Combination, Adaptation, Modification, Putting to another use, Elimination and Rearrangement.

Finally, creative thinking can be integrated into broader formal methodologies to lead to useful innovations. The most common is Design Thinking, a creative and human-centred problem-solving approach. It involves a series of divergent and convergent processes and is very often collaborative. The first step uses empathy to allow you to put yourself in the place of the target population. Then comes the exploration and exact definition of the problem to be solved. Further exploration expands the space of possible answers and then converges again towards the selected solution. A prototype is developed, and then successive iterations are carried out to improve it until a satisfactory solution is found. This methodology, which originated in the United

---

[408] This is in apparent contradiction with the view that training in creativity must be specific since creativity itself is specific. At the time of publishing we have not resolved this contradiction.

[409] See "Enhancement of Creative Thinking Skills using a Cognitive-Based Creativity Training": https://link.springer.com/article/10.1007/s41465-016-0002-3 [23].

States and is now widespread across the globe, is widely applied in the world of work, among adults; however, it is also very suitable for children. As mentioned earlier, 120 educators from Singapore's Digital Maker Programme were recently trained in it[410].

Interdisciplinary thinking

What is interdisciplinary thinking?

Interdisciplinarity in the strictest sense is the use, in a given discipline, of skills or knowledge usually specific to another discipline. For example, Henry Ford is often considered to be the inventor of the modern assembly line. The cars being assembled were moved from station to station by automated and continuous conveyer systems, while the workers, assigned to a fixed station, always performed the same tasks in the same place. This resulted in an increase in worker productivity and line throughput. This invention, in fact, does not originally come from the automotive industry. A Ford employee, William "Pa" Klann, was introduced to it during a field trip to a... slaughterhouse in Chicago. The carcasses were gradually "disassembled" on a mobile line, with the butchers remaining at their posts. Klann applied the knowledge and skills of a different discipline, butchery, to his own field, automobile assembly.

More indirectly, many researchers or inventors of exceptional quality claim to have drawn some of their inspiration from an artistic interdisciplinarity: Leonardo da Vinci, Benjamin Franklin and Alexander Graham Bell are among the talented artists who were also geniuses in their own fields.

A broader definition of interdisciplinarity also includes what is strictly speaking multidisciplinarity, i.e. the study of a specific phenomenon or subject from the perspective of multiple disciplines. Human migration, for example, has been the subject of joint studies by archaeologists, historians and linguists for decades. Archaeologists analyse the artefacts found on site and attempt to relate them to local or newly-arrived

---

[410] https://www.imda.gov.sg/digitalmaker/about-us

populations, or to trade and commerce. Historians link this to the study of states and peoples. Linguists, through very detailed comparative linguistic analysis, can determine the family tree of languages. Thus, two competing theories about the migration of proto-Indo-European peoples to Western Europe have been developed: one from Anatolian farmers 8,000 to 10,000 years ago, the other from herders in the northern Black Sea 5,000 to 6,000 years ago, with rapid expansion through the domestication of the horse and the invention of the wheel. Joining in this interdisciplinarity, geneticists were able to confirm the two waves of migration[411] by analysing the genome of the remains of individuals from these times.

While the interdisciplinary approach seems logical, it is quite a recent one in modern times. Formal interdisciplinary research only really began in the 1970s and 1980s, and met with strong resistance, with everyone involved fearing for their budget, reputation and power[412]. Today, even though the vast majority of universities and research institutes are still organised by discipline, interdisciplinarity is much more common: one third of the references in scientific articles refer to other disciplines.

Why is interdisciplinary thinking important?
Interdisciplinary thinking is important first and foremost because real human problems are not confined to one discipline: they do not conform to academic or administrative boundaries. The major issues of our time, such as global warming, are complex. They require expertise, skills, knowledge, equipment and tools that transcend disciplines. No one owns this whole toolbox by themselves, so interdisciplinary thinking and collaborative work are essential.

Artificial Intelligence is an area where interdisciplinary thinking is particularly relevant. The major advances in the field were marked by

---

[411] See "Steppe migration rekindles debate on language origin":
https://www.nature.com/news/steppe-migration-rekindles-debate-on-language-origin-1.16935
[412] See "How to solve the world's biggest problems":
https://www.nature.com/news/how-to-solve-the-world-s-biggest-problems-1.18367

the back-and-forth between the artificial and the natural. Indeed, the algorithms used for image recognition[413], invented by Yann LeCun, work in a very similar way to the visual cortex. Even more explicitly, researcher Joshua Tenenbaum, a professor of both cognitive science and computer science at MIT, draws some of his inspiration from the convergence of the two disciplines – and he is very competent in both[414]. His knowledge of the human brain and neuroscience guides him in his quest for a more advanced Artificial Intelligence. More practical applications are also a matter of interdisciplinary thinking. To create and perfect AlphaGo, the DeepMind team brought together not only brilliant computer scientists but also Go champions, including the European champion Fan Hui. To develop multiple medical applications, from the diagnosis of skin diseases to attempts at precision medicine, the expertise of medical research specialists is essential alongside that of computer scientists, both to build models and to train algorithms. Similar examples abound.

Finally, interdisciplinary thinking has a particular importance in the era of Artificial Intelligence. The ability to use knowledge and skills in multiple domains is a human characteristic. Indeed, AI today is narrow and specialised, designed and above all configured to operate in a well-defined field[415]. Thus, interdisciplinary thinking, beyond the reach of AI to date, allows us to differentiate ourselves from it and to cultivate one of our strengths.

How to teach interdisciplinary thinking

When it brings together the expertise of different individuals, interdisciplinarity is a form of collaboration – all the skills necessary for collaboration must be mastered and implemented.

But specific initiatives are beginning to emerge to strengthen interdisciplinarity in education itself. One of the most ambitious efforts

---

[413] CNN or Convolutional Neural Networks.
[414] He is one of 23 researchers cited by Martin Ford as one of the "architects of intelligence", i.e. one of the very best in AI.
[415] However, let us recognise that there is nothing to prevent us from consciously cross-referencing data from multiple disciplines and using artificial intelligence algorithms to look for correlations.

underpins all education in Finland from primary to the end of secondary school. Finland, traditionally at the top of the international PISA rankings, has declined slightly in recent years, but it claims – and we are ready to buy into the explanation – that the changes initiated were based exclusively on the real needs identified.

Finland announced in 2015 its adoption of *phenomenal education*[416]. This approach proposes to use, as a starting point, authentic phenomena from real life in their entirety and in their natural context, instead of the traditional division into separate disciplines. The subjects addressed may be the European Union, the water cycle, energy issues or, of course, climate change. Climate change, for example, can lead to approaches that include physics and climatology, natural sciences, geography, humanities and social sciences. In addition to integrating different subjects, the method aims to arouse the child's curiosity, and implements active pedagogical practices such as questioning and problem solving. The intended learning is deep – it allows for the transfer of knowledge and skills.

Contrary to what underinformed observers may have claimed, this does not mean that traditional subjects such as mathematics, English and history will no longer be taught in Finland. As a matter of fact, this new interdisciplinary approach is intended to reflect on a number of complex and multi-dimensional topics. The official guidelines require at least one extended period of interdisciplinary teaching every year in all primary and secondary schools. Like the Finnish education system itself, which is highly decentralised, implementation of phenomenal education is also defined at the local level.

Other initiatives have implemented the integration of disciplines and looked at the effects. The Board on Higher Education and Workforce at the National Academies of Science, Engineering and Medicine recently confirmed the positive impact of the integration of arts, humanities and science subjects on academic performance and career prospects[417]. In

---

[416] http://www.phenomenaleducation.info
[417] "Branches from the same tree: The case for higher integration in higher education" [25].

terms of academic performance, the addition of arts and humanities subjects contributed to superior reasoning, creative problem solving, mastery of advanced content, communication and collaboration skills, motivation and enjoyment of learning. It should be stressed that the aim here is to genuinely integrate the subjects, not just to teach them in parallel.

The author of the study just mentioned concludes his paper with an interesting quote. Drew Gilpin Faust, then President of Harvard, greeted the 2009 class with a speech making the following claim: "The best education is the one that cultivates habits of mind, an analytic spirit, a capacity to judge and question that will equip you to adapt to any circumstance or take any vocational direction."[418] What could be more relevant in the age of Artificial Intelligence?

---

[418] This quote can be read on the Harvard website:
https://www.harvard.edu/president/speech/2009/2009-baccalaureate-service-improvisation-and-art-possible

Education: Takeaways

Paradigm shift

Throughout the world, the current education system is very similar to what it was in the 19th century, with the central figure of the teacher unidirectionally imparting their knowledge to their young pupils. This system worked wonders during the first industrial revolution but is much less suited to the current one, that of Artificial Intelligence. The time has come for a complete paradigm shift.

Until recently, formal education, for those who benefited from it, occupied the initial period of life, and was sufficient to last until the end of professional life. The considerable acceleration of technological progress completely invalidates the old model. In addition to initial education, continued training, also known as lifelong learning, is now essential.

The traditional role of the school, that of transmitting knowledge, is seriously challenged. Knowledge is now a commodity, easily accessible and with an ever-shorter expiry date. Rather than focusing exclusively on knowledge, especially with the risk of it not being transferable, the most effective and robust education system focuses on cognitive and socio-emotional skills. These skills, which are much more stable, are sometimes referred to as timeless.

Skills are a practical attribute, as opposed to theoretical knowledge. They are not acquired by listening to lectures in classrooms or lecture halls. For teaching these skills and the rest of the curriculum, teachers now have a modern educational arsenal: experiential education, robust scientific learning theories, and technology – especially Artificial Intelligence.

The different approaches of school systems

Almost all school systems suffer from inertia, which limits them in their adaptation to the major changes in society. They are just starting their reforms, at varying speeds depending on the country.

The French system is taking steps in the right direction by focusing on early childhood and the acquisition of foundational knowledge, and by reforming examinations that have become obsolete in their current format. But this system remains very focused on learning.

In Singapore, major reforms are being launched to continue transforming the school system. It is, however, the very system that already enables them to top international PISA rankings in... all categories! The country realises that the current measurement scale, which is very exam-oriented, is no longer relevant and may instead prove counterproductive. The new orientation they have taken favours 21st century skills.

21st century skills lie at the heart of the IB (International Baccalaureate) system, which boasts more than 4,000 schools and one million students around the world. Teachers are obsessed with enabling each of their students to realise their full potential through the IB learner profile. They develop 10 critical skills in a proactive way, including critical thinking, curiosity, open-mindedness, attention to others and risk-taking.

The 21st Century Compass

We introduce the 21st Century Compass, both a navigation tool and an educational Swiss army knife, which everyone will benefit from being equipped with from childhood for a lifetime effect. Its design stems directly from the evolution of the world as catalysed by Artificial Intelligence and reflected in the world of work.

The compass focuses on **the ability to learn**, which is essential in a rapidly and constantly changing environment. It is now understood that learning is more science than art. Simple rules from cognitive science make it possible to drastically improve its effectiveness.

The compass is based on **foundational literacies**. They include *literacy*, or the ability to use and communicate written information in everyday life; *numeracy*, or the ability to create and use mathematical information and ideas; and *digital literacy*, or the ability to use digital tools. Digital literacy is less intrinsic than once thought amongst Millennials and later generations. Becoming digitally literate, beyond technical knowledge, implies the ability to use technology and Artificial Intelligence wisely.

The compass is flanked by two sets of skills. On the right, three essential **cognitive skills**: *critical thinking* makes it possible to disentangle the true from the false in our complicated world and to make rational decisions; *creative thinking* enables us to bring new solutions to new problems; and *interdisciplinary thinking* provides the necessary approach to solve the big problems of today's world and to develop new domains such as AI. On the left, three fundamental **socio-emotional skills**: *resilience*, essential to manage the inevitable risks to which life will increasingly expose us; *collaboration*, because almost any human output stems from collaboration and so as to benefit from the ongoing human premium; and *empathy*, a prerequisite for effective collaboration and harmonious coexistence.

Last but not least, the Compass needle points to the moral North. Our actions will be driven jointly by *ethics* and *purpose*. Ethical decisions need to be made at all stages of AI design and implementation. This is all the more essential as bad ethical choices threaten to be amplified by Artificial Intelligence. *Purpose* will clarify our *raison d'être*, our personal mission, given that the end of work will leave a huge void to fill.

All the components of the Compass can be instilled from an early age and refined throughout life. They are worked on and developed, partly in school systems that evolve at various speeds, and partly at home.

The Compass is a beginning rather than an end, a general-purpose platform that enables us to adjust in all situations and does not prohibit us from diving into any required field of expertise. All the elements of the Compass can be introduced and put in place in the early years – which are often sensitive periods for certain competencies. However, they can be further developed and refined throughout life: they can be worked on. The elements of the Compass are often – wrongly – considered natural and automatic and are thus seldom taught in most formal school systems.

The Compass was introduced to enable children to thrive in the age of Artificial Intelligence. It is not as paradoxical as it seems that it encompasses so few technical elements. But the competencies you will find in the Compass fit the specifications to enable us to use AI and, if need be, to advance it; to shield us and differentiate us from AI; and to design the world of tomorrow.

What parents need to know and do

Parents, this final chapter is dedicated to you. I'm going to take the liberty of addressing you directly.

The role of parents and school

Preparing your children for the age of Artificial Intelligence is something that must begin today. We have been caught off guard by climate change because of our inaction. The impact of AI is expected to be of a similar magnitude. Let us avoid repeating our mistake by failing to prepare either individual young adults in the making or society as a whole. There is still time, as we said in the introduction to this book, but it will not last.

Ideally, a partnership between school and you, parents, will ensure the best preparation over the long term. You complement and reinforce each other. You, parents, give a decisive boost to your children's preparation, but alone, you could end up feeling helpless in the face of the dizzying evolution of the world. As for school, it is in principle better equipped over time, but alone it can neither compete with the speed of adaptation of your family, nor do the groundwork you do. Both you and school have an important role to play in this partnership.

Yours is essential. Many of the child's socio-emotional and cognitive characteristics take shape well before school starts and are strongly influenced by the parents' daily behaviour. Some other characteristics, developed later, go beyond the scope of formal education. You, parents, are constantly solicited as your children grow up, sometimes explicitly for advice, sometimes implicitly by observing your behaviour. You set the tone.

School is obviously not to be underestimated in the transmission of knowledge to children and in developing their skills. Isn't its role to prepare today's children to be the responsible and fulfilled adults of tomorrow? It offers a well thought-out and structured approach, and inspiring coaching – when it can afford it. But as we have seen, there is great variability from one formal school system to another. Not all schools today are equally equipped to fully carry out this mission. In addition, many of them suffer from a certain inertia, due to their size and mode of operation. It is unlikely that school systems can adapt as quickly as parents to the whirlwind of Artificial Intelligence.

Some schools, however, are taking action to support their students in the rise of AI. I had the opportunity to work in partnership with the *Lycée Français de Singapour*, working with primary and secondary school pupils, and with parents like you. In two-hour sessions per class, Year 6 pupils flooded us with questions each more relevant than the last. They demonstrated a surprisingly advanced understanding of the principles, opportunities and risks of AI. We learned to identify AIs, simulated their supervised learning through role-playing, and detected bias and discrimination; and I was able to allay their fear of Terminator and reassure them that robots do not experience real emotions. With their seniors in secondary school, we talked about the jobs of the future, the technical and non-technical skills that should be acquired, the role of philosophy and humanities in the design of AI, the relevance of certain policy decisions and the meaning they might want to give to their lives. Together with their parents, gathered *en masse* in the school's large lecture theatre, we demystified AI while highlighting its exceptional power; we discussed the different scenarios for the future of society and explored how their children would contribute to it; we discussed the key points and immediate actions to be taken to put their offspring in the best possible position at the dawn of the AI era.

The trigger for this book and its *raison d'être* was precisely to help you, parents, carry out the formidable task of preparing your children. As an essential starting point, you must acquire a good understanding of what AI really is, beyond the prevailing hype or, conversely, the counterproductive denial. This allows you, as a second step, to implement some simple but decisive actions. As a conclusion, let us summarise what you need to know (AI is the new electricity) and what you need to do (prepare your children today). Let's start with the facts.

AI is the new electricity

AI is a versatile technology

No matter how breath-taking the result, there is nothing magical, mystical or supernatural about Artificial Intelligence. It is only a **technology**, implementing relatively simple mathematical algorithms. This technology is not specialised but **general purpose**. It is destined to permeate all layers of society through all kinds of physical objects or intangible services. Like electricity, Artificial Intelligence is everywhere.

AI "performs" but does not understand

Artificial Intelligence keeps rapidly increasing its level of **performance**, so much so that it has started outperforming men and women at an increasing number of mental processes. However, it has **no understanding** of the decisions it recommends, the signals or images it recognises, the sentences it translates or the answers it gives back. AI is constantly in simulation mode, and it performs its tasks with an unmatched talent.

AI is highly beneficial

Artificial Intelligence simplifies our daily lives while making them more practical and enjoyable. At work, it frees us from an increasing number of mundane or painful, menial tasks. AI is also being used to address humanity's greatest challenges: overcoming global warming, feeding and caring for people, and democratising quality education. Overall, it is highly **beneficial**.

AI also presents dangers

Like all technologies, Artificial Intelligence is double-edged. The main direct **danger** undoubtedly comes from the malevolent use that humans themselves can make of AI to deceive, manipulate, regulate, deprive or kill. In addition, the imperfect implementation of AI, at the current early stage, comes with problems such as induced biases. The loss of human control in processes that they themselves implement is also a serious cause for concern. Finally, the major indirect **risk** is a social and economic one: poor management of the transition period to a likely world without work could spell disaster.

By the end of the century, we will probably have invented Artificial General Intelligence, whereas AI is currently narrow, specialised and limited. It will then be able to do everything that humans can do, and much more. The emergence of Artificial General Intelligence will mark a major breakthrough after four billion years of evolution on Earth. Beyond the immediate benefits, the question will be asked about the new place of humans on Earth. It will also require a new model of society to be found, since the previous ones will have become ineffective.

Now that you have understood and digested these observations, which are detailed in Part 1, you can take action.

Prepare your children today

Adopt AI and talk about it

Since the spread of AI is inevitable and, moreover, largely positive, your best option is to **adopt** it frankly. There is no point in feeling hesitant or arguing that its real importance is uncertain or its deployment still risky. Frank adoption does not mean blind and unconditional adoption. It is entirely legitimate to attach ethical criteria to the deployment of Artificial Intelligence and to work with determination to make it better. It is even essential to ask the difficult but necessary questions today. We are fortunate today to be able to start thinking before the uncontrolled sequence of events decides for us or leaves us in a situation of extreme vulnerability – exactly what happened in the case of climate change.

How does this affect your children? By adopting a positive attitude towards AI, you are very clear about the meaning of history. You create a sense of enthusiasm and confidence in the future. Perhaps you will even spark careers in Artificial Intelligence. In the immediate future, by asserting your adoption of AI, you are telling your children that machines have been entrusted with the work of machines, and that humans can now foster their humanity.

Equip them for a lifetime of learning

The speed and extent of change in society will continue to increase. Your children will have to constantly adapt in their daily lives and change jobs every few years. Perpetual transformation will be accompanied by constant learning. Permanent professional reskilling will become the new norm. To successfully complete these multiple transformations, your children will need to be equipped with both the disposition of mind and the technical ability to **learn**. You can help them cultivate the former and acquire the latter through advances in cognitive and pedagogical sciences.

Develop their digital literacy

Only a small minority are destined to become Artificial Intelligence engineers, but everyone, including your children, will have to use it very widely. As such, **digital literacy** will transform them into competent and knowledgeable users of digital technologies. Remember how you taught them not to put their fingers into electric sockets when they were small, and how you yourself carefully make sure the power is off before doing any electrical rewiring. Artificial Intelligence also demands a lot of precautions.

Learning through supervised practice enables them to increase their detailed understanding of the use of digital technology, to broaden the range of tools and methods at their disposal, and to perfect their knowledge of the opportunities and risks associated with this remarkable technology. The range of learning begins with the assessment of the truthfulness of the information available with a simple click. It continues with the careful and wise use of social networks from the first encounter (a message that you must inculcate in them without delay), goes on with a clear understanding of the notion of private data, and extends to the implementation of appropriate AI models (which the school should teach in due course).

Provide them with the skills of the 21st century

21st century skills, both cognitive and socio-emotional, were already good predictors of success in life. With the advent of Artificial Intelligence, they also now allow us to make the most of Artificial Intelligence, to protect ourselves as much as possible from it, and to differentiate ourselves from it by cultivating our humanity. They are therefore essential to your children's future. We have included six of them in the 21st Century Compass; three are socio-emotional (resilience, empathy, and collaboration), and the other three are cognitive (critical thinking, creative thinking and interdisciplinary thinking). All six are extensively detailed in Part 3. Interestingly, while the crucial importance of most of these skills is now unanimously recognised, they are rarely taught, because they are – wrongly – considered natural or automatic. These skills, on the contrary, can and should be taught. Don't miss out on this opportunity! They can develop far beyond the influence you have had on your children since their early years.

Be mindful of your life and career advice
Whether they explicitly ask for it or not, your children receive plenty of **advice** from you – and may even follow some. Your influence puts you in a position of increased responsibility at a time when the world is changing at a dizzying pace and you may not have been able to update your understanding. Do you have sufficient clarity on where the world is heading? You might, if you carefully read Parts1 and 2 in detail. For career guidance, for example, you should be careful not to base your advice exclusively on your own memories: they may not be applicable in a rapidly evolving working landscape. Yes, quite a few jobs will evolve drastically or even disappear. That said, do not refrain from helping your children develop their moral North, combining ethical reference and purpose; it will guide them when they are called upon to design the world of tomorrow. You will make your children stronger by offering them unconditional love and support, expanding the range of choices available to them, encouraging their passions, and focusing on their long-term development and not just on a few grades and academic results.

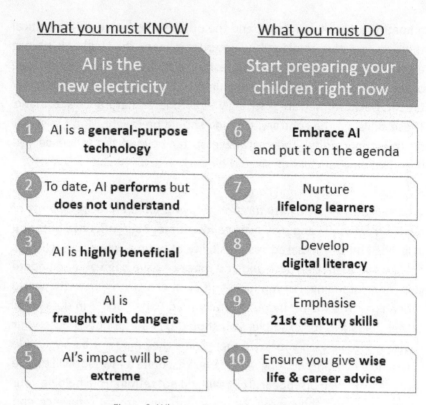

What you must KNOW	What you must DO
AI is the new electricity	**Start preparing your children right now**
1 AI is a **general-purpose technology**	6 **Embrace AI** and put it on the agenda
2 To date, AI **performs** but **does not understand**	7 Nurture **lifelong learners**
3 AI is **highly beneficial**	8 Develop **digital literacy**
4 AI is **fraught with dangers**	9 Emphasise **21st century skills**
5 AI's impact will be **extreme**	10 Ensure you give **wise life & career advice**

Figure 9: What parents need to know and do

Beyond this summary, the 21st Century Compass is a valuable reference framework to be explored – that is why it is the core of Part III of this book. Equipping your children today makes them more secure, while at the same time increasing the likelihood of a better world.

It is certainly an intense and extraordinary period that is on the horizon. Your children will make it the reality of tomorrow. You, parents, are committed to preparing them for it. Hopefully, the few pages you have just read will enable you to help your children shape the era of Artificial Intelligence to their expectations, and thrive in it.

Acknowledgements

I am greatly indebted to the small but invaluable group of people who reviewed early – and later – versions of this book. Many of their ideas and tireless input helped me refine my thinking as I was writing. Thomas Jestin contributed his encyclopaedic knowledge of AI and beyond, Marie-Agathe de Place her informed vision and human touch, Nicolas David his long-lasting wisdom, and all gave me the benefit of their sharp wit, rigorous analysis and constructive criticism.

I am extremely grateful to the experts who took the time to share their views on specific matters of interest for this book: King Wang Poon, Hélène Vauzelle, Jean-Charles Vauzelle, Corinne Rousset, Thibaud Brière, Julien Condamines, Carla Heard, Yoann Fol, Abbie Adeyeri, to name a few. I benefited immensely from Pierre Golstein's continuous scientific input and philosophical views. I was greatly inspired by Pr. Stanislas Dehaene's work, particularly in his use of cognitive psychology and neuroscience to explain Learning. I was significantly influenced by conferences highlighting the work of Pr. Raja Chatila and Dr. Christophe Habas on AI ethics. I would also like to thank all the individuals and organisations that have led me to reflect further on the topics addressed in this book and how to present them. This includes vibrant communities such as SG Innovate, Tech for Good and the "Live With AI" think tank in Singapore; high-quality interest groups and networks online; and a number of enthusiastic leaders crafting a better future such as Pierre Robinet, Eléonore Ferreyrol-Alési, Pascal Bornet, Victor Baffet, Scott Jones and many others who will undoubtedly recognise themselves.

The English version of this book would not have become a reality without the work of my editor, Rachael Churchill, whose eagle eyes and meticulousness never cease to amaze me – thank you Rachael. Others have worked hard to make this book attractive and I am grateful to them: Milan Jovanovic designed the cover and Moyez Ibrahim Khan designed most of the graphics.

I would also like to thank all the well-wishers who supported me on this journey: Greg Blackwood-Lee, Mariana Grigorian, Yoni Garbourg, Pierre Sagrafena, Olivia Dissescou Lambert, Jean-Baptiste Hazard, Yoni Rahamim, Cintia Tavella, Lucas Mirgalet, Shalini Sarin, Glenn Huybrecht, Sharon Montluc, Antonio Codinach, Frédéric Bacquet, Sarah Anglade, Jean-Christophe Bouglé – may the others know that I am thankful to them as well.

My final thanks go to my wife Simone and my children Eva and Nathan, as well my sisters and my parents. Writing a book is a long and strenuous endeavour. It could not have materialised without the generous support of those who most dread, yet accept, the author's periodic mental unavailability.

Glossary

The definitions below come from print or online dictionaries or encyclopaedias, or the author.

Algorithm

A process or set of rules to be followed in calculations or other problem-solving operations, especially by a computer.

Artificial Intelligence

The ability of machines (or the machines themselves) that can mimic human intelligence (traditional definition).

The ability of machines (or the machines themselves) that can sense their environment, think, learn, and act, in response to what they sense and their programmed objectives (modern definition).

Artificial Neural Network

A computing system representing data with multiple levels of abstraction and mimicking to a certain extent the brain's biological neural network.

Creativity

The ability to generate original ideas that have value.

Critical thinking

The analysis of facts to form a judgment.

Reasoned and reflective thinking focused on deciding what to believe or do.

Deep Learning

An algorithm learning mode — and, by extension, an algorithm class — using Artificial Neural Networks (simplified definition).

Digital literacy

The ability to use digital tools effectively and appropriately.

Duality

The quality or condition of consisting of two parts, elements, or aspects; an instance of opposition or contrast between two concepts or two aspects of something.

Empathy

The ability to understand and share the feelings of another.

Ethics

The moral principles that govern a person's behaviour or the conducting of an activity.

Interdisciplinarity

The quality or fact of involving or drawing on two or more branches of knowledge.

Job

A paid position of regular employment.

Literacy

The ability to use and communicate written information in everyday life.

Machine Learning

An algorithm learning mode — and, by extension, an algorithm class — used by machines to effectively perform a specific task without using explicit instructions (traditional definition).

An algorithm learning mode – and, by extension, an algorithm class – used by machines whose performance increases with experience (modern definition).

Numeracy

The ability to create and use mathematical information and ideas.

Paradigm

A representation of the world, way of looking at things, coherent model of the world that lies on a defined foundation.

Purpose

The central motivating aims of one's life.

Reinforcement Learning

An algorithm learning mode – and, by extension, an algorithm class – used by machines to take action so as to maximise some notion of cumulative reward, without any initial data.

Resilience

The capacity to recover quickly from difficulties; toughness.

Supervised Learning

An algorithm learning mode – and, by extension, an algorithm class – used by machines to make predictions based on an initial set of labelled training data.

Task

The smallest identifiable and essential piece of a job that serves as a unit of work.

Transfer Learning

An algorithm learning mode – and, by extension, an algorithm class – used by machines to store knowledge gained while solving one problem and apply it to a different but related problem.

Unsupervised Learning

An algorithm learning mode – and, by extension, an algorithm class – used by machines to group unsorted information according to similarities and differences even though there are no categories provided.

Index

Bibliography

[1]   M. Ford, Architects of Intelligence, Packt, 2018.

[2]   M. Tegmark, Life 3.0 : Being Human in the Age of Artificial Intelligence, Knopf, 2017.

[3]   E. J. Topol, "High-performance medicine: the convergence of human and artificial intelligence," *Nature Medicine,* vol. 25, no. January 2019, pp. 44-56, 2019.

[4]   H. S. Mohanthy, "Using Deep Learning for Image-Based Plant Disease Detection," *Arxiv temporarily.*

[5]   G. Kohs, Director, *AlphaGo.* [Film]. USA: Moxie Pictures, 2017.

[6]   ECP, "Artificial Intelligence Impact Assessment," ECP, https://ecp.nl/, 2018.

[7]   PWC, Stanford Woods Institute for the Environment and World Economic Forum, "Harnessing Artificial Intelligence for the Earth," WEF - 'Fourth Industrial Revolution for the Earth' series, 2018.

[8]   M. Ford, Rise of the Robots, One World, 2015.

[9]   Y. N. Harari, Homo Deus, Vintage, 2017.

[10] McKinsey, "Harnessing Automation for a Future that Works," Janvier 2017.

[11] McKinsey, "Jobs lost, jobs gained," December 2017.

[12] K.-F. Lee, AI Superpowers - China, Silicon Valley and the New World Order, HMH, 2018.

[13] AI100 hosted by Stanford's Human-Centered Inst., "AI Index 2018 Annual Report," 2018.

[14] C. B. Frey and M. A. Osborne, "The future of employment : How susceptible are jobs to computerisation ?," *University of Oxford,* 2013.

[15] S. Ullman, "Using neuroscience to develop artificial intelligence," vol. 363, no. 6428, p. 692, 2019.

[16] S. Dehaene, Les neurones de la lecture, Odile Jacob, 2010.

[17] S. Dehaene, Apprendre ! Les talents du cerveau, le défi des machines, Odile Jacob, 2018.

[18] A. Diamond and K. Lee, "Interventions shown to Aid Executive Function Development in Children 4–12 Years Old," *Science ,* vol. 333, no. 6045, pp. 959-964, 2011.

[19] D. Goleman, Emotional Intelligence : why it can matter more than IQ, 2009 (latest edition).

[20] Collective, The Social Neuroscience of Empathy, MIT Press, 2009.

[21] J. Bendell, "Deep Adaptation: A Map for Navigating Climate Tragedy," *IFLAS Occasional Paper 2,* 27 July 2018.

[22] J. G. Gomez, "What do we know about creativity," *The Journal of Effective Teaching,* vol. 7, no. 1, pp. 31-43, 2007.

[23] N. M. Simone Ritter, "Enhancement of Creative Thinking Skills Using a Cognitive-Based Creativity Training," *Journal of Cognitive Enhancement,* vol. 1, no. 3, pp. 243-253, September 2017.

[24] J. Baer, "The importance of domain-specific expertise in creativity," *Roeper review,* vol. 37, no. 3, pp. 165-178, 2015.

[25] D. Skorton, "Branches from the same tree : The case for higher integration in higher education," *PNAS,* vol. 116, no. 6, pp. 1865-1869, 2019.

[26] UK Universities, "Solving Future Skills Challenges," 6 August 2018.

[27] C. Rousset, "Excellence académique, joutes oratoires et pragmatisme pédagogique à Singapour," *Revue internationale d'éducation de Sèvres,* vol. 77, pp. 59-69, 2018.

[28] World Economic Forum, "The Future of Jobs," 2016.

[29] S. Nataraj, "The Need for an Introductory Computer Literacy Course at the University Level," *International Journal of Business Management and Economic Research,* vol. 5, pp. 71-73, 2014.

[30] World Economic Forum, "Future of Jobs 2018," September 2018.

[31] R. M. Ekkehard Ernst, "The economics of artificial intelligence : implications for the future of work," October 2018.

[32] Organisation Internationale du Travail, "Travailler pour bâtir un avenir meilleur," January 2019.

[33] P. Domingos, The Master Algorithm: How the Quest for the Ultimate Learning Machine Will Remake Our World, Basic Books, 2015.

[34] B. Abbott, "Deeper Learning : Machine learning makes new sense of psychiatric symptoms," *Nature Medicine,* vol. 25, no. January 2019, pp. 2-11, 2019.

[35] D. Kelley and T. Kelley, Creative Confidence : Unleashing the Creative Potential Within Us All, Currency, 2013.

[36] Y. Gurovich et al, "Identifying facial phenotypes of genetic disorders using deep learning," *Nature Medicine,* vol. 25, no. January 2019, pp. 60-64, 2019.

[37] K. Xu et al, "Show, Attend and Tell: Neural Image Caption Generation with Visual Attention," *Arxiv,* p. 1502.03044, 2015.

[38] B. Lake et al, "Building machines that learn and think like people," *Behavioral and brain sciences,* no. Arxiv 2 nov 2016, 2016.

[39] A. Melnikova et al, "Active learning machine learns to create new quantum experiments," *PNAS,* vol. 115, no. 6, pp. 1221-1226, 2018.

[40] R. Beaty et al, "Robust prediction of individual creative ability from brain functional connectivity," *PNAS,* Jan 2018.

[41] W. Stephen et al, "Trajectories of the Earth System in he Anthropocene," *PNAS,* vol. 115, no. 33, pp. 8252-8259, 2018.

[42] P. Griffin et al, Assessment and Teaching of 21st Century Skills, Springer, 2015, p. Chapter 2.

[43] T.E. Moffitt et al, "A gradient of childhood self-control predicts health, wealth, and public safety," *PNAS,* vol. 08(7):, p. 2693–2698, 2011 Feb 15.

[44] M. Komorowski et al, "The Artificial Intelligence Clinician learns optimal," *Nature Medicine,* vol. 24, pp. 1716-1720, 2018.

[45] R. Evans et al, "De novo structure prediction with deeplearning based scoring," *Yet to be published.*

[46] A. Esteva et al, "Dermatologist-level classification of skin cancer with deep neural networks," *Nature,* vol. 542, no. 02 February 2017, pp. 115-118, 2017.

[47] D. Silver et al, "A general reinforcement learning algorithm that masters chess, shogi, and Go through self-play," *Science,* vol. 362, no. 6419, pp. 1140-1144, 2018.

[48] D. Silver et al, "Mastering the game of Go without human knowledge," *Nature,* vol. 550, pp. 354-359, 19 October 2017.

[49] S. Dehaene et al, "What is consciousness, and could machines have it?," *Science,* vol. 358, no. 6362, pp. 486-492, 2017.

[50] J.F. Bonnefon et al, "The Moral Machine experiment," *Nature,* vol. 563, p. 59–64, 2018.

[51] Z. Attia et al, "Screening for cardiac contractile dysfunction using an AI-enabled electrocardiogram," *Nature Medicine,* vol. 25, no. January 2019, pp. 70-74, 2019.

[52] W.S. Kremen et al, "Influence of young adult cognitive ability and additional education on later-life cognition," *PNAS,* vol. 116, no. 6, p. 2021–2026, February 5, 2019.

[53] McKinsey, "Skill shift : automation and the future of workforce," May 2018.

[54] DARES, "Comment ont évolué les métiers en France depuis 30 ans ?," *Dares Analyses,* January 2017.

[55] National Research Council, "Education for Life and Work : Developing transferable Knowledge and Skills in the 21st century," National Academies Press, July 2012.

www.ingramcontent.com/pod-product-compliance
Lightning Source LLC
Chambersburg PA
CBHW022312070326
40689CB00049BA/784